On cover: Kash Lovec hunts sharp-tailed grouse.

Wingshooter's Guide
to
Montana

Published by Wilderness Adventures Press™
P.O. Box 1410
Bozeman, MT 59771

10 9 8 7 6 5 4 3 2 1

Printed in the United States of America

Library of Congress Catalog Card Number: 95-060557

ISBN 1-885106-13-0

To our wives, Bobbie Williams and Blanche Johnson,
for understanding and sharing our passion
for hunting and hunting dogs.

Wingshooter's Guide
to
Montana

Upland Birds and Waterfowl

Chuck Johnson and Ben O. Williams

Wilderness Adventures Press

ACKNOWLEDGMENTS

Many people have contributed to this book. Their advice and assistance have been invaluable.

First and foremost is our editor and the designer of the book, Ganay Johnson. Ganay's editing ability can make even us look good! Meagan Hassell helped with the typesetting and research.

William "Web" Parton wrote the section on preparing a bird in the field for taxidermy. Web is a bird dog trainer, taxidermist, and artist. He lives and hunts in Arizona. Web is writing *The Wingshooter's Guide to Arizona* to be published in 1996.

Gary Dusek, with the Montana Department of Fish, Wildlife, and Parks, and David Books, editor of *Montana Outdoors,* were very supportive and helpful. Lisa Landenburger of the Geographic Information Services at Montana State University provided us with many of the detailed maps. Steve Smith, the editor of *Pointing Dog Journal* and our good friend, gave us encouragement and advice. Special thanks to Charlie Waterman, the dean of outdoor writers, for being there.

Finally, to our fine dogs, the Brits and the Germans, especially Winston and Duke, our hunting partners and friends, for making our hunts special.

TABLE OF CONTENTS

Missouri Country • 89

Shelby, Toole Co. • Chester, Liberty Co. • Havre, Hill Co. • Chinook, Blaine Co. •
Malta, Phillips Co. • Glasgow, Valley Co. • Scobey, Daniels Co. • Plentywood,
Sheridan Co. • Wolf Point, Roosevelt Co. • Fort Benton, Choteau Co. • Great Falls,
Cascade Co. • Stanford, Judith Basin Co .• Lewistown, Fergus Co. • Winnett,
Petroleum Co. • Jordan, Garfield Co. • Circle, McCone Co. • Sidney, Richland Co. •
Glendive, Dawson Co. • Terry, Prairie Co.

Rocky Mountain Country • 143

Libby, Lincoln Co. • Kalispell, Flathead Co. • Cut Bank, Glacier Co. • Thompson
Falls, Sanders Co. • Polson, Lake Co. • Superior, Mineral Co. •
Missoula, Missoula Co. • Hamilton, Ravalli Co. • Deer Lodge, Powell Co. •
Philipsburg, Granite Co. • Anaconda, Deer Lodge Co. • Butte, Silver Bow Co. and
Jefferson Co. • Dillon, Beaverhead Co. • Ennis, Madison Co. •
Bozeman, Gallatin Co. • Townsend, Broadwater Co. • Helena, Lewis and Clark Co. •
Choteau, Teton Co. • Conrad, Pondera Co.

Yellowstone Country • 199
White Sulphur Springs, Meagher Co. • Harlowton, Wheatland Co. •
Ryegate, Golden Valley Co. • Roundup, Musselshell Co. • Forsyth, Rosebud Co. •
Miles City, Custer Co. • Baker, Fallon Co. • Wibaux, Wibaux Co. • Livingston, Park
Co. • Big Timber, Sweet Grass Co. • Columbus, Stillwater Co. • Billings, Yellowstone
Co. • Hysham, Treasure Co. • Red Lodge, Carbon Co. • Hardin, Big Horn Co. •
Broadus, Powder River Co. • Ekalaka, Carter Co.

Hunting on Indian Reservations • 246
Flathead • Blackfeet • Rocky Boy's • Fort Belknap • Fort Peck • Crow

National and State Wildlife Refuges • 251
Medicine Lake • Bowdoin • Charles M. Russell • Benton Lake • Freezeout Lake •
Red Rock Lakes • Lee Metcalf

Introduction

I am in love with Montana. For other states I have admiration, respect, recognition, even some affection, but with Montana it is love.

–John Steinbeck
Travels with Charley

The idea for this book came from our customers. We received many calls asking about bird hunting in Montana. What birds are available? Where do I find them? What time of year? Where should I stay? Is there a guidebook available? Unfortunately, there wasn't a guidebook available that gave all of this information. So we decided to write and publish the *Wingshooter's Guide to Montana* to fill that gap.

There is a fascination with the West and especially Montana, the "Big Sky Country." Montana is the fourth largest state in the union and one of the least populated. Eastern Montana has less than two people per square mile. There are vast grasslands, forests, wild streams, and miles of sagebrush. The combination of open land and few people provides us with ideal conditions to sustain good bird populations. You can hunt pheasants, sharp-tailed grouse, Hungarian partridge, sage grouse, ducks, and geese all in the same day. The western part of our state has excellent hunting for the three species of mountain grouse—Franklin's, ruffed, and blue. Many times we will start the morning off hunting ducks along a river and then spend the rest of the day on the prairies hunting Huns, sharptails, and sage grouse. We truly live in a hunter's paradise.

We want to welcome you to Montana and hope that you enjoy our great state and its outstanding bird hunting. We hope that you will develop a love and an appreciation for its natural beauty and abundance of birds. We need your help to preserve what is truly the best of the West. Please support the renewal of CRP (Conservation Reserve Program) lands and the preservation of our native grasslands and forests. Working together, we can sustain our gamebird populations, save our hunting areas, and maintain this wonderful way of life.

Chuck Johnson and Ben O. Williams

FOREWORD

Geese from the north wheeled, called and sought mountain passes and the mallards teetered above the cottonwoods and dropped into steaming spring creeks when the big chill came—but Montana was mostly rifle country in 1957.

The Huns I saw were bigger than quail but acted a lot like them. The huge sage hens were startling to a crawling antelope hunter pushing a rifle along a dry wash. Even then there were pheasant cackles from the shelter belts—but Montana barely noticed most of its upland game.

"There are some little chickens (Hungarian partridge) over there along the ridge but I think the big chickens (sharptail grouse) have moved. The blues (blue grouse) have already gone high and there's nothing along the creek but a lot of those little ruffled grouse," the rancher said. "What kind of a dog is that?"

But that was the year the filling station man at Clyde Park made friends with me and offered to lend me saddle horses and a stock truck—free. He said he wasn't using them and he could see that I wanted to go hunting. He did this while putting 11 gallons of gas in my car and had known me for roughly four minutes. It was in 1958 that another filling station operator in Bozeman filled my carryall, washed the windshield and invited me to hunt elk in his camp on Freezeout Mountain.

But nobody said much about shotgunnery and the long-barreled goose guns were set behind the rifles in sporting goods stores. There were two upland game events—sage hen opening and pheasant season. The pheasant business was serious, and even then no one knew why the population was spotty. There was a constant argument about whether it should be legal to shoot pheasant hens. Of course it was then.

For most Montana gunners the sage hen season was a one or two-day affair. Use your binoculars to watch the ridges for dark shadows moving under the sage bushes. March across sage hen country in skirmish order and try to keep the Labs and crossbreeds from getting too far ahead. A goose gun worked fine and everybody argued about whether sage hens were really fit to eat.

"They kept me from starving," said the old cowboy, pointing to the weathered wreckage of his old camp. "I know how to cook sage hens."

The sage hen, living in much of Montana, but with his regular short migrations, is a special bird who somehow belongs with sage country two-tracks that accommodate growling pickups and probably once carried creaking covered wagons or buckboards. He belongs in big space with ancient sheepherder monuments on the ridges, drifting coyotes, and watchful pronghorns. It is his country and he did not come from Asia with gaudy feathers, or even from Hungary by a route still not understood.

The sharptail grouse too, has watched prairie schooners, Indian cavalry, and jet airliners, fitting a changing world better than the true prairie chicken, whose world has shrunk. And the ruffed and blue grouse have watched it all from somewhat higher perches. It was in the early sixties that the Pennsylvania grouse hunter sighted a Montana bird that looked back at him from a creek bottom alder.

"It isn't a real ruffed grouse," he said. "They don't act that way."

It was a very real ruffed grouse but I didn't argue. Scare it a few times and it will act like an Eastern bird. It can go with silky setters and light double guns with scroll engraving. A ruffed grouse is a ruffed grouse and his wings can roar or whisper.

There was a day when I decided a shotgun looked as sleek as a big-game rifle while taking me to most of the same places and to a few new ones. I went pheasant hunting with people who had retrievers and I ran into Ben Williams and Brittanys. While a Southern friend I'd chased quail with shook his head at my perfidy, I began to tout Brittanys as being on the same social level as English pointers and taking up less room in motels. He said I should stick to "bird dogs."

A big-eyed quail shooter from Kansas looked me up one fall 30 years ago. What were those big things that looked like quail when they flew across the road? Would his pointers work on them? Did the ranchers care? And how should he go about hunting those Hun things, where would he stay and what kind of country did they live in? Was there a book or something that told that stuff?

I knew where there were some Huns and some sharptails and some ruffed grouse and some sage hens, and quite a few mallards, but I hadn't taken him to raise, even if I had known him for most of his life. He didn't know what a Hun was, even if he did own a bank. I had preached Montana trout fishing across the country, but I thought that for the time being I'd keep the birds to myself as much as possible. A year or two later though, I was babbling about the secret uplanders of the West.

Gamebirds of the uplands have their years of plenty and their years of loss, and while a thousand watchers count the waterfowl millions on their passages across the Big Sky, there is mystery in the welfare of the other gamebirds. Blue grouse are harder to count than pronghorns, and we are seldom sure where the sage hens went or why, even though we sometimes see them in their annual movements high over snowy mountains.

High plains and the mountains themselves are mazes of feast and famine for gamebirds, valleys of flood or drought lying but a watershed away from bumper bird crops. So the professional biologist and the hunter compare notes, each sometimes wondering where the other has spent the season.

Montana is an outstanding example of an upland bird puzzle, partly because there has never been the heavy pressure and consequent study that have attended the shooting in more populated states. Then too, commercial hunting and private management have barely touched Montana, for better or worse. It is no wonder that many visiting gunners feel like pioneers, meeting with great success, and sometimes rather hard times. Although shotgunners are often classed as best of the migratory hunters, there are landowners who make no distinctions in those matters. Anyway, the hunter should study the playing field.

A new arrival with guns and dogs is likely to contemplate the fact that there is a great deal of Montana, and if his time is limited, as it usually is, he might even feel a bit lonely at first. True, the state is now committed to tourism—from skiing to trout fishing to big game hunting, but the shotgunner is a rather recent addition to the guest list. He might even meet (as I did) someone who will say, "You mean you came clear out here to hunt *birds*?"

So the *Wingshooter's Guide to Montana* might be more than a directory. It can be an introduction to the whole works and it may come as a surprise to anyone using it that when a hunter has read most of it, there will be very, very few people who will know as much about Montana shotgunning as he or she does.

Charles F. Waterman
Deland, Florida

Charles F. Waterman puts a beeper collar on Winston.

MONTANA FACTS

Fourth largest state in the union
147,138 square miles
93,157,953 acres
550 miles across
275 miles north to south
66 million acres in farms, ranches, and CRP lands
Average ranch—2,600 acres

Elevation: 1,820 feet to 12,798 feet
Counties: 56
Towns and Cities: 126
Population (1990): 790,000
    7 Indian Reservations
    2 National Parks
    11 National Forests
    68 State Recreation Areas
    12 Wilderness Areas
    11 State Parks

Nicknames: "Treasure State," "Big Sky Country," "Land of the Shining Mountains"
Primary Industries: agriculture, timber, mining, tourism
Capital: Helena
Bird: western meadowlark
Animal: grizzly bear
Flower: bitterroot
Tree: ponderosa pine
Gemstone: Montana agate
Grass: bluebunch wheat grass

TIPS ON USING THIS BOOK

• The area code for for the entire state of Montana is 406. When no area code precedes a phone number, you can assume it is a Montana number. You must dial 1 + 406 for all in-state long distance calls.

• The towns and counties in this guide are separated into three sections: Missouri Country which covers the Missouri River drainage, Rocky Mountain Country, encompassing the western and most mountainous part of our state, and Yellowstone Country which includes the Yellowstone drainage in the southeastern and south-central regions.

• Each of the three sections includes distribution maps for all species of upland birds found in that section. These maps are based on maps issued by the Montana Department of Fish, Wildlife, and Parks (FWP). They have been updated to show current bird populations based on our personal observations over the course of many hunting seasons. These general distribution maps are only an approximation and may change due to weather conditions, habitat alterations, and farming practices.

• Although we have tried to be as accurate as possible, please note that this information is current only for 1995. Ownership of hotels, restaurants, etc. may change and we cannot guarantee the quality of the services they provide.

• Always check with the FWP for the most recent hunting regulations. Prices, season dates, and regulations can change from year to year.

• Don't forget to ask permission before you hunt on private land.

We hope that we have helped you plan an enjoyable Big Sky hunting experience.

OPENING DAY

by Chuck Johnson

No matter how old I get I still have trouble sleeping the night before the opening day of bird season. I do not need an alarm to get me up—around five I finally give up trying to sleep and start getting ready. My German wirehairs sense my restlessness. Only my wife Blanche wants to remain asleep.

Long before it's light, Blanche and I are heading down the highway on the Hi-Line toward the ranch. We drive through the wheat fields and prairie pastures as the sun pokes its head over the Rocky Mountains. We stop at the edge of the coulee and get out to glass the ranch and let the dogs take care of themselves. It's cold out—only 20 degrees. The sunrise casts a purple-red glow on the surrounding hills and prairie. From our vantage point we can see for miles. Across the creek bottom, a herd of mule deer led by a huge 4x4 buck is making its way across the breaks, drifting from the grain fields back into the side coulees for daytime cover. In the creek bottom below us, the strutting and dancing sharptails are beginning their calls. Along the dry creek, a cock pheasant chases a hen.

Chuck Johnson and Annie work Hun country.

Chuck and Blanche Johnson with their German wirehairs Duke and Cody.

The dogs have finished their business and are eagerly waiting for the hunt to begin. Several times they start down the draw and have to be called back. A covey of Huns flies out of a large coulee to our left and lights in the CRP field. Another covey about a mile up the creek flies up to the top of the grain fields. It's time to get our gear and guns and start the hunt. We head for the sharptails in the creek bottom. The Huns will be feeding for several hours and hopefully will still be there when we have finished with the sharptails. Guns loaded, dogs ready, we head down the steep draw.

When we get to the bottom of the draw we find that the sharptails have moved out into a side coulee. Duke and Cody move up the coulee and nail the birds. The birds get up—my first shot is rushed, but I hit one with my second barrel. Blanche takes one shot and drops a bird. The main covey flies up to the top of the draw. The dogs relocate them and after several flushes we manage to get one more bird.

After a short rest and some water for the dogs we go back down the draw and across the creek to work the CRP land for Huns. Running downwind, Annie and

Cody run into the Huns and flush them before we get close enough for a shot. They fly across the field and into some brush on the side hill. We heel the dogs and silently approach the hillside. Blanche crosses over to the side of the brush and settles into position as I release the dogs. They run halfway up the hill toward the brush and slam into point. The Huns explode in the air. We're ready this time and both of us get a double.

After the birds are retrieved, we break for lunch. After a chilly morning, the temperature has climbed up into the high 80s. We rest ourselves and the dogs during the heat of the day. Later in the afternoon we decide to work the side hill of a coulee. In an instant, all three dogs go on point. Duke points off to one side while Annie and Cody point straight ahead of us. We go to Annie and Cody's point and flush a covey of Huns. Blanche takes the ones to the left and I hit one flying to the right.

Soon Duke appears with his face, nose, and mouth filled with porcupine quills. True to form, Duke was pointing a porcupine. When the birds broke and the shooting started, Duke must have broken point and gone in on the porky. Fortunately for him, I have a pair of hemostats and I am able to extract the quills. He is a sweet-tempered dog and sits patiently while I work on him.

As the sun sets we work our way back to the truck. We've covered many miles and put up a number of Huns and sharptails. The cover is excellent and the birds are numerous. It looks like the start of another good season. At the truck, we sit down and watch the sun set over one of the mountain ranges some 50 miles away. The sunset casts varying hues and shadows from bright red to orange to purple. The deer start out to feed and the coyotes begin to howl. We linger awhile, thankful for the prairies, the birds, and the beautiful state of Montana.

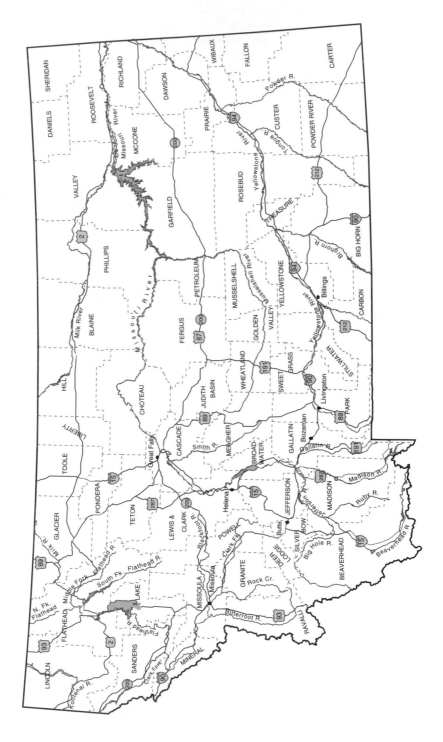

Major Roads & Rivers of Montana

MONTANA HUNTING REGULATIONS

UPLAND GAMEBIRDS

GENERAL REGULATIONS

Licenses — The following licenses are available at all Fish, Wildlife, and Parks offices and most licensing agents throughout the state. The license is valid March 1 through February of the following year.

CURRENT 1995 FEES

	Res.	Nonres.
Conservation (required prerequisite*)	$4.00	$5.00
Upland Gamebird (required prerequisite for turkey*)	$6.00	$55.00
Fall Season Turkey	$5.00	$13.00
Spring Season Turkey	$5.00	$13.00

*The resident Sportsman's License, the nonresident Big Game Combination License, and the nonresident Deer Combination License, include both a Conservation and Upland Gamebird license.

Avoid Violations of the Law — It is illegal to shoot any gamebird on, from, or across any public highway, or the shoulder, berm, borrow-pit, or right-of-way of any public highway, and/or motor driven conveyance.

Checking Stations — All sportspersons are required to stop as directed at all designated check stations on their way to and from hunting and fishing areas, even if they have no game or fish to be checked.

Hunter Education — Both resident and nonresident youths 12-17 years of age must provide a Certificate of Competency in the safe handling of firearms before they may purchase a hunting license.

Indian Reservations — Sportspersons hunting upland gamebirds on Indian reservations should check Indian reservation regulations because season dates, bag limits, licensing requirements, shooting hours, legal species, and shotshell requirements may differ from state regulations.

Landowner permission — Sportspersons are reminded that landowner permission is required to hunt on posted land. You are encouraged to "Ask First" to hunt on land not posted.

National Wildlife Refuges — More restrictive regulations may apply to national wildlife refuges open to public hunting. For additional information on federal regulations, contact Special Agent-in-Charge, U.S. Fish and Wildlife Service, P.O. Box 25486, Denver Federal Center, Denver, CO 80225, 303-234-4612.

Possession Limits — Sharp-tailed grouse, sage grouse, partridge, mountain grouse, and pheasant possession limits are 4 times the daily bag limit for each species.

Shooting Hours — Authorized shooting hours for the taking of upland gamebirds begins one-half hour before sunrise to one-half hour after sunset each day of the hunting season. See official sunrise-sunset tables for times.

Steel shot — Sportspersons are reminded that steel shot is *not* required when hunting upland gamebirds. It is required for the hunting of waterfowl (excluding snipe and mourning doves) and coots.

The U.S. Fish and Wildlife Service is considering non-toxic (i.e., steel) shot only regulations on federal refuges and waterfowl production areas in 1995. Please check with the Fish and Wildlife Service before going afield in 1995.

SAGE GROUSE
Statewide season dates: September 1—December 15
Bag Limits: 3 daily

SHARP-TAILED GROUSE
Statewide season dates: September 1—December 15
Bag Limits: 4 daily

MOUNTAIN GROUSE (Franklin's, ruffed, & blue)
Statewide season dates: September 1—December 15
Bag Limits: 4 in aggregate daily

RING-NECKED PHEASANT
Statewide season dates: October 14—December 15
Bag Limits: 3 cock pheasants daily
Transporting Pheasants: No person shall transport any pheasant within the state unless one leg remains naturally attached to each bird at all times.

GRAY (HUNGARIAN) PARTRIDGE
Statewide season dates: September 1—December 15
Bag Limits: 8 in aggregate daily.

MOURNING DOVE
Statewide season dates: September 1—October 30
Bag Limits: 15 daily and 30 in possession.
It is illegal to hunt by the use of baiting. It is illegal to shoot doves resting on utility lines or fixtures adjacent to those lines.
A Federal Migratory Bird Stamp is not required.

COMMON (WILSON'S) SNIPE
Statewide season dates: September 1—December 16
Bag Limits: 8 daily and 16 in possession

SANDHILL CRANE
Pacific Flyway season dates: Usually 2nd and 3rd weekends in September. Call FWP at 406-444-2535 for exact dates.
Bag and Possession Limit: 1 crane
Central Flyway season dates: Usually last week of September through mid-November. Call FWP at 406-444-2535 for exact dates.
Bag Limit: 3 daily and 6 in possession

MERRIAM'S TURKEY
Fall
The eastern half of Montana is open to fall turkey hunting. In western Montana, the counties of Flathead, Lake, and Sanders have a drawing for special fall permits.
Statewide season dates: September 1—December 15
Bag Limit: 1 turkey, either sex

Spring
The eastern half of Montana is open to spring turkey hunting. Flathead, Lake, and Sanders Counties in western Montana have a drawing for special spring permits. Applicants may apply for a spring permit in only one area of the state.
Spring season dates: generally 2nd week of April—1st week of May
Bag Limit: 1 male turkey.

WATERFOWL
(see Flyway map, page 82)

PACIFIC FLYWAY
Ducks
Open season: Changes each year. Approximately Oct 1–Oct 15, Oct 21–Nov 27, and mid-Dec.–Jan 1.
Bag Limit: 4 ducks and mergansers daily. Daily bag may contain no more than 3 mallards but only 1 female mallard, 1 pintail, 2 redheads, or 1 canvasback. The possession limit may not exceed twice the daily bag limit of any species and sex.

Geese
Open season: Approximately Oct 1–January 8
Bag Limit: 3 white geese (snow, blue, Ross), and 3 dark geese (all other), including no more than 2 white-fronted geese. The possession limit is twice the daily bag.

CENTRAL FLYWAY
Ducks
Zone 1 season dates: Approximately Oct 1–mid-Nov and Dec 10–Dec 26.
Zone 2 season dates: Approximately Oct 1–Oct 9 and Nov 11–Jan 1.
Bag Limit: 3 ducks and mergansers. Daily bag may contain no more than 2 wood ducks, 1 female mallard, 1 pintail, 1 canvasback, 1 redhead, and 1 hooded merganser. Possession may not exceed twice the daily bag limit of any species and sex.

Geese
Open season: Approximately Oct 1–mid-Jan.
Bag Limit: 5 white geese (snow, blue, Ross) and 4 dark geese (all other). The possession limit is twice the daily limit. *Exception: Sheridan County: 5 white geese and 2 dark geese daily and no more than twice the daily limit in possession.*

Montana Ecosystems Based on Climax Vegetation

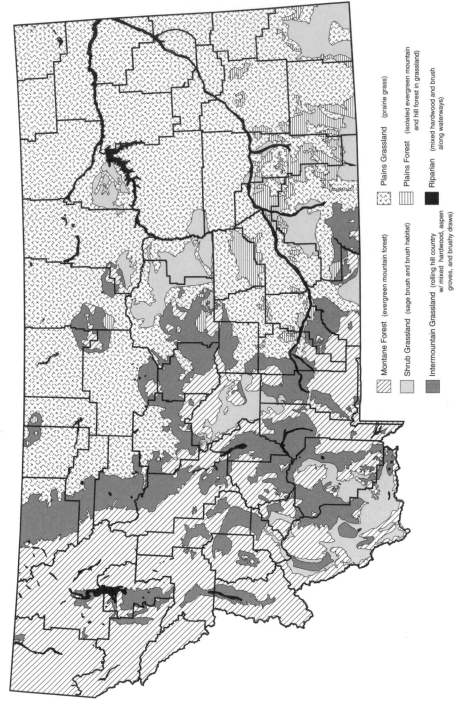

Montane Forest (evergreen mountain forest)

Shrub Grassland (sage brush and brush habitat)

Intermountain Grassland (rolling hill country w/ mixed hardwood, aspen groves, and brushy draws)

Plains Grassland (prairie grass)

Plains Forest (isolated evergreen mountain and hill forest in grassland)

Riparian (mixed hardwood and brush along waterways)

MONTANA LAND USE

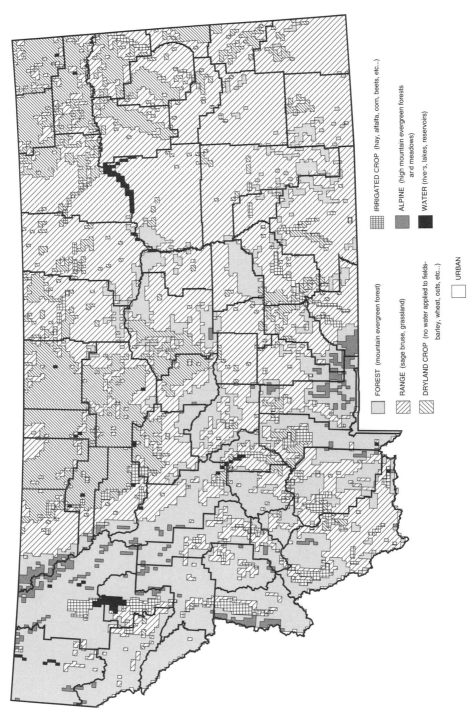

FOREST (mountain evergreen forest)

RANGE (sage bruse, grassland)

DRYLAND CROP (no water applied to fields-
barley, wheat, oats, etc...)

IRRIGATED CROP (hay, alfalfa, corn, beets, etc...)

ALPINE (high mountain evergreen forests
ar d meadows)

WATER (rivers, lakes, reservoirs)

URBAN

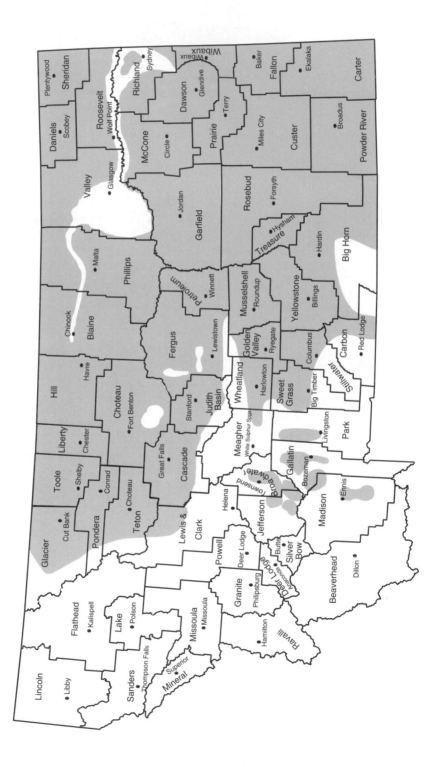

SHARP-TAILED GROUSE DISTRIBUTION

SHARP-TAILED GROUSE
Pedioecetes phasianellus

QUICK FACTS

- **local names**: grouse, sharptail, speckle-belly, pintail, prairie chicken, chicken
- **size:** both sexes average 16-20" in length and weigh 1¾–2¼ lbs. The wingspan is 26-29".
- **identification in flight:** appear almost white—have a rounded look and a short, pointed tail.

- Weather conditions are determining factors in sharptail behavior and location.
- Sharptail habitat is primarily mixed prairie rangeland interspersed with shrub and brush-filled draws and coulees.
- Number of sharptail can vary greatly between moist upland prairies and semi-arid shrub grassland.
- Sharp-tailed grouse are native to Montana and 2 subspecies remain established in the state. The Great Plains sharptail is abundant and lives in the central and eastern part of the state. The Columbian sharp-tailed grouse lives west of the Continental Divide in limited areas and is an endangered subspecies.

Color

The sharp-tailed grouse is a plump, short bird with a pointed tail. The sexes are similar in appearance, however males have yellow eye combs and pale purple air sacs on the throat. Sharp-tailed grouse are mottled black, brown, buff, and white. The feathers on the top of the head are brown and black with a black line behind the bill running through the eye. The throat and cheeks are off-white. The breast and flanks have V-shaped markings that are difficult to see from a distance. The two feathers in the center of the tail are longer. These tail feathers on the male are a neutral brown color; on the female, the feathers are cross-barred with black. Both male and female sharptails have feathered legs and small pectination, or fringe, on their toes that serves as snowshoes.

Sound and Flight Pattern

The sharp-tailed grouse's take-off is rapid. When airborne, the bird makes sharp turns with rapid wingbeats, glides for some distance, and repeats this pattern over and over. Sharptails cluck *(cac-cac-cac-cac)* loudly when flushed and in flight. Early in the season young birds usually fly only short distances. Later in the fall sharptails fly greater distances when flushed. As the hunting season progresses, the birds may not hold for dogs unless they are in heavy cover or have not been hunted.

Similar Gamebirds

Early in the season young sharptails can be confused with immature pheasants and sage grouse. A flying sharptail could be mistaken for a female pheasant, but sharptails have a shorter tail with white edging and a different wingbeat.

Flock or Covey Habits

Once the chicks hatch, the female leads them away from the nest to open areas where they can feed. If the first nest is destroyed, the hen will try to renest, but only one brood is raised each season. Before the young are half grown, they are fully feathered with their juvenile plumage. In August, the post-juvenile molt takes place producing the winter plumage, and the young bird is practically an adult by September. The female and her brood stay together during the fall. The cocks do not associate with the young throughout the brooding season.

In early autumn, loose flocks begin to form. As winter approaches, sharptails assemble in large flocks in areas that have good habitat and food supply. Sharptails will move many miles in search of these conditions.

Reproduction and Life Span

Sharptails nest in the grassland prairies close to their dancing grounds. In April or May, the hen nests on the ground in a slight depression in cover of grass, weeds, or low shrubs. The hen lays an average of 10-12 eggs and incubation takes about 24 days. From June to September, the hen and her brood will be together. From September to March, the birds are in their winter flocks.

By the time hunting season begins in September, half of the brood may have already died of natural causes. The average yearly loss of eggs and mortality of young birds can be as high as 80%. Cover and weather conditions can cause fluctuations in sharptail populations.

Feeding Habits and Patterns

Sharptail grouse are primarily vegetarians. Young chicks and adults eat many insects during the summer months, but even then their diet is mostly vegetable matter. The summer food includes large amounts of grasses, succulent forbs, seeds, and fruits. In the fall a wide variety of foods are consumed. If the sharptail's range includes farmland, wheat, barley, oats, alfalfa, clover, and many other farm crops are eaten. The winter diet of the sharptail is very different. During this season the birds feed on buds, twigs, catkins from trees, berries, rose hips, shrubs, and other woody plants.

Sharptails roost in the open prairie and on CRP tracts. They leave before sunrise to go to the feeding areas. They may feed close to the roosting area, or they may fly great distances. Most of the time the birds fly to their feeding grounds. Many times sharptails will both roost and feed in different locations within the same CRP tract. Once full, the birds will collect grit and moisture. Sharptails, like other gamebirds, rest, dust, loaf, and preen themselves after feeding. The birds spend most of their day loafing in prairie grasslands and CRP fields. Later in the day the birds move out to their feeding grounds before going to their roosting spots.

Sharptails are not as predictable as other upland birds. Look for grouse on grassy ridges during years of lush vegetation. Grouse can be widely scattered and will travel extensively to find good food and habitat.

Preferred Habitat and Cover

The core of sharptail habitat is shrub grassland and brush. Cover types used by sharptails include native grass prairie, hayfields, pasture lands, and grain fields with hardwood forest edges. Sharptails like large expanses of grasslands interspersed with shrub and brush-filled draws and coulees.

Much of this habitat in Montana has been converted to dryland farming or has been grazed intensively. To a certain degree, sharptails have adapted to modern agriculture. However, if all of the large expanses of grasslands disappear, so will the sharptails.

Locating Hunting Areas

The best sharp-tailed grouse range has large expanses of well-managed grassland and rolling hills broken by wooded and brushy draws, interspersed with cultivated fields.

1. Look for heavy cover with woody, brushy draws. It makes little difference what kind of cover, as long as there is enough of it.
2. Sharptails feed on an abundance of vegetation types, but in the fall the birds concentrate in grain fields near their summer range and will use the fields as long as the food is available.

3. Weather and seasonal food sources play an important part in location of sharptails. For example, when it is raining sharptails will not be in heavy cover.
4. Since sharptail ranges can be large, the birds usually fly to resting, loafing, and feeding areas. Traveling backcountry roads early in the morning and late in the day looking for bird movement can be effective.
5. Sharptails use trees, telephone wires, fence posts, old buildings, and other high objects to rest.
6. Use binoculars on flying or sitting birds to help locate sharptail hangouts.
7. Sharptails spend many hours resting around scattered patches of heavy cover, small tree clumps, woody reservoirs in isolated grasslands, and in croplands.
8. Knowing locations of established dancing grounds can help you find sharptails in the fall.

Don Thomas and his Lab examine a sharp-tailed grouse.

Looking for Sign

Sharptail droppings are white to green in color, much smaller than sage droppings, but only a little smaller than those of the pheasant. In roosting areas, the droppings are together in saucer-sized concentrations in many locations. Dusting bowls and resting areas will have feathers.

Hunting Methods

Even when sharptail populations are excellent, finding the birds can be difficult because their flocking habits and the variety of foods they consume contribute to their wide range and multiple movements. Once you find them, you will usually have great hunting. If you do find a large population of sharptails, take note of the type of food and habitat available. You will likely find other populations in similar areas.

On warm, sunny days sharptails can be found in clumps of brush, small pockets of trees and shrubs, on north slopes, in draws, and close to creek bottoms. Hunt these areas midday— grouse like to feed on buffalo berries and chokecherries. Late in the afternoon sharptails move to grassy areas and grain fields to feed and later to roost. Sharptails will be on fairly dense grassy hillsides and on edges of ridges in windy weather. Grouse can be in grassy flats, open ridges, and lightly grazed grasslands in wet and cool weather. Searching certain types of grasses (e.g. little blue stem) can be productive.

Successful hunters cover large areas looking for diverse types of cover—edges of fields, high stubble, high grasses, brushy draws, shallow coulees with patches of chokecherry, snowberry, and buffalo berry bushes, or large CRP tracts—and hunt the particular kinds of cover at the right time of day.

Late in the season, if sharptails have had some hunting pressure, they can be jumpy and flush wildly.

Hunting Dogs

Flushing and retrieving dogs are useful on sharptails, especially in heavy cover and narrow, wooded draws. Close-working dogs work well in CRP fields (where cover can be heavy) for flushing and retrieving downed birds.

Pointing dogs are great for sharptails. When a flock is flushed early in the season it usually doesn't fly far and can be relocated. Late in the season, if birds are in open or sparse cover feeding in hay meadows or grain fields, they tend to be wary and flush out of shooting range. I use my pointing dogs on sharptails throughout the season with fairly good results. I use more than one dog to cover lots of country.

Late in the season I hunt only heavy cover and try to find birds that have not been hunted before. Sharptails are much more likely to hold for a pointing dog in these conditions.

I also watch where the sharptails go when they flush out of range. I sometimes pursue them with success.

Field Preparations

Sharptails have dark meat. Like other wild game, people have differing opinions about its taste. Sharptail should be field drawn and cooled down as soon as possible. Hang or refrigerate birds for a few days before skinning.

Shot and Choke Suggestions

Early in the season and in close cover—No. 7½–6 shot, 1 to 1¼ oz. of shot.
    Chokes: improved and modified.
Mid-season and beyond— No. 7½–6 shot, 1⅛ to 1¼ oz. of shot.
    Chokes: modified and full.
Over dogs and all around—No. 6 shot, 1¼ oz. of shot.

SAGE GROUSE

Centrocercus urophasianus

QUICK FACTS

- **local names:** sage hen, sage cock, fool hen, sage chicken, spiny-tailed pheasant, cock of the plains, prairie bomber
- **size:** Montana's largest grouse, the cocks range 25-35" in length, have a wingspan of 36-38", and weigh 3-7 lbs. Males are often twice as large as females. Adult hens are 19-23" long, have a wingspan of 30-34", and weigh 3-4 lbs.
- **identification in flight:** mottled dark-brown back and wings, and white underwings that contrast strongly with the blackish belly. In the early season, both sexes look alike when flying. Later in the season, the males appear much darker and larger.

- Sage grouse are located in some of the most remote areas of Montana.
- In the spring and summer, sage grouse shift from a sagebrush diet to one dominated by forbs.
- There is some evidence that the strutting ground may be the hub for year-round activity, even though the range is large.
- Sage grouse may travel either long or short distances between their seasonal ranges.

Color

The female and male have similar coloring, a gray-brown mottled pattern that blends with the sagebrush. Older males are darker and have a white breast and black throat divided by a black band that is lacking in the female. Males also have a small yellow eye comb and greenish-yellow air sacs along the neck. Both sexes have long, stiff, pointed tail feathers, blackish bellies with white under the wings, and feathered legs.

Sound and Flight Pattern

Cocks have a deep, guttural clucking sound repeated slowly *(kuk-kuk kuk)* when first flushed. Females emit a cackling sound much like a chicken. However, neither sound is very noticeable. The male may run, rise slowly while keeping a straight course, and gradually ascend. Cocks will often fly long distances, tipping their wings periodically. Females rise quickly and dip side-to-side while flying. Sage grouse that are relatively undisturbed by hunting pressure will usually fly only short distances.

Sage Grouse Distribution

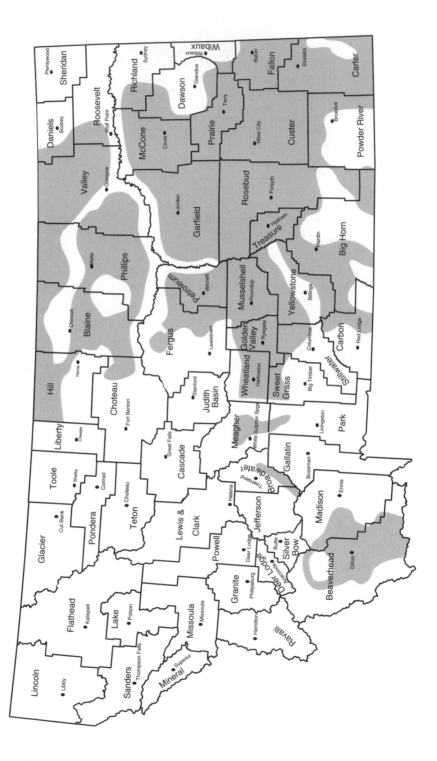

Similar Gamebirds

Very young cock and female pheasants could be confused with young sage grouse. Female pheasants have a brown belly and dark bare legs, while immature sage grouse are darker with brown-black belly patches, white under the wings, and feathered legs.

Flock or Covey Habits

In the spring, during the nesting period, hens tend to nest in colonies close to the strutting grounds (leks). The brood size is 6-8 birds. It is common for hens to exchange chicks and a female may bring up more chicks than she hatched. The cocks have no association with the young birds.

Sage grouse are gregarious and brood flocks often have close associations. The family groups break up in late summer to form loose, fragmented flocks. Immature birds form the biggest flocks. The adult males stay in separate groups. Young birds do not attain full growth until November.

Flocking begins in mid-autumn in preparation for winter. As winter approaches, the birds gather in groups numbering anywhere from 12 to 100. Sage grouse are not migratory, but as winter approaches, may travel considerable distances to lower elevations or high sage areas where food is not covered with snow.

Reproduction and Life Span

Sage grouse prefer tall sagebrush for nesting because it creates a high canopy that completely camouflages them. The hen lays 6-8 eggs and incubation takes 25 days. Hatching takes place mid-May through mid-June.

Sage grouse broods prefer open stands of sagebrush to feed on succulent forbs and insects. If this is unavailable, they will move to relatively moist areas of alfalfa fields, barrow pits, hay meadows, and creek bottoms.

Mortality is low during the early brood period unless weather conditions become severe. Natural mortality will bring the brood size down to 3 or 4 birds by September. The average annual turnover rate for young juveniles is about 65%.

Land allowed to remain in good vegetative condition is the important factor for sage grouse survival. The use of range by livestock and wild game must be kept within the carrying capacity of the land.

Feeding Habits and Patterns

No other upland gamebird obtains so much of its food from so few vegetation types. Only from spring until fall do the grouse feed on a variety of foods. Seventy percent of the sage grouse's diet is the leaves and blossoms of the sagebrush. Sage grouse do not have a thick-walled gizzard and lack the grinding capacity for breaking down seeds and other hard food.

When spring arrives sage grouse broaden their diet, adding numerous other greens and insects. Legumes (alfalfa, clover, and vetch), weeds (dandelion, salsify, wild mustard, and prickly lettuce), and a variety of grasses are utilized until late fall.

Juvenile sage grouse, like other gamebirds, eat insects in great numbers when first hatched, but soon add succulent forbs to their diet. Toward the end of summer, sage grouse will congregate during feeding time in alfalfa and clover fields if they are close to sagebrush tracts. As green vegetation declines, the diet is progressively one of sagebrush throughout the winter.

Sage grouse are fairly early risers; they feed and gather moisture for several hours in the morning. As summer progresses the birds will select moist areas or water sites to feed on green plants. Open water is used by the grouse when available; dew and moist vegetation suffices when there is no free water. Snow is used in the winter, although sage grouse can go many days without drinking water or dew. The birds usually fly to favorite watering places. They spend considerable time traveling to reach water areas in their range. Late morning and midday, the grouse retire to rest, dust, and sit in the shade. In winter they like to sun themselves in open areas. Late in the afternoon the grouse will start to move and will often seek moisture again before roosting.

Preferred Habitat and Cover

It is impossible to consider sage grouse distribution without considering sagebrush. Common sagebrush *(artemisia tridentata)* is a woody, strong-smelling, gray-green shrub of variable size. Common sagebrush grows from 2-7 feet, and has been labeled the most abundant shrub in North

Tony Route with a large male sage grouse.

America. There are many species of shrubby artemisia in the West, but only common sage has three-lobed leaves. Common sagebrush is found mainly in semi-arid country at an altitude of 2,000-8,000 feet. The shrub grassland in Montana includes arid lowland prairies and well-watered basins broken up by mountains. It is windy country and temperatures can change rapidly to produce extreme conditions.

Sagebrush range has other associated shrubs (rabbit brush, greasewood, and winter fat) and numerous grasses (western wheat, needle-and-thread grass, and blue bunchgrass). Many forbs (fringed sage wort, dandelion, yarrow, and vetch) make up the understory. These combine to make a variety of mixtures that are most useful to the sage grouse. The different types of sagebrush cover are used for various purposes: sparse or open areas for strutting grounds; tall and thick cover stands for loafing, roosting, and winter feed areas; medium-low and open cover for nesting.

A lot of shrub grassland has been converted to irrigated crops such as alfalfa and hay meadows. In places where these changes have not been too extensive, the habitat is still suitable for the sage grouse.

Locating Hunting Areas

Sage grouse are tied to large blocks of shrub grassland. This sagebrush vegetation is found in Montana in the eastern half and southwestern corner of the state. (See sage grouse distribution map.)

1. In early September, sage grouse will be in moist areas where there are green plants.
2. Sage grouse gather near permanent water sites even though they don't need free water.
3. When the range has an abundance of vegetation and moisture, birds can be scattered throughout the sage. In dry years the bird will be concentrated in green belts.
4. Increased moisture in the fall can make sagebrush more palatable, shifting birds to a wider area.
5. Areas with water, sagebrush, and hay meadows often have concentrations of juvenile sage grouse.
6. Creek bottoms and irrigated channels through large sagebrush areas hold pockets of sage grouse.
7. CRP fields adjacent to sagebrush tracts are used for feeding on greens.
8. Sage grouse rest, dust, and preen at midday and will be in their sagebrush loafing areas.
9. Be aware of weather conditions and seasonal changes as fall progresses. Sage grouse have a large range and move to taller sagebrush cover types as the weather gets colder.

Looking for Sign

Sage grouse have large pale-green and white chicken-like droppings. Accumulation of droppings is an indication of loafing or roosting areas. Favorite preening and dusting areas will have feathers. Fresh droppings are firm, moist, and bright, while older droppings are dull and crumble easily. Dark black tarry deposits are also secreted by sage grouse. The discharge is called caecal droppings. This material from the caecal ducts does not last as long as other droppings and can indicate a sage grouse's recent presence.

Hunting Methods

Sage grouse live in big, open country and there is a lot more sagebrush than there are sage grouse. If unfamiliar with the area, drive to a hilltop or walk to a high ridge and survey the country with binoculars, looking for green belts, ponds, creeks, reservoirs, CRP or alfalfa fields, different type of sage cover, and habitat that is not over-grazed.

Sage grouse hunting takes a lot of walking, but by carefully examining the country, time can be saved. Early in the season, hunt moist areas in the morning and evenings looking for sage grouse sign. Hunt the higher sage midday looking for resting areas and dusting places. Hillsides can be productive in warm weather.

Most successful hunters cover large areas in basins not more than a mile from a water source.

Sage grouse will be on their winter grounds later in the season. Look for heavy, high vegetation.

Hunting Dogs

Since large areas have to be covered for sage grouse, dogs are an important part of the hunt. Flushing and retrieving dogs will save you many miles of walking when looking for birds and do a great job on sage grouse once the birds are located.

My personal preference is to hunt sage grouse with pointing dogs. I use two or three dogs and cover lots of country. Sage grouse leave good scent, but scenting conditions can be poor in arid sagebrush country. When conditions are good, dogs can pick up the scent at great distances. Young and adult birds that have had no hunting pressure hold well for pointing dogs.

Field Preparations

People have very different opinions about eating sage grouse. Some find only young birds in early season palatable. Others think all sage grouse is bitter. I think sage grouse is delicious if proper care is taken in the field. In warm weather, field draw* the birds as soon as possible and put in a cool place so air can circulate around them, or put them in a cooler with ice. I like to hang my birds or place them on a refrigerator rack for several days. I do not remove the feathers until I prepare them for the table or the freezer. Most sage grouse I skin and cut into pieces.

Shot and Choke Suggestions

Early in the season: No. 6 shot, 1¼ oz. of shot.
Chokes: modified and full.
Mid-season and beyond: No. 6-5 shot, 1¼ oz. of shot.
Chokes: modified and full.
Over dogs and all around: No. 6 shot.

---

* To field draw a bird, use a pair of game shears or a knife with a gut-hook blade. Cut an incision of 2-3" at the bottom of the breast. Remove the stomach, windpipe, and entrails. Wipe the cavity with a paper towel before hanging.

FIRST SAGE GROUSE
by Ben O. Williams

It was late in the year for sage grouse, but Chuck had never had the opportunity to hunt this magnificent prairie bird. We drove to the top of the hill to one of my favorite sage grouse hangouts and stopped to look over the vast country. The pale blue sky was all around us; the air was crisp with a slight northerly, moist wind in our faces; the frost sparkled on the sagebrush waiting for the morning sun to give warmth. In the distance were two large reservoirs, tiny specks in this expansive wilderness. We walked down the narrow gumbo road, looking over both sides of the ridge down into the large sagebrush basins.

"Chuck," I said, "I think the birds are gone. They must have left their summer range."

Disappointed, we drove back to the main highway, the sun reflecting off our rearview mirror, and stopped to talk to a rancher fixing fence. We kicked dirt for a while and talked about weather, cattle prices being down, the high school baseball team, and the lack of sage grouse. The rancher said, pointing, "They went that way over a week ago, but I did see some a mile off the highway by the gumbo buttes two days ago when I was looking for strays."

We thanked him and told him we would stop by to see him before we left the country. We got back in the rig and turned south toward the buttes. I looked at Chuck and said, "They must be on their wintering grounds. I'll bet we can find them."

I had hunted the area before and had a fairly good idea where the grouse would be. Chuck and I hunted around the gumbo buttes with three pointing dogs for about an hour without success, but we did see three big male sage grouse get up wild. I watched them set their wings going over the low ridge. "Chuck, let's go back to the pickup," I said. "The birds may have told us something."

We drove three miles back down the country road, turned left onto a BLM dirt road, and headed in the general direction the sage grouse had flown. After a mile, the sagebrush looked high and thick against the hillsides.

"Good winter range," I thought. I stopped and pulled the outfit off the trail. A lone deer hunter in a faded yellow pickup drove by as we were parking, looking at us and our dog hunting rig with either disgust or amusement, I don't know which. He was heading for a distant stand of bull pines on the ridge line, thousands of sage bushes away.

It was big country, but a place to start. We got out of the pickup, stretched our legs, and poured ourselves a cup of coffee. "No hurry," I said. "It's going to be a long day."

Sage grouse rise in a sagebrush basin.

After coffee Chuck asked, "Which dogs do you want out?"

"Let's start with Winston and I'll think about the other two." I got out the beeper collars. Chuck put a collar on Winston and put him on the ground. He turned to get another collar, and before Winston had a chance to christen any sage plants, he was on point.

"Chuck, you'd better get ready. Winston's on point!" Winston moved 20 yards up the hill and froze. The scenting conditions were perfect. Chuck grabbed his vest and, with shells falling everywhere, fumbled for his gun. Winston stood firm. Chuck followed. Thirty sage grouse boomed out from the hillside, flying across the sagebrush basin.

Chuck shot his first sage grouse that day.

GRAY PARTRIDGE
Perdix perdix

QUICK FACTS

- **local name:** Hungarian partridge, Hun, Hunkie, European partridge
- **size:** Montana's only true covey bird. Both sexes are 12-13" in length, have a wingspan of 15-17", and weigh 13-16 oz.
- **identification in flight:** Huns are strong flyers with rapid wingbeats. They make quick turns in flight. Early in the season, they usually fly short distances making right or left turns, frequently flying to a knoll or ridge and then dropping out of sight. Their bright, rusty tail is conspicuous in flight.

- The gray partridge, usually referred to as the Hungarian partridge, is not native to North America.
- If good habitat is maintained in a particular location, it will support a covey of Huns year after year.
- In Montana's big, open country, the grasslands and associated cover types have to be well managed to carry Hungarian partridge populations.
- Huns, like most covey birds, are limited to their occupied range, but have some movement during their pairing break up.
- Old abandoned homesteads with shelter belts are excellent Hun hangouts.
- Climate, soil, and topography are important factors in gray partridge habitat.

Color

The sexes are similar in color. The adults have reddish-brown and gray backs, cinnamon heads, gray breasts, gray sides with wide vertical chestnut bars, and often a dark brown horseshoe on the lower breast. Both males and females can have a horseshoe, but it is more common on the male. During breeding season, males have a red ring around their eyes. The center two tail feathers have bars, and the outer tail feathers are bright, rusty red.

Sound and Flight Pattern

Coveys rise in a single noisy burst of whirring wings and loud, harsh shrieks that sound like a rusty gate being opened *(keee-uck-kuta-kut-kut)*. Huns have rapid wingbeats alternating with glides.

Similar Gamebirds

Hungarian partridge are the smallest and only covey upland gamebird in Montana. When a covey is scattered, a single Hun could be confused with a young sharp-tailed grouse.

GRAY PARTRIDGE DISTRIBUTION

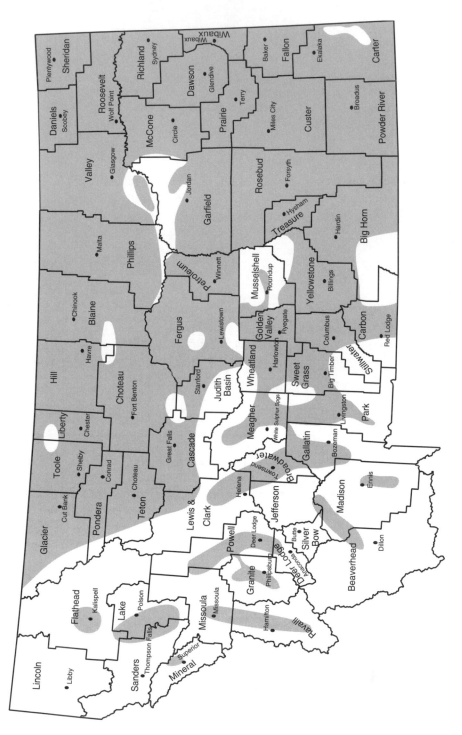

Flock or Covey Habits

The entire covey generally takes off together and flies in a tight formation. If the covey is broken up, birds will call and assemble as soon as possible. Coveys are family groups and remain together until spring breakup. In late fall and winter, more than one covey may band together.

Reproduction and Life Span

The hen partridge makes a simple nest—a slight depression in the ground with a few leaves, grass, and feathers. It is usually in bushes (snowberry), long grass, or under other plant cover (lupine). During the egg laying process, which can take up to 3 weeks, she will carefully cover the eggs with grass or dead leaves. The average number of eggs is 15, but can be anywhere from 5 to 22. If the first nest is destroyed, the hen may renest at least once, but she will lay fewer eggs. The incubation period is 24 days and the peak hatching time in Montana is from mid-June to mid-July. Only the hen sits on the eggs, but the male remains in the area. When the chicks are hatched, the parents share the chore of raising the brood.

If disturbed, the young birds freeze and the parents attempt to draw the intruder away. As summer progresses, the brood becomes more mobile and moves about freely, extending their range. They roost in a circle, much like bobwhite quail.

The brood is the fall covey, but adults that have no young will sometimes join a covey. Vegetation, climate, and seasonal weather conditions are the important factors in population fluctuation from year to year. The annual mortality rate of Hungarian partridge can be over 70%.

Feeding Habits and Patterns

Huns are early risers and will start moving long before sunrise. They are primarily vegetarian. The main sources of food are cropland grains, seeds of herbs, and leafy greens, although young Huns eat many insects during their growth period. Adults will also eat insects when available. In some areas of Montana, waste grain may make up 60% or more of the birds' diet. In prairie grasslands or large CRP tracts where grain is not available, Huns will feed on a wide range of seeds, forbs, and grasses. Greens are probably taken as soon as they become available. Many greens in CRP tracts start early in spring and remain late in the fall due to protective cover overhead, thus giving wildlife an extended period to feed on green vegetation.

During the winter, Huns can work down through the snow in search of food. Huns living in open grassland remain on the prairie as long as food is available. When it is not, they move to heavier brush draws or open areas without snow. Windy winters can be beneficial to grassland partridge.

As fall approaches, Huns feed on mature weed seeds and cereal grains. The birds' main moisture comes from dew, rain droplets, snow, and greens. Standing water is used by partridge at times, but is not essential. Regardless, many times Huns are found around an open water source because water complexes usually have useful Hun habitat associated with them.

If the weather is warm, Huns look for shady places to hang out. In cool or cold weather, they will move into denser cover.

Grit is definitely essential to Huns and is collected in many different places. In the fall and winter, when the birds' diet is mainly grain and/or seeds, grit is particularly needed.

In the late afternoon they move out again to their feeding areas. Resting and feeding areas can be close together or a considerable distance apart. When close, the birds may walk to and from these spots.

Preferred Habitat and Cover

Gently rolling topography—bare knolls, draws, and shallow depressions—seems to suit the gray partridge best. Soils that are sandy, loamy, loose, and highly fertile make good Hun habitat. The highest population of partridge may be on the northern plains where the grasslands collide with the Rocky Mountain front. Only the higher elevations and montane forests do not support Huns. Climate that is cool and moderately dry appears to be best for the Huns.

Important habitat needs are related to vegetation combinations. Two essential types of cover are needed by partridge; grassland and cropland combination and grassland herbaceous cover (native grasses, hay, alfalfa, and other weed seed vegetation). I have found that Hun coveys are not as plentiful in grassland/herb habitat

Eliza hunts gray partridge (Huns) in a CRP field.

combinations and their daily movements encompass a larger area than coveys occupying grassland/cropland combinations.

As long as the grasslands have plenty of brushy, woody draws with large amounts of weedy herbs and other cover types that are well-managed, Huns will occupy these areas.

Locating Hunting Areas

As mentioned above, hunting areas have to be linked to habitat combinations. Montana has thousands of square miles that fit this formula. To locate Hun country look for:

1. Grasslands and dryland crops interrupted by draws, grassy slopes, and rolling hills;
2. Irrigation projects with grain crops and other agricultural crops interspersed with cover types;
3. Grasslands with multiple vegetation types and cover that is not overgrazed. The more cover, the better;
4. CRP fields surrounded by cover and croplands;
5. Areas used by both sharptails and pheasants.
6. Hungarian partridge, early in the morning or evening, along established roadways collecting grit and flying to different areas. (If a covey is found in this manner, more than likely other coveys will be in the same area.) Montana has regulations that forbid shooting right along these roads. Always ask permission before hunting private land along roadways.

Looking for Sign

Gray partridge droppings are the smallest of any gamebird in Montana. They are pale green with a dark green end. Droppings will be in large circular deposits in roosting areas because the covey sleeps in a circle. Huns will usually roost in the same area for many nights. CRP fields are excellent places for Huns to roost. Dusting bowls and relaxing areas will have scattered droppings and feathers. Hun droppings do not last as long as other gamebird droppings—if found, you can be assured the birds are in the vicinity.

Hunting Methods

When Hungarian populations are excellent, the birds are not hard to find. They are very active early and late in the day while feeding and moving about. They glean food at a fast pace. Early in the season hunt likely feeding stations along the edges of crop and hay fields, and CRP fields that have green herbs available.

Young Huns' movements are relatively short—usually flights are less than a quarter-mile. As the birds mature and become stronger, their flights will increase.

I think of a covey's lifetime range as a circle. When the Huns are plentiful or the habitat is excellent, covey circles overlap. The circles become larger and do not overlap as much in sparse years. Once you learn where covey circles are, finding the

HUN COUNTRY
by Ben Williams

The Hungarian partridge was not here when the Bird People (Crow Indians) traveled the foothills of the lofty mountains. Gray partridge came from central Europe and were introduced into the Northwest around 1900. In the early days, Alberta and Saskatchewan established the largest Hun population, and as the populations grew, the Huns moved south to Montana.

The birds live in grainfields and high grasslands. The best Hun hunting is where the grainfields meet high pasture country and the sagebrush draws run into grainfields, leaving long open strips that converge like a large mosaic.

* * * * * * * *

The Brittanys didn't seem to mind the warm weather. The air was clear, a little windy, with no threat of rain. It wasn't really cold enough to be a good hunting day for dogs.

I breed my Brittanys primarily for Hun hunting. By Brittany standards my dogs are large, leggy, and wide ranging. I also like more white in their coats so I can see them from farther away.

The three Brittanys were turned out and Eliza uncased her 20-gauge over/under. Eliza and I walked the rolling country for several miles. We started up the creek following the edge of sagebrush. Winston's cast was across the wide golden field. He turned back along the old wooden post fence crosswind and stopped. Muffin cut out of the tall grass draw and slammed into a back. Shoe was on the other side of the creek. He saw Muffin stop and he pulled up and honored.

Eliza had never hunted with so many dogs before, and seeing the three dogs on point was exciting. No matter how many years I devote to hunting and dogs, I am still awed by this. Eliza's pulse quickened as she moved up fast, breathing deeply. There was plenty of time. Huns don't run like pheasants or set like bob-whites; they just jog a little and fan out. The Huns burst into the sky.

Eliza shot a pair of Huns that warm autumn day.

birds becomes easier. I have hunted many of the same circles (where the habitat has not changed) for over 30 years. That is one of the ways I predict the population density for the upcoming season.

Once the covey is found and flushed, the birds will stay together as long as possible. Most of the time the same covey can be pursued over and over. When the covey is finally separated, like any other covey bird, the singles will sit tight and the birds will call each other, trying to assemble. Quite often they will run or fly back to their original flushing point.

After feeding, Huns will return to an open area to loaf and find grit. If the weather is warm, Huns will gather in shady cover such as juniper bushes or chokecherry bushes. Huns may occupy a rock outcropping to sun themselves in cool weather. They will relax along creek bottoms, bushy draws, and cool, moist areas midday. Huns also like to use steep hillsides to rest or relax.

Hunting Dogs

If the Huns have an excellent hatch and the coveys are numerous in the fall, hunting without a dog can be good. If you do not have a dog, follow along the edges of fields, fence rows, patches of cover, or creek bottoms.

Retrievers and flushing dogs can be very effective when hunting Huns along weedy draws, CRP fields, brushy bottom lands, or any area with heavy cover that will help to hold the bird close to the hunter. In most cases, Huns will flush at a greater distance when they are hunted with flushing and retrieving dogs.

Close-working pointing dogs can be outstanding, especially if the hunter has slowed down a bit and would just like to hunt short distances. When the Huns are pointed and flushed, close-working dogs can do wonders finding singles and locating the covey again.

I have had my own Brittany blood lines for over 40 years. I use more than one dog at a time with beeper collars so I can hear the dogs in this rolling terrain and coulee country.

I prefer a partridge dog to hunt wide because there is more country than there are Huns. Many coveys live in big, rolling hill country. I walk the highest points along ridge lines or tops of sloping hills. When I'm in more level terrain, I still try to seek the highest ground. Using this method, I can scan miles of country and see the dogs working. Also, I can get to the dogs faster by going downhill, and see where the coveys go if they happen to leave before I arrive. If hunting Hun country with many draws leading down to a main water course, I hunt the draws from ridge to ridge instead of following them. It may make your blood pump a little faster, but you'll have a better chance of locating the covey. Hun hunting can be tough no matter what you do, but it is worth the effort.

Table Preparations

Gray partridge have medium-dark meat on their breast and legs. Draw the birds as soon as possible in warm weather. Hanging in a cool place or refrigerating for a few days seems to help the flavor and reduce stringiness. I skin the bird just before preparation for the table.

Shot and Choke Suggestions

Early hunting season: No. 7½ shot, ⅞-1¼ oz. of shot.
Chokes: improved and modified.
Late in the season: No. 7½ shot, 1¼ oz. of shot.
Chokes: improved, modified, or full.

PHEASANT

Phasianus colchicus

QUICK FACTS

- **local names:** ring-necked pheasant, ringneck, Chinese pheasant, chink
- **size:** adult cocks are 30-36" in length—unlike other gamebirds, the tail accounts for almost ⅔ of their length. Cocks have a wingspan of 32-34" and weigh 2½-3½ lbs. Adult hens are 20-25" long with a wingspan of 24-29" and an average weight of 2-2¼ lbs.
- **identification in flight:** brightly colored male appears much darker than the female. Other features of the cock are the white collar around its neck and long dark tail. The male will sometimes cackle in flight, but this is not a sure identification factor. Following a pheasant in the sun or in low light can confuse the identification of the sexes. *When in doubt, don't shoot!* Hunting in Montana is for male pheasants only.

- Distribution of food and cover is important. Twenty acres of cover scattered throughout a crop field is more effective than 20 square acres.
- CRP has been a boon to pheasant populations. In Montana, 2.7 million acres have been taken out of agricultural production and planted to permanent cover.
- Pheasants Forever, Inc. is an organization that was formed to protect land and enhance pheasant and other wildlife populations throughout North America through public awareness and education, habitat restoration, development and maintenance, and improvements in land and water management policies. I highly recommend that all upland bird hunters join Pheasants Forever. Membership is $20 a year and includes $5 for the magazine, *Pheasants Forever, The Journal of Upland Game Conservation*, published 5 times a year. Contact your local chapter or write: Pheasants Forever, Inc., 3522 La Bore Road, St. Paul, MN 55110.

Color

Many Montana upland bird hunters consider the adult male pheasant the handsomest of all gamebirds. It is certainly a magnificent, brilliantly plumed bird. Well established in North America, the wild pheasant was introduced in Montana in the late 1800s following the plowshare and agricultural development in the state.

The cock has ear tufts and bright-red cheek patches around its eyes forming wattles around much of the head. The beak is bluish-white and chicken-like. The rest of the head and neck is iridescent green separated from the body by a white collar. The body is colorful with many rich metallic, bronze, brown, red, black, and gray

PHEASANT DISTRIBUTION

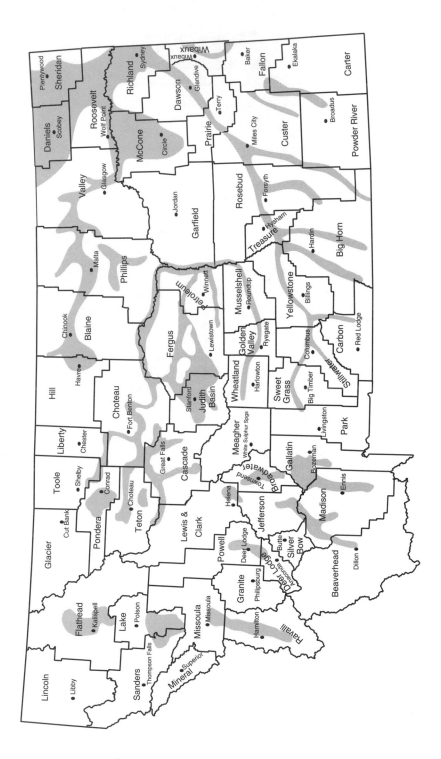

markings. The long, pointed tail is light brown with dark bars. The legs lack feathers but have spurs.

The hen is smaller and has several shades of mottled light browns, with dark markings throughout her body. She does not have a white ring around her neck. The female has a pointed, light brown, barred tail that is shorter than her partner's. The hen's legs are bare and lack spurs.

Sound and Flight Pattern

Cocks will often utter a coarse cackle when flying *(cuct-et, cuct-et, cuct-cuct).* Hens are mostly silent but can make a high pitched *queep-queep.*

Although pheasants would rather run than fly, they are strong flyers for short periods. They take off explosively in any direction except the one you are expecting. The rounded wings are short compared to their body size. The wings are cupped and built for sudden power strokes. Within seconds, pheasants can hit speeds of up to 35 miles per hour. The pheasant locks its wings and can glide up to a quarter-mile, flap its wings, and start the glide again. Many cock birds will fly and glide nearly a mile before landing with their running gear down. The distance of the flight depends on the proximity of cover the bird is looking for as an escape route.

Similar Gamebirds

Early in the season, young pheasants of both sexes can be confused with young sharp-tailed and sage grouse. Young pheasants have brown bellies with bare legs and long tails. Sharptails have shorter tails, white bellies with feathered legs, and a plump shape. Young sage grouse have feathered legs and black belly patches. All three species have different flight patterns, wingbeats, and vocal sounds. With a little practice, it is easy to identify these characteristics.

Flock or Covey Habits

By fall, young birds have reached adult size and the broods have broken up for pre-winter conditioning. Pheasants are in mixed-sex pairs, singles, or small flocks in late fall. In years of high pheasant populations, large flocks of 40 or more birds will remain in protective cover close to food sources.

Winter is a critical time for pheasants in Montana. Great losses can occur during severe winters. It's important for pheasants to have heavy protective cover and adequate winter food to minimize losses and achieve a breeding population.

Reproduction and Life Span

Pheasants nest on the ground in a wide variety of cover types—open grassland, CRP fields, ditch banks, fence rows, hay meadows, alfalfa fields, or any brushy area with heavy cover. Nests in undisturbed cover have the best chance for success, while nests in sparse habitat have little chance of survival. Pheasants lay 8-12 eggs with an incubation period of 23 days. If the nest is destroyed, the hen is quite persistent and will renest. Pheasants raise only one brood each year, but during the early fall you may see birds of different sizes because of renesting.

Hatching activity peaks in mid-June, coinciding with the mowing season for alfalfa and hay in many Montana counties.

Clutches of eggs differ in number. The average is 8-12, but usually only 30% or less of young pheasants survive to the following spring. A two-year old pheasant is comparatively old. Studies have indicated that less than 4% of the pheasant population is over three years old.

Pheasant population numbers are affected by diversity of cover crops, weather, seasonal changes, and longterm land practices. The quantity and quality of the habitat is the determining factor in the population numbers for any species. The CRP has contributed greatly to higher nesting success.

Feeding Habits and Patterns

Pheasants normally roost on the ground in cover such as CRP fields or grassy draws. In cold weather, they roost in cattails and other dense cover. Pheasants leave their roosting place at daybreak and begin feeding after sunrise. During overcast days or bad morning weather, they may change their feeding habits considerably. If there is a change in weather or a front approaching, the pheasant will feed longer to take advantage of the light.

At daybreak, pheasants gather along edges of roads, rock outcroppings, or in grain fields to feed and collect grit. Daybreak and sunset are excellent times to drive gravel roads and spot birds for the next day's hunt. Once full of food and grit, the pheasant seeks denser cover along waterways and draws, preferably with a canopy of cover such as willows, cattails, rose bushes, or other high vegetation to rest. In the middle of the day, birds may move to dusting areas for short periods, and on cool days, occasionally lie out in the open to sun themselves. Later in the day, the birds begin moving to feeding grounds and grit spots before returning to their roosting places.

Young pheasant chicks eat insects to get protein needed for growth. Soon they learn to eat a wide variety of foods. Young and adult Montana pheasants dine mostly on cereal grains. Wheat, barley, oats, corn, beans, peas, sorghum, weed seeds, grasses, wild oats, thistle, sunflower seeds, fruits, dandelions, sweet clover, insects, snails, and many other plants and animals are consumed by pheasants. Pheasants obtain water in many forms, including insects, fruits, green vegetation, rain, dew, and snow. Creeks, ponds, and ditches are useful but not necessary. Wetlands are used by pheasants mostly for protection.

Lyn Grinstein works three Brittanys in a CRP field.

Preferred Habitat and Cover

Ideal pheasant habitat has a balance between non-cultivated land and cultivated land. Large blocks of dryland farming provide a food source for pheasants but lack cover for protection. Large areas of shrub grasslands and plains grassland have cover but no food.

Diverse cover types and food crops perform a variety of functions in pheasants' lives. Trees, shrubs, woody plants, and thorny bushes found mostly around waterways provide the pheasant with shade and protection from wind, sun, and predators. Undisturbed vegetation provides nesting and brood cover. Wetlands, cattail marshes, weedy patches, and brushy draws are used for loafing, dusting, and roosting. Edges of fields, fence rows, ditches, narrow draws running into grain fields, and roadsides provide travel lanes for food or escape.

While training dogs one August, I observed through my binoculars, a red fox with pups by her den beside a creek bottom. The willows were high and the cover heavy. Around the den was a large mound of open grassland about 30 yards square. There was a group of young pheasants chasing grasshoppers, paying little attention to the vixen and the pups rolling around in the dirt. After a time, the female fox got up, stretched her front feet forward and yawned, sending the pheasants back into the cover. I approached the site with my dogs, putting the fox family down the hole and the pheasants on the run for heavy cover. The dogs pointed several birds, but most of the pheasants funneled down along the creek. I returned to the den and examined the bones and fox scat scattered around the site. I did find a number of pheasant bones, but to my surprise the scat was mostly rodent bones, grasshopper wings, fruits, and other vegetation I could not identify. The habitat provided the young birds with an escape route, thus keeping them safe from the fox. That fall the pheasant hunting on this stretch of creek bottom was outstanding. The combination of different vegetation cover in an area is the key to good pheasant populations and pheasant hunting.

Locating Hunting Areas

In Montana, the hunter will find the right combination of cover types plus croplands together:
1. along major river bottom lands and their tributaries;
2. around irrigation projects;
3. in grain croplands, dryland areas interrupted by brushy draws and steep grassy slopes, marshes, reservoirs, and other terrain unsuitable for tillage;
4. in CRP tracts (many CRP fields are bordered by grain cropland);
5. near large water impoundments with cover and adjacent croplands.

Looking for Sign

Pheasant droppings are similar to those of chickens. The birds scratch the ground to uncover food and make well-defined dusting bowls. Favorite loafing places will have feathers.

Hunting Methods

There are possibly as many ways to hunt pheasants as there are pheasant hunters. Here are some things that work for me. Learn the birds' daily routine (feeding habits, roosting areas). Early in the morning when the birds are feeding, hunt along the edges of grainfields, old homesteads adjacent to crops, draws running into croplands, high-cut stubble fields close to vegetation areas, cover along fence rows with feed, and reservoirs and stock ponds located near food sources. These are the places where birds have food and escape routes.

It may take only an hour or so for the pheasant to get enough grain and grit. After they loaf, the pheasants will move into CRP tracts, high cover, and weedy hangouts. Later in the season, due to hunting pressure or cold weather, pheasants will hide in heavier cover like cattails. Hunt the CRP fields, creek bottoms, large draws, and woody thickets in the middle of the day. Late in the afternoon, as birds move back to feeding areas, hunt the same cover as you did in the morning.

Hunting large fields of CRP or croplands without dogs can be futile, but hunting the same area with a good dog can be outstanding. Two or more hunters can walk the fields from opposite ends, cutting the edges of the field. This prevents pheasants from running out. Another approach is to move along in a zig-zag pattern, stopping often to give the pheasants a chance to flush. Pheasants often circle around and are pushed into the trailing person. The important thing about this maneuver is that each hunter remains aware of the others' locations.

When hunting creek bottoms and long draws, blocking by two or more hunters with or without dogs can be effective. Meandering creeks, oxbows, and turns can provide a place to cut off birds. Isolated patches of cover should be approached from different ends.

One of my favorite ways to hunt pheasants is to follow a creek bottom with my dogs, running the birds ahead and forcing them into the small side draws that either run out or lead to stubble fields. Later, I hunt the small draws slowly. Some of the pheasants will hold for the dogs.

Hunting with Dogs

A dog that hunts close and likes to retrieve birds is the best kind of pheasant dog. Fast-moving pointing dogs occasionally pin down pheasants, but many good pointers have a lot of trouble with them. While the dog is on point, the pheasant runs out. Pointers that work close or trail are worthwhile pheasant dogs.

Flushing and retrieving dogs are the best all-around pheasant dogs. A dog working back-and-forth in front of the hunter within 25 yards will be successful. It takes a smart pheasant to escape a flushing dog.

After shooting a pheasant, the first responsibility is to find the bird. Any well-trained bird dog, whatever the breed, will save many downed and crippled birds.

A good water dog often comes in handy.

Table Preparations

Pheasant breasts are white meat and the legs are medium-dark. I draw my birds as soon as possible and hang them in a cool place for at least a week. This seems to reduce stringiness and add flavor. Pick or skin the bird just prior to cooking.

Shot and Choke Suggestions

Early in the season and in close cover: No. 7½-6 shot, 1⅛-1¼ oz. of shot.
Chokes: improved and modified.
Mid- and late season: No. 7½, 6, or 5 shot, 1¼ oz. of shot.
Chokes: improved, modified, and full.
Over dogs and all around: No. 6 shot.

PLEASANT PHEASANTS
By Ben Williams

*There are times when western pheasants hold well
and the heart beats a little faster.*

The country of the wild, western pheasant rolls from the Dakotas to the lofty Rocky Mountain front.

Like all pheasants, Montana birds love to run. But here, the birds prefer to run uphill when pursued. And these long-legged track stars can cover a lot of ground whether horizontal or vertical. In hill country it is critical to get the pheasant to stop and hold for a pointing dog.

I use Brittanys to hunt pheasants as well as other upland gamebirds. My dogs handle pheasants well despite the birds' tendency to run. Three and sometimes four dogs can be effective as long as the dogs honor each other.

In the pheasant country of Montana a hunter might find a mixed bag of birds—Huns, sharptails, and even a sage grouse—and climbing to upper draws can yield anything. Huns and sharptails will fly from draw to draw but the pheasant flies back to the creek bottom and the work begins again. The western pheasant is indeed a challenge.

* * * *

Flying connections were made on time and the big jet landed at Billings airport on schedule. Tom and Ken, Virginians, walked off the aircraft and greeted me with big smiles and handshakes. The Billings airport is not large and by the time we arrived at the baggage room the guns and gear were on the conveyer belt. The grips were loaded in the back of the Wagoneer above the dog boxes while my three Brittanys—Shoe, Muffin, and Winston—gave Tom and Ken a happy vocal greeting.

Billings is the largest city in Montana, but is not big by most standards, and we were out of the city limits in a short time. Two hours and a small-town lunch later (Tom and Ken think small-town cafes are the best places to eat in Montana and I have to agree), we bounded along a gumbo dirt road, following the rolling contours across the golden bench land. Tom looked at Ken and asked, "Have you ever seen this much wheat with grassy draws running through it?"

Ken shook his head and said, "I wonder how many birds are out there."

I said, "Hungarian partridge should be on the bench. But I believe the pheasants will be in the main creek bottom, around the heavy cover and willows." It was the time of day pheasants like to congregate, dust, and rest. Willows provide a good canopy cover, and the understory was clear, giving the birds protection from overhead predators and a view of potential danger.

I drove the Wagoneer off the bench, down the winding road, and eventually turned into the ranch yard. On the way down, we could see pheasants in the willows. After stopping briefly to talk to the rancher, I continued for a half-mile and parked near the creek.

The ranch was typical of many in central and eastern Montana. It had six miles of meandering creek bottom, and beavers had flooded parts of the low areas, creating thick cover of willows, cattails, and bulrushes.

The combination of marshy areas and clusters of woody vegetation made this excellent pheasant habitat. The valley we were hunting was not wide, stretching at most a half-mile on each side of the creek. The creek had many oxbows and deep-cut banks. The hills gave way to the rolling bench land and from the valley floor to the top of the grain fields the elevation was 200 to 300 feet. Long coulees started at the creek and ran like fingers up into the fields. The coulees were very steep at the bottom of the drainage and shallow out into long grassy draws extending to the grain fields. Early morning and late afternoon always found pheasants using the coulees to get to the grain.

The plan was simple—start hunting the creek, working the dogs along the willows and heavy brush to move the birds into the coulees ahead. Some birds would try to cut around us, we reasoned, but with three dogs it would be difficult. There were places along the creek where dogs might pin pheasants, but our objective was to drive birds up the coulees and into the grassy draws.

The back window of the Wagoneer was open and the three Brittanys smelled the crisp air. Shoe, Muffin, and Winston were getting impatient. Ken, Tom, and I sat in the vehicle for a few minutes watching pheasants moving away from us along the willows.

"Well, gentlemen," I said, "I think it's time you get into your hunting gear. I'll take my camera this trip." Tom carried a light over/under, Ken a side-by-side; both 12-gauge, improved and modified. Hunting gear in place, dogs ready, we headed for the willows.

The hunters moved along the drainage. Winston, the youngest dog, was excited, moving too far ahead but still pushing pheasants into the coulees. Shoe and Muffin trapped several birds on the inside of an oxbow. Shoe swung to the left, then slammed into a classic point. Ken hustled over and up came a big rooster. At the same moment, Muffin locked up tight and Tom moved in—rooster number two! The Brittanys retrieved the pheasants. Ken and Tom walked back and we shook hands, praised the dogs, and admired the birds. Winston returned, having missed all the action.

We spent the afternoon walking long coulees, following the escape route, the three dogs working hard in grassy draws and isolated cover. Some birds flushed wild, but others jumped at our feet, just in front of rigid dogs. Finally the shadows from the hills grew long, and we could feel the cool air of evening moving in.

Ken said, "What a pleasant day to hunt pheasants!"

Tom smiled and nodded.

RUFFED GROUSE DISTRIBUTION

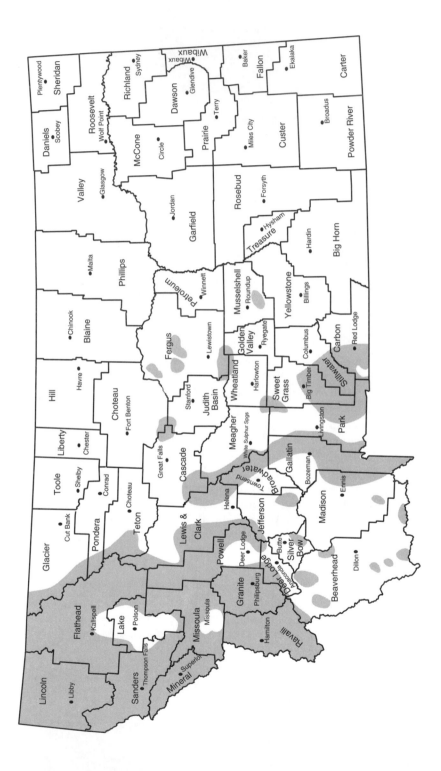

RUFFED GROUSE
Bonasa umbellus

QUICK FACTS

- **local names:** wood grouse, partridge, mountain chicken, birch partridge, mountain pheasant
- **size:** Ruffed grouse are fairly large—15-19" long, with a wingspan of 23-25" and a weight of 1½-2 lbs. Adult males are usually larger and heavier than females.
- **identification in flight:** Chicken-like in size, and has a thunderous roar of wingbeats when flushing from the ground or a tree. In flight, the dark bars on the side are very prominent, as is the long, dark, fanned tail.

- Ruffed grouse are native to Montana.
- In Montana, ruffed grouse, Franklin's (spruce) grouse, and blue grouse are all referred to as mountain grouse. There is a mixed bag limit for all mountain grouse, rather than a per-species limit.
- Adult ruffed grouse spend most of their lives in a small area.
- Plant succession is important in ruffed grouse ecology. Grouse cover is always changing.
- Perfect cover for ruffed grouse is predominantly mixed woodland.

Color

Montana has the gray phase ruffed grouse, which is common in the Northwest and at higher elevations. Both sexes have "ruff feathers" on each side of the neck. The head, back, and upper body are gray-brown, brown, black, and white with oval spots. Ruffed grouse have a long, fan-shaped tail with narrow bands of blackish-brown and one wide band at the end of the tail. The side and the breast of the grouse is light gray with large dark bars and fading narrow lines through the breast. The legs are feathered to the toes.

Sound and Flight Pattern

The adult males will usually climb steeply, while the adult female will fly lower to the ground. Ruffed grouse can fly fast and will twist and turn, dodging brush and trees that are close together. Grouse will try to quickly get some obstruction between the hunter and themselves.

Similar Gamebirds

Young blue and Franklin's grouse can be confused with ruffed grouse. Early in the season, they occupy some of the same cover.

Flock or Covey Habits

After hatching, the ruffed grouse brood stays together until early fall. At this period in September, often after a storm, grouse may go through their fall shuffle of crazy flights to find a home range. There are many theories about the cause of this phenomenon, but none have been proven. Grouse do a lot of walking during this period, intermixed with short flights. There is some evidence of grouse regrouping in the winter, forming flocks of 3-8 birds.

Reproduction and Life Span

The nest of the female ruffed grouse is usually located against a stump, clump, or tree to protect her back. Her camouflaged colors blend into the material of the nest. The hen may put leaves over her back to further conceal herself. She lays 8-12 eggs with an incubation period of about 22 days.

Young grouse are the size of marshmallows when hatched. The hen will leave the nest as soon as possible to get her brood into open areas where more insects are

available. She can spot danger quickly and will call her chicks to scatter and use the "broken-wing" trick to distract an intruder. Within a few days the young birds are able to fly up to low branches with much greater protection to roost.

In winter, ruffed grouse habitat is often covered with snow. If the snow is wet, birds will roost on top of it or in trees. When temperatures are cold and the snow is deep and powdery, the grouse will sleep beneath the snow for protection and warmth. In winter, grouse movements are restricted to a few acres as long as food is available.

The young ruffed grouse has a high mortality rate, with habitat and weather conditions contributing to large losses. Population levels vary with the carrying capacity of the habitat. Ruffed grouse population will increase steadily for many years, decline, then rise again. Ruffed grouse numbers vary greatly from year to year due to this cycle. Mortality of adult grouse from all causes can be more than 40%. The average life expectancy of a ruffed grouse is 2-4 years.

Feeding Habits and Patterns

Young birds eat many insects, which are vital to their growth. Late in the summer, the poults eat about the same amount of animal matter as the adults. Juvenile birds do not eat the variety of foods the adults consume.

The ruffed grouse diet varies greatly, the bulk being vegetable matter. Grouse and white-tailed deer are browsers and can be in competition with each other. In summer and early fall, the adults eat tender shoots, green leaves, insects, berries, and fruits. Later, the birds will add nuts, grain, and seeds to their diets. In winter, ruffed grouse will feed on many kinds of buds.

The feeding patterns of ruffed grouse are like most gallinaceous birds. Feeding starts at daybreak and continues until mid-morning, then the birds seek cooler covered spots to rest and dust. Late in the afternoon, the grouse will feed again until low light, and go to roost at dusk.

Preferred Habitat and Cover

Ruffed grouse live most of their lives within about two square miles, as long as there is an ample food supply.

The grouse inhabit brush, woodlands of dense cover, mixed evergreens, and hardwoods. The cover is often along small streams, creeklets, springs, open grassland parks on steep hills, mountainsides of quaking aspen stands, and drainages coming out of mountains. Cover type used by ruffed grouse can vary greatly during feeding periods and seasons. Open grasslands have good supplies of insects and greens during the summer. Brushy and overgrown areas have seeds, fruits, and greens in the fall. Mixed woodlands of conifers and deciduous trees have fewer food supplies, but are used in winter and spring feeding for fruits, nuts, and buds.

Locating Hunting Areas

Ruffed grouse are common on both sides of the Continental Divide and also in a few mountain ranges in central Montana.
  1. Intermountain grasslands and montane forests are the best hunting areas for ruffed grouse.
  2. Much ruffed grouse hunting is on state and federal lands.
  3. Many county and Forest Service roads follow drainages across the intermountain grasslands leading into the mountains. Most of the ruffed grouse are in this range where the hardwood draws, steep rolling hills, and waterways disappear into the evergreen forests.

Looking for Sign

Ruffed grouse droppings are about ¾-1¼" long and the diameter of a pencil. One grouse can produce many droppings, because much of what they consume has little nutritional value. Dusting spots can be along old roads and open places that are dry. A few feathers are left behind.

Hunting Methods

Ruffed grouse are always easier to find in the early morning or late afternoon. Midday, the birds are often in very dense cover or holding up in trees. Hunt along the forest edges of open parks, hayfields, pastures, berry patches, or brushy draws during feeding times. Hunt hardwood creek bottoms, moist areas that have springs, aspen groves, and bushy hillsides in the afternoon. Look for grouse sign and if found, cover the area completely, walking slowly and looking up in trees for movement.

Hunting Dogs

Retrievers and flushing dogs help tremendously in finding birds in heavy cover. The closer the dog works, the better. Winged ruffed grouse run after falling and can be very difficult to find due to their camouflage coloring. A good retriever in ruffed grouse country will rarely lose a bird because scenting conditions are usually better in the moist habitat.

Pointing dogs do well on ruffed grouse, as most birds hold and leave a good scent. Big running dogs hold birds well, but my experience has been that grouse will sometimes fly into a tree before the hunter arrives.

When working dogs on ruffed grouse, bells and beepers are important.

Table Preparations

I believe young ruffed grouse are the most tender of all upland gamebirds. The breast and legs are white meat. In warm weather, field draw and wash out with cold water, hang, or place in a cooler with ice. I hang my birds for several days and either pick or skin them, depending upon how I am going to prepare them for the table.

Shot and Choke Suggestions

All season: No. 8-7½ shot, ⅞-1¼ oz. of shot.

Chokes: improved and modified

BLUE GROUSE
Dendagapus obscurus

QUICK FACTS

- **local names:** dusky grouse, fool hen, gray grouse, pine grouse, pine hen, sooty grouse.
- **size:** largest of the mountain grouse (blue, ruffed, and Franklin's). The male blue grouse is 20-22" long, has a wingspan of about 28", and weighs up to 4 lbs. The female blue grouse is 17-18" long and weighs about 3 lbs.
- **identification in flight:** adult male appears very dark gray, showing a long, wide gray tail. Females and juveniles appear similar in flight but are smaller.
- Blue grouse are native to Montana.

- In Montana there is a mixed bag limit for all mountain grouse.
- Blue grouse are the only upland gamebird that move to a higher location in winter.
- When flushed, blues will usually fly downhill to gain speed and have an advantage over the hunter.
- Blue grouse are associated with Douglas fir throughout most of their range.
- Many times blue grouse will sit up in trees out of sight and scent of man and dogs.

Color

The male has mostly grayish or slate-colored plumage with a yellow and orange comb above the eyes and a slightly crested head. The female is somewhat smaller and different in coloration with more mottled brown overall. Both sexes have long, square, unbarred tails. Northern Rockies blue grouse lack the gray band at the end of the tail. Blue grouse have leg feathers extending to the toes.

Sound and Flight Pattern

Blue grouse are not very vocal when alarmed and prefer running to flying. When flushed, blues have a loud, rapid take-off, and try to put a tree between themselves and the hunter. When flushed on a ridge, they pitch down over the side to gain speed. On hillsides, they prefer to fly around the hill going slightly downward until out of sight. Blues have fast wing motions and can maneuver around branches and trees.

BLUE GROUSE DISTRIBUTION

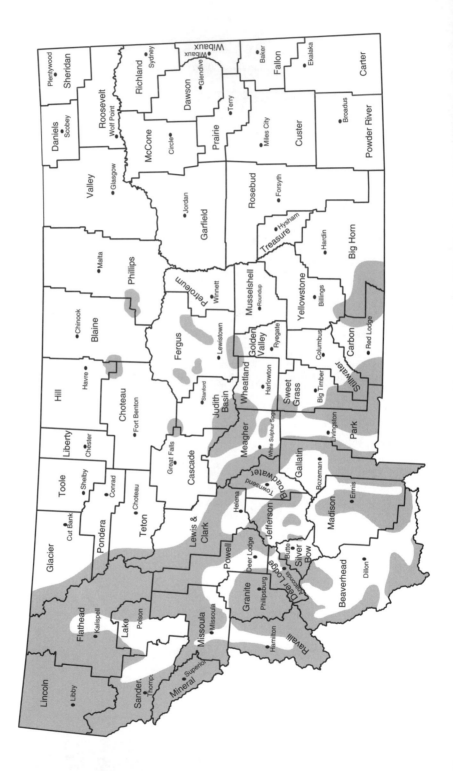

Similar Gamebirds

Female blue grouse may be confused with ruffed or spruce grouse. Young ruffed, blue, and spruce grouse share the same habitat at certain times of the year and look similar when flying.

Flock or Covey Habits

After hatching, the female and her brood will stay together as a family group or small flock during the summer and fall. The male blue grouse does not help raise the young. After breeding, males are fairly solitary and may move to higher timbered areas in late summer. In early autumn, depending on weather and availability of food, the female and juvenile birds will move to higher areas.

Reproduction and Life Span

Female blue grouse nest and raise their broods at a much lower elevation than that of their winter range. The hen blue grouse makes a shallow bowl-shaped nest on the ground, lined with grasses, needles, and leaves in or around aspen groves, cottonwood mixed forest, shrub grasslands, or bunchgrass prairies.

The hen's clutch consists of 7-10 eggs with an incubation period of about 23 days. Blue grouse chicks are fairly independent and can fly in about a week. If her chicks are in danger, the female will distract the intruder by pretending to have a broken wing.

The young chicks feed on insects at first and then turn more to vegetation like the adults. Adult blue grouse will feed on insects too, if available. I have hunted blues in September around open forest parks (mountain meadows) and found after shooting a bird that its crop was full of grasshoppers.

During the summer months, the young primarily use mixed grass-forb cover. Later, the birds will use brushy hardwood thickets and begin to abandon their brood range. Some females leave the brood behind when they travel to their wintering grounds. The juveniles will begin to move singly or in groups, making their way up to wintering areas.

As with all upland gamebirds, the mortality rate of blues is high. Studies indicate 50-65% of young grouse do not live through their first fall and a third of the adults die annually. However, the blue grouse's life expectancy is longer than most upland gamebirds. Research has shown that birds can live 10 or 12 years. Hunters usually have little effect on the yearly mortality rate of blue grouse.

Feeding Habits and Patterns

Adult blue grouse feed mostly on vegetation. Only in summer and early fall do the adults and young feed on animal food. During this short period, looking for concentrations of insects can help you find the birds. The rest of the year blue grouse feed on berries, fruits, leaves, seeds, flowers, and many herbaceous plants. Blues do not migrate, but from spring to late fall, shift to higher elevations and different food types. In winter blue grouse are usually associated with Douglas fir. The major food source in winter is needles of the Douglas fir, ponderosa pine, and hemlock. In fall,

grouse feed early in the morning, then rest, and sometimes feed again midday. The most intense feeding time for all ages of blue grouse is the three hours before dark.

Preferred Habitat and Cover

Blue grouse will be found early in the hunting season on their summer range. Many times they are in the same habitat and location as ruffed grouse (intermountain grassland and parts of the montane forest). In fall, the grouse family will occupy areas of more open woods, lower slopes, foothills, and isolated open parks below the dense conifer forests. In these areas, look for long mixed hardwood and evergreen draws with creeks, sidehills of sagebrush, steep slopes with brush, patches of berries and fruit, aspen groves, and edges of summer pasture lands.

As winter approaches and brings frost and cold nights to their summer range, the birds move to higher elevations. The winter habitat is mixed conifers (Douglas fir) with open parks and edges of ridge lines. Much of the blue grouse's winter range is in national forest areas.

Locating Hunting Areas

Blue grouse are widespread in the coniferous forests of western Montana and also in isolated mountain ranges in the center of the state.

1. During the first month of the mountain grouse hunting season, the young blue grouse will be in the lower intermountain grasslands. Many private, county, state, and federal roads cross the intermountain grasslands leading into the mountain forests. If traveling private roads, landowner permission is required.
2. Young blue grouse that have not moved to their winter range overlap into ruffed grouse area.
3. As the blue grouse's summer diet (insects, berries, tender plants, and seeds) disappears due to weather conditions and other factors, the blues will move to their winter ranges at higher elevation.
4. Walking to and finding winter ground can be difficult at times, but the birds are more concentrated here than on their summer range.
5. Blue grouse are most often associated with Douglas fir forests. Hunt the mountain ridge lines.
6. Many Forest Service roads follow drainages into the mountains. These roads give good access to ridges and open parks where blue grouse winter.

Looking for Sign

Blue grouse droppings are like those of a chicken in size and light to dark green in color. Look for droppings on roads, trails, open grasses, ridges, and under roosting trees. Dusting spots can be hard to find, but feathers are sometimes present in open areas.

Hunting Methods

Early in the season when the grouse are on their summer range, hunting methods are much like those used on ruffed grouse. Hunt berry patches, side hills, and around open, low mountain meadows early in the morning or late afternoon. During the middle of the day, hunt creek bottoms and moist draws with mixed forest types.

The winter areas are my favorite blue grouse haunts. Mountain ridges that are fairly wide with mixed coniferous forest, open meadows (parks), and rocky outcroppings seem to be the best. Many times the birds will be along the edges of the ridge not far from rock outcroppings with steep slopes. Blues will spend many hours feeding and resting in trees. Hunting the same location at different times of the day can be rewarding.

The hardest part of hunting blue grouse is climbing the mountains in search of them. Walk slowly—the scenery and the birds are well worth the effort.

Hunting Dogs

Any breed of hunting dog can be beneficial to the blue grouse hunter. Birds that dive over a hill or ridge can be difficult to find. When birds are winged or shot in heavy cover, they will run and are hard to locate without a dog. Flushers and retrievers are helpful in brushy cover. Pointing dogs are useful in open meadows and brushy slopes where large areas need to be covered.

Table Preparation

In early fall, blue grouse feed on many berries and fruits. Consequently, their white meat is considered superior to most other grouse. I think blue and ruffed grouse are equally delicious. In warm weather, field draw, wash out with cold water, and place in a cooler with ice. I hang my birds for several days before picking or skinning them.

Shot and Choke Suggestions

All hunting seasons: No. 8-7½ shot, ⅞-1¼ oz. of shot.

Chokes: improved and modified.

FRANKLIN'S GROUSE

Dendragapus canadensis
franklinii

QUICK FACTS

- **local names:** spruce grouse, black grouse, spotted grouse, Canada grouse, wood chickens, wood partridge, fool hen, swamp partridge
- **size:** medium-sized mountain grouse, averaging 15-17", with a wingspan of 23-24", and a weight of 1¼-1½ lbs.
- **identification in flight:** both sexes have dark backs and a long, wide, black tail. Their scarce white marking are not usually visible in flight.

- Franklin's grouse are native to Montana.
- Franklin's spend many hours in trees out of sight of ground dwellers.
- Although Franklin's grouse are often referred to simply as "spruce grouse," the spruce is actually a subspecies of the Franklin's. The lack of a rust-colored band on the tip of the tail distinguishes the Franklin's from the true spruce grouse.
- Franklin's inhabit remote regions of Montana and the encroachment of civilization may be the greatest threat to this bird.
- Lewis and Clark were the first to describe the Franklin's grouse.

Color

The male Franklin's grouse is barred with black and gray on the back and a white and black lower belly. The breast and throat are black bordered with white. The Franklin's tail is completely dark, without a rust band like its subspecies, the spruce grouse. Males have a red comb.

The female is mottled black and brown on the back, copper and black on the throat and upper breast, and brown, black, and white on the belly.

Both male and female have leg feathers to their toes.

Sound and Flight Pattern

Franklin's grouse make a loud whirring sound when flushed from the ground or a tree. The birds fly to the heaviest cover available, twisting and turning through the timber. This grouse, sometimes called the fool hen, has earned the name more than any other upland gamebird. Franklin's grouse often refuse to fly from a tree or flush off a trail or road.

Similar Gamebirds

Ruffed and blue grouse are sometimes in the same general area as the Franklin's grouse and are hard to distinguish when flying. All young mountain grouse appear

FRANKLIN'S GROUSE DISTRIBUTION

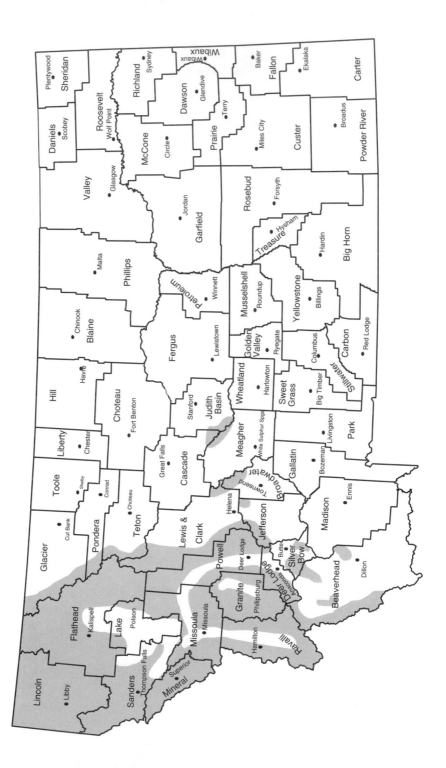

similar, but are rarely together. Montana hunting regulations allow a hunter to have a mixed bag limit of mountain grouse.

Flock or Covey Habits

Franklin's grouse do not form flocks. The birds stay in scattered loose family groups in the fall, often in singles or pairs over a wide area.

Reproduction and Life Span

In Montana, breeding starts in late April and lasts through the end of May. The Franklin's hen nests in June and the brood is hatched around the first week of July. Nests of the Franklin's grouse are usually well concealed under low branches or brush, often in evergreen thickets. The hen lays 4-10 eggs. Incubation is about 21 days. The female grouse can be highly aggressive toward intruders.

Young birds develop rapidly and in a week, can fly short distances. At 2-3 weeks, they can easily fly from danger. Young birds on the ground will usually fly into trees or thickets.

The young Franklin's grouse mortality rate is about the same as other mountain grouse, depending on habitat and weather conditions. The yearly cycle numbers can vary greatly. There is very little information about the longevity records of Franklin's grouse, but like other mountain grouse, they probably live 3-5 years.

Feeding Habits and Patterns

The food of the Franklin's grouse varies with the seasons. During late spring and summer, leaves, berries, forbs, and insects are consumed. From fall to spring, the largest part of their diet is conifer needles. The kind of needles used depends on the area where the birds live, but can include larch, pines, fir and spruce.

The Franklin's grouse does not migrate but is subject to seasonal shifts. In cold weather, the grouse seeks out dense covers of evergreens.

The feeding pattern of Franklin's grouse is about the same as other mountain grouse. Feeding starts at daybreak and continues for several hours. In the late afternoon, the grouse will feed for a longer period of time before going to roost. Since they mostly eat conifer needles, much of their feeding time is spent in trees. The grouse will move to open areas or roads to collect grit and other foods from the ground.

Preferred Habitat and Cover

The Franklin's grouse occupies boreal forests and favors the heavy mature conifers of the Rocky Mountains. It is associated with different forest types ranging from high-elevation spruce, fir, and lodgepole pines to mixed coniferous forests at lower elevations. In summer the grouse will often use creek bottoms, brushy draws, and slopes at high elevations.

In winter, Franklin's will use covers of Douglas fir, western larch, lodgepole, and ponderosa pine. Most of the year the birds live at an elevation of 3,000-6,000 feet. In fall and winter, Franklin's seem to prefer southern slopes and exposures.

Locating Hunting Areas

Franklin's grouse live primarily in the counties west of the Continental Divide, although some eastern slope counties have birds. (See distribution map.)

1. Much of the Franklin's grouse habitat is on state and federal lands. Use Forest Service roads to locate hunting areas.
3. Hunt dense forests of conifers on southern exposures
4. Walk old logging roads and skid trails to locate birds and sign.

Looking for Sign

Franklin's grouse droppings are different shades of green. The birds spend a great deal of time in heavy cover and trees, therefore spotting droppings can be difficult. Along roads and clearings in the forest floor are the best places to find dropping and feathers.

Hunting Methods

The Franklin's grouse has short, cupped wings typical of all mountain grouse. The wings are designed for quiet take-off and acrobatic mobility, but not suited for long flights. Franklin's flight speeds are fairly slow and they usually fly short distances from ground to tree. When the bird is in a tree, it can be difficult to get it to fly. If the hunter throws sticks or shakes the branches, the bird will usually fly out the other side of the tree.

The most important factor when hunting Franklin's is finding the right habitat type. In early fall that could be berry patches, south slopes, or along moist areas with heavy cover. Be sure to stay in the 3,000-6,000 foot range.

Hunting Dogs

All mountain grouse will run when pursued, usually into heavy cover. I work more than one pointer at a time on Franklin's grouse to cover more acres. Bells or beepers are a must when hunting any mountain grouse in Montana.

Once birds are located, close-working dogs of any breed can be very beneficial to the hunter. Even if Franklin's are flushed out of range, they usually don't fly very far and are easy to relocate.

Dogs that retrieve or track wounded birds are essential because the cover is so heavy.

I once hunted with a man who had a Lab and a pointer. I was working two of my wide-running Brittanys across the creek from him. Both of us were hunting steep, brushy, mixed forest slopes. One of the dogs found the birds, and they scattered into a thicket on the side of a steep slope. The four dogs went to work on the birds, but only the close-working Lab got the job done. My friend's game bag had more lumps in it than mine.

Table Preparations

In early fall, when the birds are young and are feeding on vegetation other than needles, their white meat is better than later in the season, although all mountain grouse are excellent table fare anytime. Proper preparation and cleaning improves the bird for the table.

Shot and Choke Suggestions

All hunting season: No. 8-7½ shot, ⅞-1¼ oz. of shot.
Chokes: improved and modified.

MERRIAM'S TURKEY DISTRIBUTION

Special Permit-Only Hunting Areas

General Hunting Areas Spring & Fall

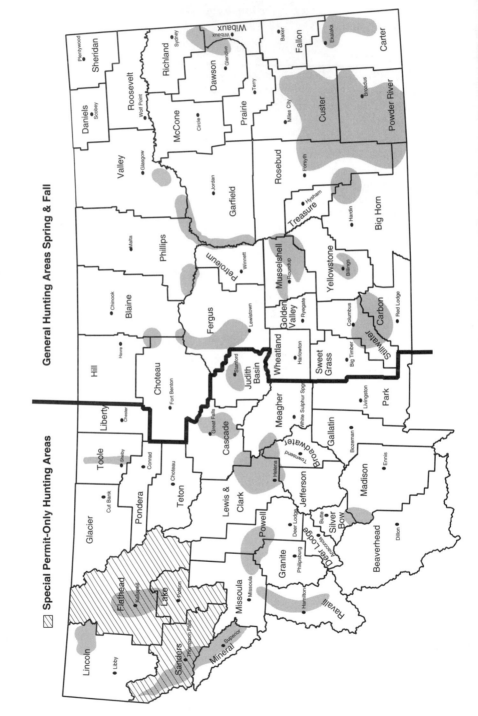

MERRIAM'S TURKEY

Meleagris gallopavo merriami

QUICK FACTS

- **local names:** tom, gobbler, wild turkey, American turkey
- **size:** largest North American upland gamebird. The male is 3½-4' long, has a wingspan of 4-5', and weighs 15-20 lbs. The adult hen is 2½-3' long, has a wingspan of 3-4', and weighs 7-10 lbs.
- **identification in flight:** Turkeys prefer running to flying. They have powerful legs, and can reach speeds of 20 miles per hour on the ground. They are strong flyers and can clear a treetop easily and glide for long distances. Turkeys are easily distinguished in flight because of their large size.

- The Merriam's turkey is not native to Montana.
- Montana has a spring gobbler season and an either-sex fall season. (Hunters must have a conservation license, an upland bird license, and a turkey tag for each season.)

Color

The male's body plumage is brilliant metallic bronze with a rainbow of reflections. The wings are dark with white bars and the back and breast feathers are tipped with black. The head is mainly red with fleshy snood above the bill. The males have a long tassel (beard) that hangs from the breast and can be 10-12" long on an older male. The medium-long tail is bronze with darker bars, white tail coverts, and cream tail tips. Males have spurs.

The female is lighter and less brightly colored. The breast feathers have buff tips. The hen's head is darker than the male's and blackish blue. Females lack spurs and rarely have beards.

Sound

Turkeys learn early in life to communicate and have many different calls and sounds. Males, females, and young poults all have variations of tones, pitches, and rhythms. The early morning call by the hen is a soft tree yelp. The gobbling of the male is mainly used during the mating season, but occasionally a tom will gobble during the fall and winter.

Other calls that turkeys use are the yelp, the lost call, the cluck, the *kee-kee*, the cackle, the *pit-pit*, the *purr*, and the alarm *putt*. Seven of these calls are used by hunters, but this is only a small part of the turkey vocabulary.

Flock or Covey Habits

After hatching, the hen and brood stay together and are sometimes joined by other broods to form larger flocks. By fall, the juvenile gobblers have outgrown the hens and disrupt the social order of the flock. Some of the young males separate from the brood and band together. In winter, there can be many different kinds of flocks—brood hens with offspring, hens without broods, young gobblers separated from the brood, and adult males. In Montana, Merriam's turkeys often form large droves and move to lower riparian habitat or seek out food around ranching operations.

Reproduction and Life Span

Breeding season starts in April and lasts into May. The hen makes or finds a depression in the ground for her nest that is well concealed under branches, logs, or other thick cover. The nest is lined with leaves or grass and when she is not present, the hen will cover the eggs with leaves. The number of eggs the female lays can be as few as 8 or as many as 20, but is usually 10-12. The incubation period is about 28 days.

As soon as the eggs are hatched, the hen leads the poults away from the nest in search of food and protection. Poults learn to fly in about two weeks. The period before they fly is a dangerous time in their lives. The mortality rate of young birds depends on the weather, habitat, and other factors. The turkey's life expectancy is 6-10 years, although birds older than 8 years are rare.

Feeding Habits and Patterns

Wild turkeys may have the most varied diet of any animal. It is easier to list what they don't eat than what they do. It has been said if turkeys can catch it or swallow it, they'll eat it. The most important plant foods eaten by turkeys are mast, fruits, and seeds. These foods are not produced in abundance each year. There are many other factors that affect birds' feeding habits, such as snow, ice, drought, fire, and flooding conditions along rivers. Turkeys may remain in trees for several days without feeding during heavy snow or rain. In winter, turkey droves will feed around cattle, ranch buildings, hay stacks, and grain bins.

Turkeys fly down to feed at daybreak. In spring, hens will fly down first and call. The gobbler may stay on the roost and call for up to an hour before flying down. By mid-morning, feeding has tapered off and the birds begin moving about. Around noon, the turkey usually spends time resting, dusting, and preening. Turkeys spend a lot of time dusting in sandy areas, under trees with soft soil, and even in anthills. In the summer and fall, when the weather is hot, the birds will be in cool, shady locations. In the early afternoon, the flock increases its movements and feeding picks up for 2-3 hours before roosting.

Preferred Habitat and Cover

Habitat used by Merriam's turkeys in Montana is of two types—riparian hardwood along streams adjacent to farmlands and ponderosa pine forests. Much of the ponderosa pine forest is rugged terrain with brushy hardwood draws, steep slopes, and long ridges with open meadows and mixed prairie vegetation.

Locating Hunting Areas

A great deal of the pine forest turkey habitat is on public land and most of the riparian forest is private.

1. After driving to a likely hunting spot, walk to a ridge, sit, listen, and glass the area for turkeys or turkey habitat.
3. Walking logging roads and trails is helpful in locating sign and bird habitat.
4. Many county roads follow riparian drainages. When good habitat is located, get permission from the landowner before hunting.

Looking for Sign

Droppings can reveal sex. Gobblers make large-diameter droppings that are "J" shaped. Hen droppings are corkscrewed or piled.

Turkeys shed each feather on their body once a year, so looking for feathers is usually productive.

Footprints along trails, roads, and moist areas are easiest to spot. An adult male's tracks are much larger than a hen's. Piles of leaves that have been scratched or disturbed can indicate feeding places. Dusting areas will have many feathers and droppings. Waterholes have numerous tracks, feathers, and droppings. Finding turkey sign can be more helpful than any other method for locating the birds in an area.

Hunting Methods

1. Learn to use a turkey call.
2. Wear camouflage or clothing that blends with the foliage.

3. For spring hunting, be in the woods before dawn.
4. If you hear a gobble (it can be audible a half-mile away), move to within 200 yards and set up.
5. When calling to a tom on the roost, a *cluck* works best.
6. If no turkeys are heard or found in the morning, walk a ridge slowly, listening, glassing, and looking for turkey sign.
7. In the fall, walk logging roads and ridges and view wide areas with binoculars.

Table Preparations

Wild turkey is outstanding table fare. Draw the turkey as soon as possible. I like to hang my birds for a few days and pick them just before freezing or eating.

Shot and Choke Suggestions

Rifles are legal for taking turkeys in Montana: the .222, .223 or .22 mag are very effective.

I prefer to use a 12-gauge shotgun with a full choke with loads of 4, 2, and B.B. Many books do not recommend these loads, but I have found that they work well in the open forests of Montana.

Ken Farmer bags a big Merriam's gobbler.

WATERFOWL

Waterfowl are managed by the Department of the Interior's Fish and Wildlife Service. The migratory waterfowl in Montana are swans, sandhill cranes, geese, and ducks. Ducks are divided into two groups: puddle (dabbling) ducks and divers. Montana is surrounded by some of the best breeding range in North America. In spring and summer, Montana has over 20 species of waterfowl nesting across the state. The number and distribution changes from year to year due to varying water conditions. Two species of ducks (mallard and goldeneye) winter in Montana along warmwater springs, open water areas, and large lakes. Weather conditions and available food play an important part in determining the numbers of waterfowl residing here in winter.

Canada geese and mallard ducks are the major waterfowl hunted in Montana. However, early in the season when water is not frozen, hunting for other species of ducks can be outstanding.

Montana has many miles of rivers, streams, spring creeks, reservoirs, refuges, lakes, and other types of open water. Almost every county in the state has good waterfowl hunting at certain times of the year.

Habitat, flock action, color, shape, sound, and voice are factors to consider when identifying ducks and geese. Identification is essential when hunting waterfowl.

Montana is located in both the Central Flyway and the Pacific Flyway. The Pacific Flyway extends to the eastern boundaries of Liberty, Pondera, Teton, Cascade, Judith Basin, Meagher, and Park counties. The Central Flyway includes all the counties east of that line. (See map.)

Generally, the best hunting occurs late in October and November when the birds are migrating. I found the following to be the most productive counties for hunting waterfowl during migration:

Missouri Country
Choteau (Fort Benton), Cascade (Great Falls), Fergus (Lewistown), Phillips
    (Malta), Valley (Glasgow), Sheridan (Plentywood), Roosevelt (Wolf Point)

Yellowstone Country
Custer (Miles City), Rosebud (Forsyth), Treasure (Hysham), Sweet Grass (Big
    Timber), Park (Livingston)

Rocky Mountain Country
Teton (Choteau), Broadwater (Townsend), Gallatin (Bozeman), Ravalli
    (Hamilton), Beaverhead (Dillon)

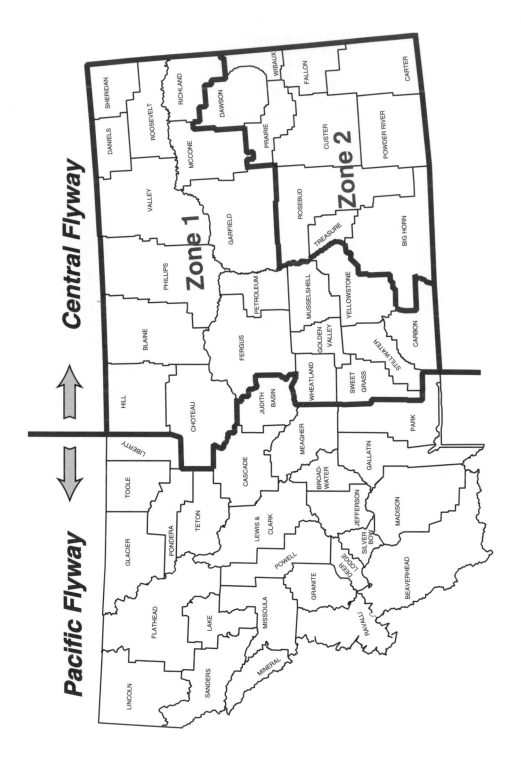

DUCKS

PUDDLE DUCKS

Mallards, teal (blue-winged, cinnamon, and green-winged), gadwall, and wigeon make up the majority of the puddle ducks hunted in Montana. Other puddle duck species are available, but not in large numbers and some leave fairly early in the hunting season.

Puddle ducks (dabbler) are birds of fresh water, rivers, potholes, and marshes that feed in the water. Puddle ducks also feed in croplands on vegetable matter and grains. These ducks take off vertically and do not skim the water.

DIVING DUCKS

Barrow's goldeneye, bufflehead, canvasback, shoveler, common merganser, ruddy duck, lesser scaup, and other diving duck species are available in Montana. Hunting pressure is light in Montana for diving ducks.

Divers frequent large bodies of water and deep rivers and, as their name suggests, feed by diving. Most diving ducks feed on aquatic life and are not hunted because their diet makes them less palatable than other species. Canvasbacks and redheads are the exception, but there aren't large numbers of these here in the fall hunting season.

Divers take off by scooting across the water.

Hunting Methods

Ducks usually have two distinctly different stops and can be counted on to move between these spots in the morning and evening. Hunting activities function around these movements. Puddle ducks feed around water and grain fields and always rest on the water.

There are three ways to hunt puddle ducks: jump shooting, pass shooting, and staged shooting (over decoys). Jump shooting can be very effective in

Waterfowl laying over during migration.

Barrow's gold-eneye landing on a spring creek.

Montana because there are many small stock dams with high brims, numerous small creeks, irrigation ditches, spring creeks, and rivers with oxbows and high banks. Pass shooting is achieved by concealing yourself with camouflage or using cover between duck feeding and resting routes. Ducks that have not been hunted will use the same route day after day. Migrating ducks establish their own patterns as a result of weather and feeding conditions and their routes are not as predictable. Ducks should be studied with binoculars for the exact route they are using.

Much of the duck hunting in Montana is with decoys. The number of decoys used depends upon the places hunted. Large numbers are usually not necessary

because there are many places to set up decoys, few hunters, and the ducks are not decoy-shy. The biggest concentration of duck hunters is in the established wildlife areas and refuges.

Mallard drake.

GEESE

Canada Goose (Western)
Branta canadensis moffitti

Local Names: honker, Canada

Identification

There are many subspecies of Canada geese. Their size can vary from the small cackling goose *(B.c. minima)* that weighs about 3 lbs to the giant goose *(B.c. maxima)* that can weigh up to 12 lbs. The predominant subspecies in Montana is the western Canada goose. The lesser Canada goose migrates through the state.

Both sexes have a black head, long, black neck, and a distinctive white chin strap from ear to ear. The body and wings are gray-brown. In flight, the birds show large, dark wings, a black tail, and white rump. Flocks usually fly in "V" formation or in a long line. Canada geese are very vocal with clear, honking calls.

Geese taking off in eastern Montana.

Hunting Methods

Many counties in Montana have excellent goose hunting and only light hunting pressure. Part of the Yellowstone River is closed to waterfowl hunting, so consult the hunting regulations.

The best way to locate Canada geese is by scouting the big grain fields adjacent to major rivers for feeding geese or driving around looking for geese flying to their feeding areas. When found, wait until the geese return to water. Get permission to hunt, dig a pit or set up a blind, spread out decoys, and return that evening or morning depending on the time of day you spotted the birds. Decoys can also be set up on a gravel bar or reservoir when the birds are out feeding. This works best in the mornings because birds usually return to their resting areas after sunset. Binoculars and spotting scopes are extremely helpful when looking for geese.

Jump shooting can be productive on small rivers, ponds, and reservoirs.

Other Geese

Lesser Snow Goose *(Anser c. caerukescers)*
Local names: blue goose, snow, white, white goose
Identification

The lesser snow goose has two color phases—bluish-white and white. Both phases have black primary and gray covert feathers. Birds of the different color phases intermix when flying. Snows are gregarious when migrating and the birds may fly in flocks of several hundred. They are often confused with swans, but the snow goose has a shorter neck. The feet and legs are scarlet and the bill is pink with a black patch. The juvenile of the species is sooty gray. The snow goose call is a high-pitched yelp similar to the bark of a small dog.

Ross's Goose *(Anser rossii)*
Local Names: arctic goose, white, white goose, little wavie, horned wavie
Identification

Identical to the snow goose, except slightly smaller. The Ross's goose is often seen in association with the snow goose.

White-Fronted Goose *(Anser albifrons frontalis)*
Local names: specklebelly, laughing goose
Identification

The adults are brown with irregular brownish bars on their breasts. White-fronted geese are brownish gray at a distance and tend to fly in loose formations of lines or "V"s. Their most distinguishing feature is their high-pitched, laughing call.

Geese moving along a large western river.

Hunting Methods (Snows, Ross's, White-Fronted)

Snow geese, Ross's geese, and white-fronted geese are often seen in flocks together. Many thousands of geese migrate to staging areas north of Fairfield on Freezeout Lake in the fall. Benton Lake near Great Falls, Bowdoin Refuge east of Malta, and Medicine Lake refuge east of Wolf Point will also host a few thousand snow geese in the fall.

Predicting the arrival of big flocks of geese moving into Montana in the fall can be very difficult due to agricultural practices and weather conditions in Canada. Staging of snows can start as early as October or as late as November. It is essential to get information on goose movement. Contact the wildlife management area or wildlife refuge you plan to hunt.

Hunting the big flocks is best done using field shooting techniques, much like hunting Canada geese. Snows can range many miles to the wheat and barley field and birds are usually followed from a vehicle, using binoculars to locate their feeding areas. Many different flocks of geese will use the same place to feed on a given day, so watching or following the birds is not difficult. Snows are not as predictable as Canada geese and may not return to the same field.

Using large spreads of decoys is the most successful method of hunting the whites. Use floating decoys on bodies of water or other wetlands areas where geese are resting. Back shooting (birds coming back to their resting area from feeding) or pass shooting can be productive. Boats and decoys are useful on large bodies of water, but not always necessary. Lots of hunters use shoreline or shallow water areas to hunt geese and ducks.

MISSOURI COUNTRY

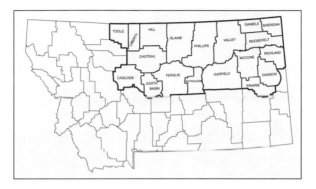

S mall farming and ranching communities form the heart of the Missouri Country, the least populated part of Montana. The dryland farming communities along the Hi-Line (the area that borders Canada), scenic Rt 2, the Missouri River, and the vast C.M. Russell Wildlife Refuge are the major features of this area.

Pheasants are plentiful in northeastern Missouri Country. They can also be found along the rivers of the area. The dryland farms and the deep coulees along the Hi-Line provide excellent hunting for Hungarian partridge, sharp-tailed grouse, and sage grouse. The C.M. Russell Refuge has great hunting for sharptails and contains pockets of sage grouse and pheasants. The prairie counties south of the Missouri River also provide hunting for Huns, sharptails, pheasants, and sage grouse. The pothole ponds, the rivers, and the wildlife refuges have great waterfowl hunting. Missouri Country is truly a wingshooter's paradise.

PHEASANT DISTRIBUTION

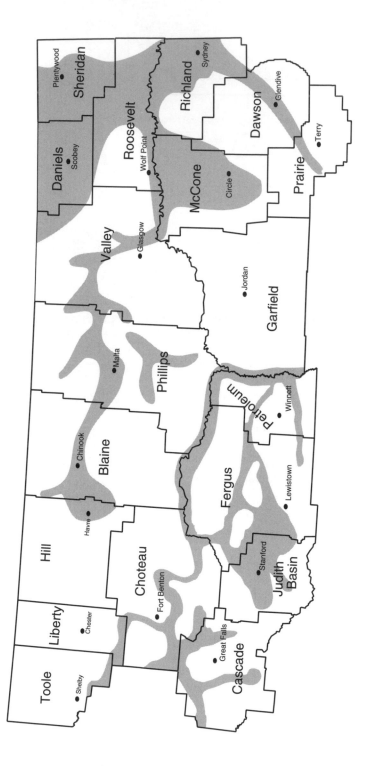

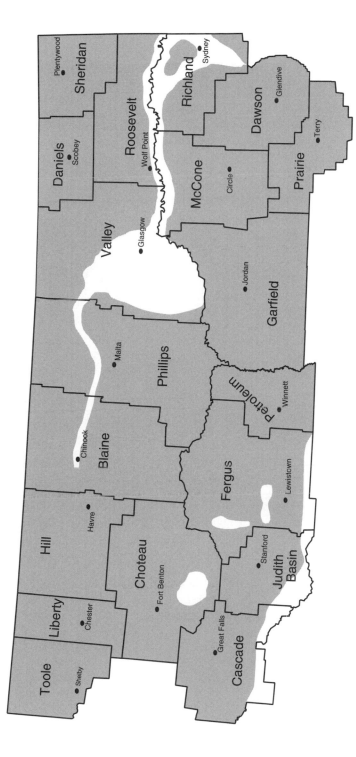

SHARP-TAILED GROUSE DISTRIBUTION

SAGE GROUSE DISTRIBUTION

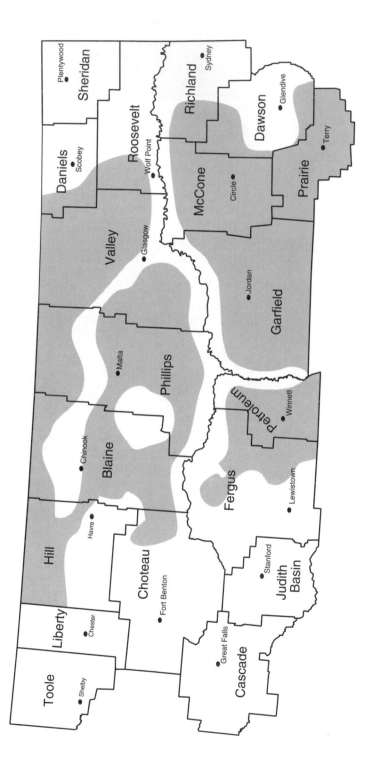

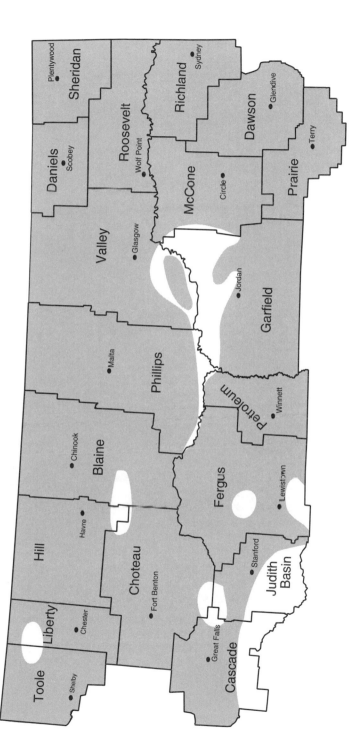

GRAY (HUNGARIAN) PARTRIDGE DISTRIBUTION

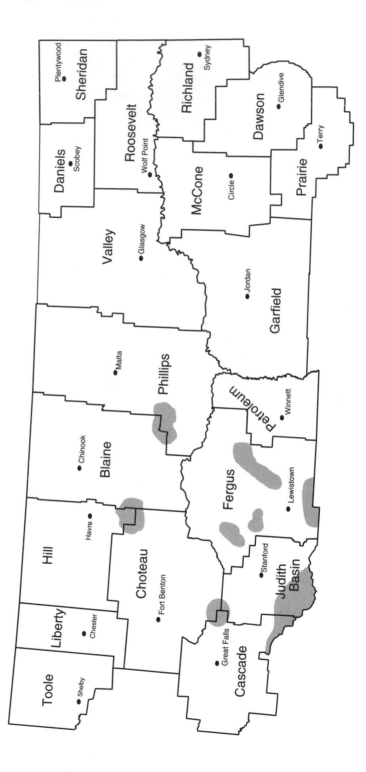

BLUE GROUSE DISTRIBUTION

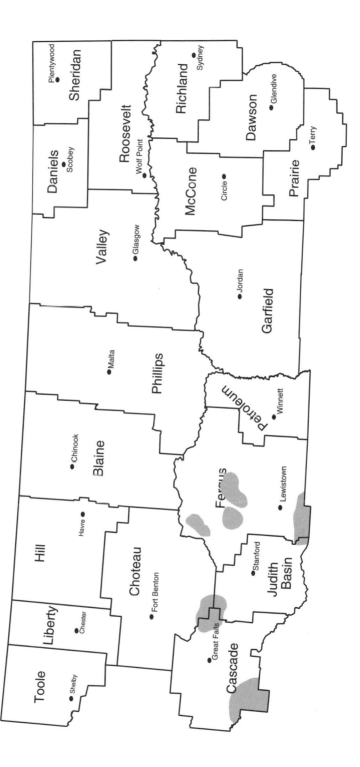

RUFFED GROUSE DISTRIBUTION

MERRIAM'S TURKEY DISTRIBUTION

General Hunting Areas Spring & Fall

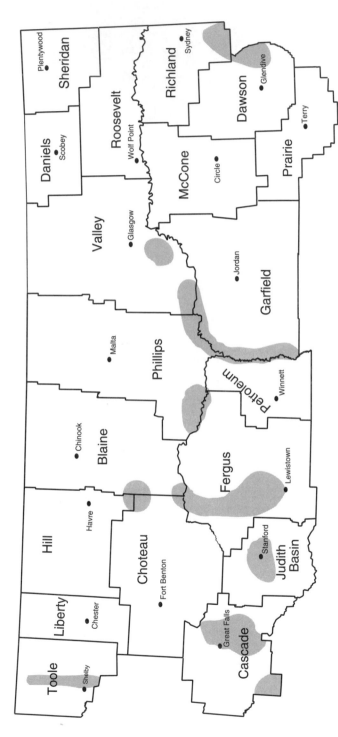

Leigh H. Perkins with a large rooster.

SHELBY
AND TOOLE COUNTY

Population– 2,763	October Temperature–47.8
Elevation– 3,450'	Annual Precipitation– 11.31"
County Population– 5,046	Acres in CRP– 134,844
County Area– 1,911 sq. mi.	FWP Region 4

Shelby is a city with a colorful past and a bright future. It is located at the cross-roads of Interstate Rt 15 and Rt 2 in the northern plains of the Hi-Line. The community is in the center of some of the best grain producing land in the nation. Shelby has many conveniences and its warm and friendly people enjoy a great quality of life in this unique western atmosphere.

UPLAND BIRDS
pheasant, Hungarian partridge, sharp-tailed grouse
The large grain fields of the area provide very good hunting for Hungarian partridge. Pheasants can be found along the Marias River, the Tiber Reservoir, and the numerous streams and agricultural land. Sharptails can be located in the CRP land and in the brushy coulees in the northern part of Toole County.

WATERFOWL
ducks and geese
Toole County is in the Pacific Flyway. The Marias River, Tiber Reservoir, and the stock ponds and streams of the area provide good waterfowl hunting.

ACCOMMODATIONS
Crossroads Inn, 1200 West Hwy 2. 434-5134.
  52 units, cable, coin operated laundry, continental breakfast. Dogs allowed in smoking rooms only.
O'Haire Manor Motel, 204 2nd St South. 434-5555.
  40 rooms, cable, coin operated laundry, hot tub. Dogs allowed in rooms, $5 a night. Hosts are Kevin and Elaine Mitchell.
TownHouse Inn, 50 Frontage Rd. 434-2212.
  72 rooms, cable, coin laundry. Dogs allowed in smoking rooms, $5 a night.

CAMPGROUNDS AND RV PARKS
Lewis and Clark RV Court, North on Hwy 91. 434-2710.
  65 spaces, water and electric hookups, showers, dump, laundry, store.

RESTAURANTS

Pat's Diner, 742 Oilfield Ave. 434-5452.
Open 6AM–10PM, 7 days. Serving fine home-cooked meals.
Sports Club Lounge and Dining Room, 210 Main. 434-7224.
Open for dinner. Great steaks.
Town Pump Travel Plaza and Restaurant, I-15 and Hwy 2. 434-5491.
Open 24 hours.

VETERINARIANS

Marias Veterinary Clinic, East of Shelby. 434-5176.
Clark Hardee, D.V.M.

SPORTING GOODS

Coast to Coast Hardware, 175 Main St.
Pamida, 1950 Roosevelt Hwy.

AUTO REPAIR

Appley Repair, 902 Birch Ave. 434-2915.

AIR SERVICE

County airstrip, Jerry Larson. 434-2462.

MEDICAL

Toole County Hospital, 640 Park Dr. 434-3200.

FOR MORE INFORMATION:

Shelby Chamber of Commerce
Box 865
Shelby, MT 59474.
434-7184.

CHESTER
AND LIBERTY COUNTY

Population– 950	October Temperature– 44.7
Elevation– 3,132'	Annual Precipitation– 15.20"
County Population– 2,400	Acres in CRP– 81,000
County Area– 1,458 sq. mi.	FWP Region 4

Liberty County is characterized by rolling prairies. The terrain is plains grassland and intermountain grasslands in the northwest part of the county. Three major streams—Cottonwood Creek, Eagle Creek, and Sage Creek—along with the Marias River, break up the terrain. In the northwest part of the county, the Sweetgrass Hills rise to nearly 7,000 feet. Farming and ranching are the principal industries of Liberty County with 97% of its land area active in grain and cattle production, 67% in dryland farming, and 37% in rangeland. Chester is the largest town and the county seat. This small farming town is located on Hwy 2.

UPLAND BIRDS
Hungarian partridge, sharptails, pheasants
Hungarian partridge hunting is excellent in the grasslands and dryland farming areas. Sharptails are found throughout the county in the grasslands, coulees, and the lower areas of the Sweetgrass Hills. Pheasants are found along the creek bottoms and adjacent to the Marias River.

WATERFOWL
ducks and geese
Both ducks and geese gather at Lake Elwell and feed in the surrounding grain fields. The creeks and the Marias River provide excellent jump shooting for ducks and geese during the fall migration.

ACCOMMODATIONS
MX Motel, 759-7165.
18 rooms. Dogs allowed for small charge. Store, casino, and bar. Rates very reasonable.
Wheat Sheaf Motel, 759-7166
8 rooms. Dogs allowed in one room.

CAMPGROUNDS AND RV PARKS
Tiber Marina, 20 miles south of Chester on Hwy. 223. 759-5200.
20 tent and 5 RV spaces. Open all year. Water, electric, dump, shower, and store.

RESTAURANTS
DJ's Golden Harvest Cafe, 759-5418.
8AM-9PM, 7 days. Breakfast, lunch, and dinner.

VETERINARIANS
The nearest vet is in Shelby:
Marias Veterinary Clinic, Clark Hardee, D.V.M. 434-5176.

SPORTING GOODS
Coast to Coast Store, 759-5415.

AUTO REPAIR
J&R Automotive Repair, 759-5655.
Chester Motors, 759-5431.

AIR SERVICE
Frontier Aviation, 759-5431. Call for information.

MEDICAL
Liberty County Hospital, Hwy. 223 and Monroe. 759-5181.

FOR MORE INFORMATION:
Liberty County Chamber of Commerce
Box 632
Chester, MT 59522.

HAVRE
AND HILL COUNTY

Population– 10,500	October Temperature– 45.5
Elevation– 4,167'	Annual Precipitation– 15.35"
County Population– 17,654	Acres in CRP– 167,045
County Area– 2,896 sq. mi.	FWP Region 6

Havre is located on the rolling plains of northcentral Montana. It is the largest town on the Hi-Line. The city of Havre is the focal point of commercial activity in the area and is home to Northern Montana College. The city is surrounded by the Milk River, golden wheat fields, and the rising peaks of the Bear Paw Mountains that tower several thousand feet above the plains. While providing excellent services, Havre still maintains the charm and friendliness that is the trademark of Montana.

Chuck Johnson's Annie pointing a pheasant.

UPLAND BIRDS
pheasants, Hungarian partridge, sharp-tailed and sage grouse

Pheasant hunting is very good along the Milk River and its tributaries. Good populations of Huns are found throughout the county, mostly on private agricultural grain fields and CRP land. Sharptails are found throughout the county in the brushy coulees. Sage grouse numbers are limited due to the small amount of sagebrush habitat that remains in the county.

WATERFOWL
ducks and geese

Geese are numerous in the grain fields. Both ducks and geese can be found on the many farm ponds in the area.

ACCOMMODATIONS

Budget Inn, 114 9th Ave. 265-8625.
  39 units, some with kitchenettes. Dogs allowed. Rates are reasonable.
El Toro Motel, 521 1st St. 265-5414.
  41 units, all with refrigerators and micro-ovens. Dogs allowed. Coin laundry. Very nice accommodations at reasonable rates. Your hosts are Norm and Sandy Larson.
Super 8 Motel, 901 Hwy 2 West. 265-1411.
  64 units. Dogs allowed. Nice accommodations at reasonable rates.

CAMPGROUNDS AND RV PARKS

Havre RV Park, 1465 1st St. 265-8861.
  59 spaces. All season, full hook-up, tent space, free showers, deli, saloon, Conoco food and fuel store.
Evergreen Campground, 2 miles west of Havre at Junction 87.
  22 full hook-ups, unlimited tent space, laundry, shower, dump.

RESTAURANTS

Andy's Supper Club, 658 West 1st St. 265-9963.
  Open for lunch and dinner. Cocktails, steak and lobster.
Duck Inn, 1300 1st St. 265-6111.
  Two restaurants. Mediterranean room has gourmet dining, cocktails. Main dining room open for breakfast, lunch, and dinner.
4B's, 604 1st St West. 265-9721.
  Breakfast, lunch, and dinner.
Naliuka's, 415 1st St West. 265-5426.
  Open 11AM–10PM, 7 days a week.

VETERINARIANS

Bear Paw Veterinary Service, 5051 Hwy 2 East. 265-8901.
Shambo Veterinary Hospital, 6751 West. 265-4514.
  Frank Meiwald, D.V.M.

SPORTING GOODS
Bing 'n Bob's Sport Shop, 316 3rd. 265-6124.
Stromberg's Sinclair and E-Fish-Hunt Sports, 1200 1st St. 265-3441.

AUTO REPAIR
G and B Toyota, Hwy 2 West. 265-2205.

AIR SERVICE
Havre City County Airport, Airport Rd. 265-4671.
Serviced by Big Sky Airlines, 265-5494.

MEDICAL
Northern Montana Hospital, 30 13th St. 265-2211.

FOR MORE INFORMATION
Havre Chamber of Commerce
P.O. Box 308
Havre, MT 59501.
265-4383.

CHINOOK
AND BLAINE COUNTY

Population– 1,512	October Temperature– 45.4
Elevation– 2,340'	Annual Precipitation– 14.78"
County Population– 6,728	Acres in CRP– 119,999
County Area– 4,226 sq mi.	FWP Region 6

Chinook is a cattle town on the Hi-Line. The Milk River runs just south of town. The Chief Joseph Battlefield, where the Nez Perce Indians fought their final battle, is just 16 miles to the south.

Agricultural land and rangeland comprised of shrub grassland make up most of Blaine County's terrain. The northern part of the county is cattle country with rolling hills and coulees. The Bear Paw Mountains are in the southern region.

UPLAND BIRDS
Hungarian partridge, sharp-tailed grouse, pheasant

Milk River country provides excellent cover for pheasants. They can also be found on the CRP land throughout the county. Most of the prime pheasant hunting is on private land. Permission is required. Good numbers of Huns are found throughout the county near grain fields. Again, most of this land is privately owned. Sharptails can be found in brushy coulees on private lands in the foothills of the Bear Paw Mountains. They also appear in smaller concentrations on the BLM lands and the coulees in the northern part of the county.

WATERFOWL
ducks and geese

The Milk River and its tributaries hold large numbers of ducks. Large quantities of geese can be hunted in the fields on private lands. There are several BLM reservoirs throughout the county that provide excellent hunting for ducks and geese.

ACCOMMODATIONS
Chinook Motor Inn, 100 Indiana Ave. 357-2248.
   38 rooms, restaurant, lounge, cable. Hunters welcome and dogs allowed in rooms. Reasonable rates.

RESTAURANTS
Chinook Motor Inn, 100 Indiana Ave. 357-2248.
   Open 6AM–9PM for breakfast, lunch, and dinner.
Pastime Lounge and Steakhouse, 326 Indiana Ave. 357-2424.
   Open for lunch and dinner.

VETERINARIANS
Blaine County Veterinary Services, SE of Chinook. 357-2279.
  Roger Baxter, D.V.M.

SPORTING GOODS
Paulfon's Hardware, 420 Indiana Ave. 357-3350.

AUTO REPAIR
Jamieson Motor, 100 Pennsylvania St. 357-2470.

AIR SERVICE
Chinook Airport, 357-2429.

MEDICAL
Sweet Medical Center, 419 Pennsylvania St. 357-2294.

FOR MORE INFORMATION
  Chinook Chamber of Commerce
  P.O. Box 744
  Chinook, MT 59523.
  357-2313.

MALTA
AND PHILLIPS COUNTY

Population– 2,400	October Temperature– 46.5
Elevation– 2,300'	Annual Precipitation– 15.57"
County Population– 5,163	Acres in CRP– 123,288
County Area– 5,140 sq. mi.	FWP Region 6

Malta is a small, friendly Hi-Line town located on Hwy 2 in the center of Phillips County. Just east of town is the Bowdoin National Wildlife Refuge. The refuge consists of 15,500 acres. One-third of the refuge is protected, but the other two-thirds has excellent hunting for waterfowl and good hunting for pheasants. Malta also is adjacent to the 1.1 million-acre C.M. Russell National Wildlife Refuge. The Milk River runs through the center of town. Malta is one of the stops on the northern Amtrak route. Cattle ranching is the primary source of income in Phillips County.

UPLAND BIRDS
pheasant, sharp-tailed and sage grouse, and Hungarian partridge
The majority of the county is private land, however there is a large amount of BLM land, mostly in the northern and extreme southern parts of the county. The C.M. Russell Wildlife Refuge is on the southern border of the county. Pheasants are abundant along the Milk River. Sharptails can be found in the CRP grasslands and the brushy coulees. Their numbers have been down the past several years and hunting is only fair. There are good pockets of sage grouse located in the sage-brush areas. Huns can be found in the agricultural areas, but presently their populations are low.

WATERFOWL
ducks and geese
The Bowdoin National Wildlife refuge provides excellent hunting for puddle ducks, diving ducks, and geese. There is very little hunting pressure on the refuge. For a complete description of the refuge see page 252. There is also good jump shooting on the stock ponds throughout the county.

ACCOMMODATIONS
Edgewater Inn, Hwy 2 across from the Westside restaurant. 654-1302.
32 units, many with refrigerators. Cable, indoor pool, and sauna. No dogs allowed in rooms. Nice accommodations at reasonable prices.
Riverside Motel, Hwy 2 West. 654-2310.
21 units. Dogs allowed in some rooms. Reasonable rates.

CAMPGROUNDS AND RV PARKS
Edgewater Campground, Hwy 2 West.
60 tent sites, 40 RV spots. Full hook-up facilities. Laundry, indoor pool, and sauna.

OUTFITTERS
Tripple Creek Outfitters and Whitcomb Lodge, Box 1173, Malta, MT 59538.
654-2089 or 658-2550. Contact Roy Ereaux. Hunt sharp-tailed and sage grouse, Hungarian partridge, pheasant, and waterfowl on 65,000 acres. Includes all guiding, lodge accommodations, and meals. Full kennel facilities. Reservations required.

RESTAURANTS
Westside Restaurant, Hwy 2 West. 654-1555.
Open 5AM–Midnight. Good food, good service, and good prices.
Roger's Saloon and Chuck Wagon, 139 South 1st Ave East. 654-9987.
Open for lunch and dinner. Good steaks. Bar and live music on weekends.
Hitchin' Post Cafe, Hwy 2 East.
Open 6AM–9PM for breakfast, lunch, and dinner.

VETERINARIANS
Phillips County Veterinary Clinic, located 2 miles south of Malta on Hwy 191.
654-1794.

SPORTING GOODS
Westside Sporting Goods, Hwy 2 West. 654-1661.
Complete line of hunting gear, ammo, and licenses.

MEDICAL
Phillips County Hospital, 417 South 4th St East. 654-1100.

FOR MORE INFORMATION:
Malta Chamber of Commerce
Drawer GG
Malta, MT 59538.
654-1776.

GLASGOW
AND VALLEY COUNTY

Population– 3,600	October Temperature– 46.8
Elevation– 2,612'	Annual Precipitation– 11.57"
County population– 8,239	Acres in CRP– 144,862
County Area– 4,936 sq. mi.	FWP Region 6

Glasgow is a ranching community located in a lovely river valley on the Hi-Line of Montana in the northeast section of the state. It is 12 miles west of the Fort Peck Indian Reservation and 15 miles north of the Fort Peck Recreation Area. The Milk River runs through town. There are a number of block management hunting areas in Valley County. Large blocks of BLM land are situated in the northern and southern part of the county.

The Fort Peck Recreation Area is located in the C.M. Russell National Wildlife Refuge. The Fort Peck Reservoir is 245,000 acres, making it the second largest reservoir in the U.S. The C.M. Russell Wildlife Refuge extends 125 miles up the Missouri River. It contains native prairies, forested coulees, river bottoms, and badlands in its million acres.

Don Thomas and his Lab hunt in pheasant habitat.

UPLAND BIRDS
sharp-tailed and sage grouse, pheasant, Hungarian partridge

The wide variety of terrain—prairie, river bottoms, and forested coulees—provide an abundance of different birds. Sharptails are the leading gamebird. They can be found in the native grasslands and in the brushy coulees. There is an excellent population of pheasants along the Milk River. The large areas of sagebrush and grassland in the southern half of the county have the best habitat for sage grouse. The agriculture lands in the northern part of the county provide spotty hunting for Hungarian partridge.

WATERFOWL
ducks and geese

The Fort Peck Reservoir and the Milk River provide excellent hunting for ducks and geese. The reservoir is public land and provides easy access. However the roads to and from the area are dirt and difficult to travel when it rains. The Milk River flows through private land and permission is required for access. There is also good jump shooting for ducks on the stock ponds scattered throughout the county.

ACCOMMODATIONS

Cottonwood Motor Inn, located on Rt 2, ½ mile east of town. 228-8213.
Best Western, 71 units, coin laundry, restaurant. Dogs allowed. 28 units with refrigerators. Indoor pool, sauna, cable. Very nice accommodations at reasonable rates.

LaCasa Motel, 2381 Ave North. 228-9311.
13 units. Two rooms have 4 double beds each. Refrigerators in some rooms. Cable. Hunters welcome and dogs allowed. Rates very reasonable. Your hosts are Doug and Sharon Adophson.

Star Lodge, Hwy West Rt 2. 228-2494.
30 units, cable, refrigerators in some rooms. Hunters and dogs welcome. Rates very reasonable. Your hosts are Bill and Shirley Fewer.

CAMPGROUNDS AND RV PARKS

Shady Rest RV Park, Rt 2 East. 228-2769.
4 tent sites, 40 RV. Water, laundry, electric, sewer, shower, store.

Trails West Campground, 1½ miles west of Glasgow on Rt 2. 228-2778.
15 tent sites, 35 RV. Water, electric, sewer, dump, shower, store.

OUTFITTERS

Antelope Creek Outfitters, Rt 1. 367-5582.
Paul Cornwell. Full accommodations. Sharptails, sage grouse, Huns, and pheasant are available.

Billingsley Ranch Outfitters, Box 768. 367-5577.
Jack Billingsley. Upland birds and waterfowl.

RESTAURANTS

Cottonwood Inn Dining Room, located on Hwy 2 in the Cottonwood
Motel. 228-8213. Open for breakfast, lunch and dinner. Prime rib served every
evening. Cocktails available, rates reasonable.

Sam's Supper Club, 307 1st Ave North. 228-4614.
Sam's is a popular spot for the local ranchers and town people. They specialize
in Montana beef. Cocktails. Very good food at reasonable rates.

Johnnie's Cafe, 433 1st Ave South. 228-4222.
Open 24 hours. This diner is a favorite for Glasgowites.

VETERINARIANS

Glasgow Veterinary Clinic, 2 miles east of Glasgow on Hwy 24. 228-9313.

SPORTING GOODS

D&G Sports and Western, 215 4th Ave South. 228-9363.
Hunting, fishing, guns, and ammo.

AUTO REPAIR

Dan's Auto Clinic, 802 Second Ave South. 228-2604

AIR SERVICE

Glasgow International Airport, east of town. 228-4023.

MEDICAL

Community Memorial Hospital, 216 14th Ave South. 482-2120.

FOR MORE INFORMATION:

Glasgow Chamber of Commerce
110 5th St South
Glasgow, MT 59230.
228-2222.

Dept. of Fish, Wildlife, and Parks
Hwy 2 West
Glasgow, MT 59230.
228-9347.

BLM Office
Hwy 2 West
Glasgow, MT 59230.
228-4316.

PLENTYWOOD
AND SHERIDAN COUNTY

Population– 2,136	October Temperature– 43.5
Elevation– 2,024'	Annual Precipitation– 15"
County Population– 4,732	Acres in CRP– 171,445
County Area– 1,677 sq. mi.	FWP Region 6

Plentywood, in the extreme northeastern corner of the state on Hwy 16, is the trading center for the people living in this area. It is 16 miles south of the 24-hour Port of Entry of Regway and only 2 hours from Regina, Saskatchewan. Plentywood is the hub of northeast Montana and the "gateway" to Canada.

Plentywood is the county seat of Sheridan County. The residents of Sheridan County call this area the "Land of the Lazy Mountains." These peaceful "mountains" are really beautiful rolling hills. The main industry is agriculture, with wheat farming and cattle ranching comprising most of the activity. In the early 1900s Sheridan County had many homesteaders. As a result, there are a great number of county roads along the section lines. Medicine Lake (and Medicine Lake National Wildlife Refuge) lies in the old channel of the Missouri River. This wide valley is dominated by numerous shallow lakes and is a prairie lake ecosystem. Medicine Lake National Wildlife Refuge contains 31,000 acres of water, prairie, and wetlands.

UPLAND BIRDS
sharp-tailed grouse, Hungarian partridge, pheasant

Pheasants occupy much of the county. The return of marginal grain fields to grasslands (thanks to the Conservation Reserve Program) has greatly increased the upland bird population in many areas. Hungarian partridge and sharp-tailed grouse are established in all parts of Sheridan County, but numbers fluctuate from year to year depending on the weather conditions.

WATERFOWL
geese and ducks

Medicine Lake and other shallow-water lakes in the old (before the ice age) channel of the Missouri River provide excellent duck and goose hunting. The refuge is home to an enormous number of ducks and geese. Sheridan County has all the requirements that waterfowl need for breeding and migration.

ACCOMMODATIONS

Sheridan Inn, 515 1st Ave. 765-2810.
65 rooms, dogs welcome. 24-hour desk service. Coffee, laundry, bird cleaning table, Fryer Tuck's fine dining, and the Robin Hood Lounge. Reasonable rates.

Plains Motel, 626 1st Ave West. 765-1240.
50 rooms. Reasonable rates.
Grandview Hotel, 120 South Main St. 765-2730.
13 rooms, lounge, bar. Reasonable rates. Dogs allowed.
Plentywood Can-Am RV Park, MT 16, 203 Raymond Rd. 765-2121.
Open all year. RV and tent spaces available. Full services.

RESTAURANTS
Cassidy's Bar and Lounge and The Loft Supper Club, 105 South Main St.
765-2350. Lunch, 11AM–2PM; dinner, Thurs–Sat, 5PM–10PM.
Blue Moon Supper Club, east of Plentywood on Hwy 5. 765-2491.
Steaks and seafood.
Laura Belle's, 121 North Main St. 765-1080.
Coffee shop, daily specials, soup. Open 8AM–4PM.
Alta Vista Cafe, 564 West 1st Ave. 765-1690.
Fine food. Smorgasbord on Sundays.

VETERINARIANS
Plentywood Veterinary Clinic, 622 Sunnyside Ave. 765-1760.
Robert Kane, D.V.M.

SPORTING GOODS
Hi-Line Sports, 558 West 1st Ave. 765-1522.

AUTO REPAIR
Ray's Exxon, 321 West 1st Ave. 765-1180.

AIR SERVICE
Sherwood Airport, Harold DeSilva. 765-1400.

MEDICAL
Sheridan Memorial Hospital, 440 West Laurel Ave. 765-1420.
Emergency response: 765-1234.

FOR MORE INFORMATION:
Chamber of Commerce
501 West 1st St.
Plentywood, MT 59254.
765-1320.

SCOBEY
AND DANIELS COUNTY

Population– 1,154	October Temperature– 41.3
Elevation– 2,800'	Annual Precipitation– 17.20"
County Population– 2,266	Acres in CRP– 143,014
County Area– 1,426 sq. mi.	FWP Region 7

Scobey is in the northeast corner of the state, 14 miles from Canada and 48 miles north of Wolf Point on Hwy 13. Scobey is a trading town for the local farmers, ranchers, and neighbors from Canada and has Montana's only curling ring.

It is the county seat of Daniels County. This is grain and cattle country, rich in farmland and rolling grass prairies.

UPLAND BIRDS
sharp-tailed and sage grouse, Hungarian partridge, pheasant

With many acres of cropland in CRP cover, habitat has increased for pheasants, Hungarian partridge, and sharp-tailed grouse. Pheasant are the most numerous. Huns and sharptails are established in all regions, but their numbers fluctuate depending on weather conditions. Sage grouse are in the southeast corner of the county in limited numbers.

WATERFOWL
geese and ducks

The meandering Poplar River, with its many tributaries, marshes, and potholes, and the cropland throughout the county make this an attractive area for waterfowl on the move. Canada geese requirements are similar to mallards, but they are associated with larger areas of water. There is early season hunting along the river and waterways. Farm country can offer outstanding waterfowl hunting if water conditions are good.

ACCOMMODATIONS
Cattle King Motor Inn, Hwy 13 South. 487-5332 or 1-800-502-2775.
   29 rooms. Dogs allowed. Reasonable rates.
Juel Motel, 524 Main. 487-2765.
   9 rooms. No dogs. Reasonable rates.
The Lodge, P.O. Box 1009. 487-5349.
   4 bedrooms, 2 baths, full kitchen. No dogs. Single groups, call for reservations.

RESTAURANTS
The Silver Slipper, Hwy 13 South. 487-9973.
Lounge and supper club, lunch 11:30AM–1:30PM, dinner 5PM–10PM.
Ponderosa Bar and Pizza, 102 Main St. 487-5954.
Bar, grill, and pizza.
Whiskey Buttes Club, 45 Four Buttes. 487-5318.
Steak, seafood, full bar, lunch and dinner.

VETERINARIANS
Kenneth Lee, D.V.M. 1 mile west of Scobey. 783-5201.

SPORTING GOODS
Coast to Coast, 24 Main St. 487-2628.
Gary's Sports Equipment, 406 1st Ave West. 487-5485.

AUTO REPAIR AND RENTAL
Solberg Chevrolet, Buick, GMC, 106 1st Ave East. 487-2821.
Dan's Auto and Cycle, Hwy 5 East. 487-2670.

AIR SERVICE
City and County Airport, Trower Aviation. 487-2725.

MEDICAL
Daniels Memorial Hospital, 105 5th Ave East. 487-2296.

FOR MORE INFORMATION:
Scobey Chamber of Commerce
P.O. Box 91
Scobey, MT 59263.
487-5502.

WOLF POINT
AND ROOSEVELT COUNTY

Population– 2,880	October Temperature– 45.7
Elevation– 2,004'	Annual Precipitation– 15"
County Population– 10,999	Acres in CRP– 141,017
County Area– 2,356 sq. mi.	FWP Region 6

Wolf Point, located on Hwy 2, is home of the "Wild Horse Stampede," the oldest rodeo in Montana. The town is on the mainline of the Burlington Northern Railroad, which services the large grain elevators and farms in the region. Wolf Point is a trading town for farmers and ranchers. It is on the Fort Peck Indian Reservation and home to many Sioux and Assiniboines. The Wolf Point Historical Society exhibits artifacts of the early settlers and Native Americans. The town has grown into a modern shopping center with many services and facilities.

Wolf Point is the county seat of Roosevelt County. East of the Fort Peck Dam, the Missouri River flows down a wide valley lined with cottonwood trees. Hwy 2 also follows the river, which is the southern boundary of Roosevelt County. Wolf Creek, Poplar River, and the Big Muddy flow into the Missouri from the north. In the early 1900s, homesteaders poured into the surrounding area for the "last of the free land," making agriculture the major economy.

UPLAND BIRDS
sharp-tailed and sage grouse, pheasant, and Hungarian partridge

The Poplar River, Big Muddy Creek, the Missouri River, and the adjacent farmland provide excellent habitat for pheasants. Hungarian partridge are well established in the entire region, but numbers will vary from season to season. Sage grouse are in the northwestern part of the county, but they are very dependent on the sagebrush habitat. Distribution of sharp-tailed grouse in the county is mainly in the agricultural and CRP grassland.

WATERFOWL
geese and ducks

With the combination of water and croplands in Roosevelt County, hunting for all species is excellent along the waterways as well as in the fields.

Accommodations
Sherman Motor Inn, 200 East Main. 653-1100 or 800-952-1100.
46 rooms, restaurant, lounge. Dogs allowed. Reasonable rates.

Homestead Inn, 101 US 2 East. 653-1300.
  22 rooms. Dogs allowed. Reasonable rates.
Big Sky Motel, US 2 East. 653-2300.
  22 rooms. Dogs allowed. Reasonable rates.
RBW Campground, 7 miles east on US 2. 525-3740.
  Open from 5/1-10/1. 10 tent and 14 RV spaces. Full services.

RESTAURANTS
Sherman Motor Inn, 200 East Main St. 653-1100.
  Full menu, 6AM–10PM.
Stockman's Bar and Cafe, 217 Main St. 653-2287.
Wolf Point Cafe, 217 Main St. 653-9610.
Elk's Club, Main and 3rd. 653-1920.
  5PM–10PM for dinner.

VETERINARIANS
H. A. Hopson, D.V.M., P.O. Box 302. 653-1821.

SPORTING GOODS
Hi-Line Sports, 420 Hwy 2. 653-2276.
  Complete sportswear and equipment. 8:30AM–5:30PM, Mon-Sat.

AUTO REPAIR
K&J Repair, Hwy 2 East. 653-3103.
Peter's Auto Service, 225 Hwy 2. 653-1652.

AIR SERVICE
Wolf Point Airport, 653-1621.
Big Sky Airlines, 653-2250.

MEDICAL
Northeast Montana Medical Group, 301 Knapp. 653-2260.
Trinity Hospital, 315 Knapp. 653-2100.

FOR MORE INFORMATION:
Wolf Point Chamber of Commerce
P.O. Box 237
Wolf Point, MT 59201.
653-2012.

FORT BENTON
AND CHOTEAU COUNTY

Population– 660
Elevation– 2,600'
County Population– N/A
County Area– 3,973 sq. mi.

October Temperature– 48.8
Annual Precipitation– 15"
Acres in CRP– 151,254
FWP Regions 4 and 6

Fort Benton is 44 miles northeast of Great Falls on US 89. It is the county seat of Choteau County and the gateway to the upper Missouri River. There are 50 miles of beautiful scenery, fishing, and big game, upland bird, and waterfowl hunting along the waterway. The Teton and Marias Rivers come in from the north. The Shonkin Sag area in the southwest has a 500 foot deep, mile-wide, u-shaped valley along the Square Butte and the Highwood Mountains. Once a huge river, it is now a series of shallow lakes and scattered farms and ranches. In Choteau County, the Missouri River leaves its valley to form deep canyons and high eroded walls known as the Missouri Breaks. The Highwood Mountains in the southern area of the county, part of the Lewis and Clark National Forest, are surrounded by intermountain grassland. The majority of the county is plains grassland and crops.

UPLAND BIRDS
ruffed, blue, sage, and sharp-tailed grouse, Hungarian partridge, pheasant
The Highwood Mountains, with their aspen and evergreen forests, provide mountain grouse habitat. Sage grouse are found only in the northwest corner of Choteau County. Hungarian partridge and sharp-tailed grouse are well established in most of the grassland and agricultural country. The three main river systems and adjacent bottomland produce excellent pheasant habitat.

WATERFOWL
geese and ducks
Choteau County has numerous rivers, streams, creeks, lakes, reservoirs, potholes, and marshes, as well as large agricultural land use. This makes ideal habitat for breeding and migratory waterfowl. When migration is in full swing, decoying waterfowl on the rivers and in the stubble fields can be outstanding.

ACCOMMODATIONS
Pioneer Lodge, 1700 Front St. 622-5441.
9 rooms. Reasonable rates. No dogs.
Fort Motel, 1809 St. Charles. 622-3312.
11 rooms. Dogs allowed. Reasonable rates.

OUTFITTERS
Perry Hunts and Adventures, P.O. Box 355, Fort Benton, MT 59442.
622-5336. Shooting preserve for upland gamebirds.

RESTAURANTS
3-Way Cafe, 2300 St. Charles. 622-5681.
Breakfast and lunch, 7AM–3PM.
L&R Sandwich Shop, 1310 Front St.
Open for lunch.
Banque Club, 1318 Front St. 622-5272.
Dinner and spirits, 5PM–1AM.
CJ's Diner, 1402 Front St. 622-5035.
Breakfast and lunch, 7AM–3:30PM.
Overland Bar, 14th St.
Sandwiches.

VETERINARIANS
Animal Medical Center, P.O. Box 1105. 622-5027.
Benton Vet Clinic, 999 St. Charles Ave. 622-3732.

SPORTING GOODS
Coast to Coast, 1422 Front St. 622-5042.
Guns and ammunition.

AUTO REPAIR
Fort Benton Motor, 2520 St. Charles St. 622-5131.

AIR SERVICE
County airstrip, Rick Zanto. 622-5249.

MEDICAL
Missouri River Medical Center, 1501 St. Charles St. 622-3331.

FOR MORE INFORMATION:
Fort Benton Chamber of Commerce
Karen Bryant
Karen's Insta-Print
1402 Front St.
Fort Benton, MT 59442.
622-5634.

GREAT FALLS
AND CASCADE COUNTY

Population– 55,000	October Temperature– 46.2
Elevation– 3,333'	Annual Precipitation– 23.01"
County Population– 77,000	Area in CRP– 65,617
County Area– 2,698 sq. mi.	FWP Region 4

Great Falls is located in northcentral Montana at the confluence of the Missouri and Sun Rivers. It is Montana's second largest town and home to the famous Charlie Russell Museum. Cascade County provides ample opportunity for both upland and waterfowl hunting. The Lewis and Clark National Forest lies to the south and the rest of the county consists of intermountain and plains grasslands. Agriculture is one of the main industries of the county.

UPLAND BIRDS
Hungarian partridge, pheasant, sharp-tailed, blue, and ruffed grouse
Pheasant hunting is excellent along the rivers and in CRP and agricultural lands. Huns can be found in the plains grasslands and adjacent agricultural areas. Sharptails are located in the intermountain grassland, CRP tracts, and coulees. There is good hunting for all three species of grouse in the Lewis and Clark National Forest in the southern part of the county.

WATERFOWL
geese and ducks
The agricultural areas provide excellent field hunting for geese. The rivers and the Benton Lake National Wildlife Refuge in the northern part of the county offer excellent hunting for both geese and ducks.

ACCOMMODATIONS
Budget Inn, 2 Treasure State Dr. 453-1602.
   60 rooms. Dogs allowed, grassy area. Rates moderate.
Comfort Inn, 1120 9th St South. 454-2727.
   64 rooms. Dogs allowed in smoking rooms only, $5 charge, grassy area. Spa. Rates moderate.
Edelweiss Motor Inn, 626 Central Ave West. 452-9503.
   20 rooms. Hunters and dogs welcome, grassy area. Rates very reasonable.
Super 8 Lodge, 1214 13th St South. 727-7600.
   117 rooms. Dogs allowed, grassy area. Rates moderate.

TownHouse Inn, 1411 10th Ave South. 761-4600.
108 rooms. Dogs allowed, $5 charge per dog. Grassy area, pool, restaurant. Rates moderate.

CAMPGROUNDS AND RV PARKS

Dick's RV Park, ½ mile east off exit 278 on 10th Ave South. 452-0333.
Open all year. 10 tent and 140 RV spaces. Showers, laundry, and store.

Great Falls KOA Campground, SE edge of town at 10th Ave South and 51st. 727-3191. Open all year. 22 tent, 116 RV spaces. Showers, laundry, store, and cabins.

RESTAURANTS

4B's, 4610 10th Ave South. 727-3366. Open 24 hours.

Elmers Pancake and Steak House, 1600 Fox Farm Rd, next to Budget Inn. 761-2400. Open 6AM–10PM for breakfast, lunch, and dinner.

El Comedor Mexican Restaurant, 1120 25th St South. 761-5500.
Open 7 days,11AM–11PM for lunch and dinner. Imported beers.

Jaker's Steak, Ribs, and Fish House, 1500 10th Ave South. 727-1033.
Open for lunch and dinner.

VETERINARIANS

Rocky Mountain Medical Center, 1401 Northwest Bypass. 727-8387.
24-hour emergency service,

Skyline Veterinary Clinic, 15th St North, Junction Havre Hwy and Bootlegger Trail. 761-8282. 24-hour emergency service.

SPORTING GOODS

Big Bear Sports Center, 4800 10th Ave. 761-6300.

Prairie Sporting Goods, 802 2nd Ave North. 452-7319.

AUTO RENTAL AND REPAIR

Budget, Great Falls International Airport. 454-1001.

Hertz Rent-A-Car, Great Falls International Airport. 761-6641.

Carl's Exxon, 2300 10th Ave South. 761-1342.
Open 7 days. Towing.

Westgate Exxon, 416 Smelter Ave NE. 452-1271.
Open 7 days. Towing.

AIR SERVICE

Great Falls International Airport, 15 South. 727-3404.
Serviced by Northwest, Delta, and Horizon airlines.

MEDICAL

Columbus Hospital, 500 15th Ave South. 727-3333.

Montana Deaconess Medical Center, 1101 26th St South. 761-1200.

FOR MORE INFORMATION:
Great Falls Chamber of Commerce
P.O. Box 2127-A
Great Falls, MT 59403.
761-4436.

Montana Dept. of Fish, Wildlife, and Parks, Region 4
4600 Springs Rd
Great Falls, MT 59406.
454-3441.

Bureau of Land Management
812 14 North
Great Falls, MT 59406.
727-0503.

Benton Lake National Wildlife Refuge
922 Bootlegger Trail
Great Falls, MT 59406.
727-7400.

STANFORD
AND JUDITH BASIN COUNTY

Population– 529
Elevation– 4,200'
County Population– 2,282
County Area– 1,869 sq. mi.

October Temperature– 45.5
Annual Precipitation– 15"
Acres in CRP– 20,684
FWP Region 4

Stanford is 60 miles southeast of Great Falls on Hwy 200. The town's wide streets and well-kept homes make it a peaceful, pleasant place. At the turn of the century, Stanford was an important trade center for ranchers and farmers.

Stanford is the county seat of Judith Basin and is bounded on the southwest by the Little Belt Mountains in the Lewis and Clark National Forest. The land gives way to the broad Judith River basin, which has some of Montana's most fertile farmland.

The county has more diversity of habitat than most, with its montane forests, intermountain grasslands, plains grasslands, dryland farming, croplands along the Judith River, and numerous small creeks.

UPLAND BIRDS
ruffed, blue, sharp-tailed, and spruce grouse, Hungarian partridge, pheasant

The wide variety of habitat types support many species of upland gamebirds. There are mountain grouse in the national forest lands and intermountain grasslands and spruce grouse in denser forests. Sharp-tailed grouse and Hungarian partridge are scattered throughout the county, except in the high mountain forest. The pheasant distribution is mostly in the northeastern half of the county in the croplands and water systems.

WATERFOWL
geese and ducks

Judith Basin County is too far south for most waterfowl activities, but provides fair shooting along the small reservoirs, potholes, creeks, and the Judith River before freeze-up.

ACCOMMODATIONS
Sundown Motel, 200 West, P.O. Box 126. 800-346-2316.
    10 rooms, 1 house. Dogs allowed. Very reasonable rates.
By Way Motel, South of Stanford on Hwy 200. 566-2943.
    5 rooms. No dogs allowed. Very reasonable.

RESTAURANTS
The By Way Cafe, South of Stanford on Hwy 200. 566-2631.
  Truck stop, restaurant, and liquor store.
The Sundown Inn, west of town. 566-9911.
  Lunch and dinner, 5PM–10PM daily, 5PM–12PM weekends.
Wolves' Den, 81 Central Ave. 566-2451.
  Breakfast, lunch, and dinner, 6AM–10PM.

VETERINARIAN.
John Gee, D.V.M., 566-2687.

AIR SERVICE
Big B Flying Service, 566-2236.
  Mike Biggerstaff. Airstrip paved and lighted.

MEDICAL
Judith Basin Medical Center, 566-2773.

FOR MORE INFORMATION
  Stanford Chamber of Commerce
  P.O. Box 222
  Stanford, MT 59479.
  566-2300 or 566-2714.

LEWISTOWN
AND FERGUS COUNTY

Population– 6,051
Elevation– 3,960'
County Population– 12,083
County Area– 4,339 sq. mi.

October Temperature– 44.2
Annual Precipitation– 20.97"
Acres in CRP– 68,6078
FWP Region 4

Lewistown, 128 miles northwest of Billings and 105 miles west of Great Falls, is nestled at the foot of the Judith, Moccasin, and Big Snowy Mountains, along Big Spring Creek. This hub of central Montana is in the exact center of the state. It is a trading center for the ranchers and farmers in the area.

Lewistown is the county seat of Fergus County. Fergus County, like most of central Montana, produces bccf cattle and grain products in the form of wheat and barley. The county is large and has a wide variety of terrain and vegetation types including mountains with montane forest and intermountain grassland, and rolling hill country with shrub and plains grasslands. Both are interspersed with ranch and farmland. The northern boundary of Fergus County is the Missouri River. The Judith River and its tributaries flow north into the Missouri River system. The county has numerous other creeks and small streams with mixed types of habitat along their water courses.

UPLAND BIRDS
ruffed, blue, sharp-tailed, and sage grouse, Hungarian partridge, pheasant

The Big Snowy and the Judith Mountains with their montane forests provide habitat for mountain grouse. Sharp-tailed grouse and Hungarian partridge are throughout the county, but numbers vary greatly between dry sagebrush and moist grassland prairies. Croplands, heavy cover along the many waterways, dryland farming, and CRP fields have contributed to the excellent pheasant population. Turkeys are found in the area that extends from the Judith River to the Missouri River.

WATERFOWL
geese and ducks

During migration, the Missouri River and the adjacent dryland farming country provide outstanding hunting for mallards and geese. The numerous rivers, creeks, potholes, and marshes support good duck populations early in the season.

ACCOMMODATIONS

Mountainview Motel, 1422 West Main St. 538-3457 or 800-862-5786. Reservations suggested. 31 rooms, 3 kitchenettes, 1 house (day or week). Dogs allowed. Reasonable rates. Your hosts are Jim and Virginia Woodburn.

Yogo Park Inn, 211 East Main. 538-8721 or 800-437-PARK.
Reservations suggested. 124 rooms, dogs allowed. Moderate rates. Golden
Spike Lounge and Yogo Steak House.
B&B Motel, 420 East Main. 538-5496.
36 rooms, kitchenettes. Dogs allowed. Reasonable rates.

OUTFITTERS
Montana Outdoor Expeditions, 76370 Gallatin Rd, Gallatin Gateway, MT 59730.
763-4749 or 580-1799. Upland gamebird and big game hunting. Call for reservations. Bob and Patti Griffith.
Pigeye Basin Outfitters, Peter B. Rogers, HCR 81, Box 25, Utica, MT 59452.
423-5223. Blue, ruffed, and sharp-tailed grouse, Hungarian partridge, pheasant.
Pete also has a private pheasant preserve. Accommodations and meals. Call for
reservations.

RESTAURANTS
Snow White Cafe, 122 West Main St. 538-3666.
Daily specials 5:30AM–10PM. Closed Mondays.
Sportsman Restaurant and Casino, top of the hill. 538-9053.
Dining, 6PM–10PM. Lounge, 8AM–2AM.
Pete's Fireside Dining Room and Drive-In, 1308 West Main. 430-9400.
Open 7 days a week.

VETERINARIANS
Lewistown Veterinary Service, Fairgrounds Road. 538-3663.
Dr. Vischer.

SPORTING GOODS
The Sports Center, 320 West Main St. 538-9308.
Hunting and fishing headquarters. 8:30AM-6PM.

AUTO REPAIR AND RENTAL
Dean Newton Olds, 519 West Broadway. 538-3455.

AIR SERVICE
Lewistown Airport, Big Sky Airlines. Daily service. 538-3264.

MEDICAL
Central Montana Medical Center, 408 Wendall Ave. 538-7711.

FOR MORE INFORMATION:
Chamber of Commerce
P.O. Box 818
Lewistown, MT 59457.
538-5436.

WINNETT
AND PETROLEUM COUNTY

Population– 188   October Temperature– N/A
Elevation– 2,906'   Annual Precipitation– N/A
County Population– 519   Acres in CRP– 17,874
County Area– 1,654 sq. mi.   FWP Region 4

Winnet is 54 miles east of Lewistown and 98 miles north of Billings on Highway 200. A small family town, the area's primary economy is farming and ranching. Winnet is the county seat of Petroleum County, one of the most sparsely populated counties in the state. The eastern line of Petroleum County is bordered by the Musselshell River. The Crooked Creek Recreation Area, northeast of Winnet, is the western entrance to Fort Peck Lake, which is in the C.M. Russell National Wildlife Refuge. Most of the county is shrub grassland interspersed with plains grassland, but it does have considerable dryland farming with hay meadows along the water courses. The off-road, backcountry byways through the rolling sage country can be rough. Do not attempt these routes if they are wet.

UPLAND BIRDS
sharp-tailed and sage grouse, Hungarian partridge, pheasant
The shrub grassland supports populations of sage grouse, and the mix of agricultural land, CRP, plains grasslands, and vast rolling sagebrush country provides good habitat for sharp-tailed grouse and Hungarian partridge. The region can be very arid at times, causing the upland bird population to fluctuate considerably. Pheasants will mainly be in agricultural areas and riparian habitat.

WATERFOWL
geese and ducks
Ducks and geese migrate and winter in large rivers that have open spaces adjacent to a food source. Petroleum County has limited open water during the late hunting season, but does have early waterfowl hunting on the potholes and reservoirs and along the Musselshell River.

ACCOMMODATIONS
The Northern Hotel, 429-7781.
22 rooms. Rates very reasonable. No dogs allowed.

RESTAURANTS
Kozy Korner, 429-2621.
Full menu, 6AM–9PM, bar 10AM–2PM.

Winnet Bar, 429-2221.
Hamburgers and sandwiches, 10AM–2PM.

VETERINARIANS
The closest veterinarian is in Lewistown
Lewistown Veterinary Service, 538-3663.

SPORTING GOODS
Gerfhmel General Store, 429-5571.
Hardware, ammunition, groceries, cafe.

AUTO REPAIR
Ray Bern Oil Co, 429-2961.
Gas station and repair.

MEDICAL
Winnett does not have medical service. Emergency care can be found in
Lewistown, Billings, or Round-up. Call 911 for ambulance.

Chuck Johnson connects with a sage grouse in typical sage country.

JORDAN
AND GARFIELD COUNTY

Population– 485	October Temperature– 46.8
Elevation– 2,800'	Annual Precipitation– 13"
County Population– 1,589	Acres in CRP– 77,703
County Area– 4,668 sq. mi.	FWP Region 7

Jordan is 130 miles east of Lewistown and 84 miles northwest of Miles City on Hwy 200. It is the county seat of Garfield County, nicknamed the "Big Lonesome." The county has the lowest population density in Montana, one person to every three square miles. The C.M. Russell Wildlife Refuge and Fort Peck Lake cover a large portion of Garfield County. The rest of the county is large ranches, plains grassland, gumbo buttes, mixed sagebrush prairie, and Missouri Breaks badlands.

UPLAND BIRDS
sharp-tailed and sage grouse, Hungarian partridge, pheasant, Merriam's turkey

Sharp-tailed grouse are established in all parts of Garfield County. The shrub grassland provides habitat for sage grouse. Hungarian partridge are found in the lower two-thirds of the county, but coveys are widely spaced due to habitat and terrain. Pheasant habitat is confined to the Musselshell River bottoms and adjacent croplands. Wild turkey habitat is along the Musselshell and Missouri River systems.

WATERFOWL
geese and ducks

Fort Peck Reservoir, one of the largest artificial lakes in the world, is an important migratory route and staging area for waterfowl. Small grains such as wheat and barley are raised on large dryland ranches in Garfield County. Field shooting for ducks and geese can be excellent. Garfield County is in the Central Flyway.

ACCOMMODATIONS
Fellman's Motel, Hwy 200, Box 89. 557-2209 or 1-800-552-2689.
16 rooms. Dogs allowed. Reasonable rates.
Garfield Hotel and Motel, Hwy 200 and Main, Box 374. 557-6215.
12 rooms. No dogs allowed. Reasonable rates.

CAMPGROUNDS
Kamp Katie, west of the bridge on Big Dry Creek. 557-2851.

OUTFITTERS

Twitchell Bros. Snap Creek Ranch, Rt 2, Box 23. 557-2554.
J. Twitchell. Waterfowl and upland birds.
Hell Creek Guest Ranch, P.O. Box 325. 557-2224.
John and Sylvia Trumbo. Turkey and big game hunting.

RESTAURANTS

QD's, west of Jordan on Hwy 200.
Full service, 6AM–10PM.

VETERINARIANS

The closest veterinarian is in Circle.
Circle Veterinary Clinic. 485-2610 or home, 485-2828.

SPORTING GOODS

Fellman's Ace Hardware, 557-2206.

AUTO REPAIR

Pioneer Garage, 557-7263.

AIR SERVICE

Garfield County Airport, Vivienne Schrank. 557-2565.

MEDICAL

Doctor's Clinic, 557-2500.

FOR MORE INFORMATION:

Chamber of Commerce
P.O. Box 370
Jordan, MT 59337.
557-2248 or 557-2232.

CIRCLE
AND McCONE COUNTY

Population– 805	October Temperature– 44.2
Elevation– 2,450'	Annual Precipitation– 20.31"
County Population– 2,275	Acres in CRP– 133,542
County Area– 2,643 sq. mi.	FWP Region 6

Circle is halfway between Fort Peck and Glendive, 47 miles south of Wolf Point on Hwy 200. The town was named for the simple circle brand of the Mabrey Cattle Corp. On the edge of town is the McCone County Museum with over 5,000 items on display. Circle has overnight accommodations, a campground, restaurants, service stations, and all other facilities necessary for a relaxing stay.

Circle is the county seat of McCone County, with the Missouri River as its northern border and a leg of Fort Peck Lake on the western boundary. The county is mostly plains grassland, mixed with over a million acres of grain farmland. The northern area is broken up by the Missouri Breaks along the river.

UPLAND BIRDS
sharp-tailed and sage grouse, pheasant, Hungarian partridge
The pheasant population extends from the Redwater River bottoms across McCone County to the Missouri River. Sharp-tailed grouse and Hungarian partridge are established in this region, depending on available habitat. Sage grouse can be found where there are large expanses of sagebrush.

WATERFOWL
geese and ducks
The large bodies of water on the western and northern border and extensive amounts of grain production make this county well-suited for waterfowl. Field shooting can be extremely productive during waterfowl migration.

ACCOMMODATIONS
Traveler Inn Montana, P.O. Box 78. 485-3323.
14 rooms. Dogs allowed. Reasonable rates.

RESTAURANTS
Tastee Freez, east end of town. 485-3674.
Wooden Nickel, Main Street. 485-2575.

VETERINARIANS
Circle Veterinary Clinic, 485-2610 or home, 485-2828.

SPORTING GOODS
Larson True Value Hardware, 485-2690.

AUTO REPAIR
Community Auto Repair, 485-2630.
Exxon Service Center, 485-3663.

AIR SERVICE
County airstrip, Jeff Skyberg. 485-2481.

MEDICAL
McCullum County Hospital, 485-3381.

FOR MORE INFORMATION:
Circle Chamber of Commerce
Box 321
Circle, MT 59215.
Orville Quick, 485-2414.

Ben Williams and his Brittanys working a grassy coulee.

SIDNEY
AND RICHLAND COUNTY

Population– 5,217
Elevation– 1,928'
County Population– 10,716
County Area– 2,084,151 sq. mi.

October Temperature– 45.1
Annual Precipitation– 15"
Acres in CRP– 74,794
FWP Region 6

Sidney is nestled in the fertile valley of the lower Yellowstone River, on Hwy 16 in northeastern Montana, five miles from the North Dakota border. Five motels and hotels provide over 250 rooms. There are many restaurants and a wide variety of stores.

Sidney is the county seat of Richland County and offers a wide scope of recreational opportunities and varied landscapes. There are rugged badlands to the east, while the Yellowstone flows northward towards a majestic confluence with the Missouri River. The Missouri also forms the northern border of Richland County. The western reaches of the county have open grasslands and rolling hills. The county is rich in agricultural lands and has a growing season of 140 days.

UPLAND BIRDS
sharp-tailed and sage grouse, Hungarian partridge, pheasant

The lower Yellowstone River bottoms and the Missouri River offer good pheasant hunting. The Yellowstone River enters from the south and the Missouri enters from the west, forming a triangle. This triangular region supports a strong population of pheasants and Hungarian partridge. The distribution of the sharp-tailed grouse in Richland County is mainly in the western part of the triangle. The western third of Richland County with its sagebrush grassland prairie, supports pockets of sage grouse. Hungarian partridge are established in all of the region.

WATERFOWL
geese and ducks

This triangular region is rich in waterfowl, not only because two major rivers come together, but because the whole lower region of the Yellowstone and Missouri River system has numerous islands, creeks, springs, and marshes, in addition to the agricultural land that waterfowl need during migration. Open water and an abundance of food hold the birds in this area.

ACCOMMODATIONS

Richland Motor Inn, 1200 South Central Ave. 482-6400.
62 rooms. Dogs allowed. Reasonable rates.

Angus Ranchouse Motel, 2300 South Central Ave. 482-3826.
  32 rooms, kitchenettes. Dogs allowed with deposit. Very reasonable rates.
Lalonde Hotel, 217 South Central Ave. 482-1043.
  24-hour desk, 32 rooms. No dogs allowed. Very reasonable. Yellowstone
  Lounge, dining room.
Lone Tree Motor Inn, 990 South Central Ave. 482-4520.
  40 rooms, continental breakfast. Dogs allowed. Reasonable rates.

OUTFITTERS
Montana Experience, Rt 1, Box 1495, Fairview, MT 59221. 798-3474.
  Scott Sundheim, licensed guide for upland birds and big game.

RESTAURANTS
Eagle Cafe, 102 East Main. 482-1839.
  Breakfast, lunch, and dinner. 5AM–10PM, M-Thurs. Fri. and Sat., 24 hours.
Triangle Night Club, Southeast of Sidney. 482-9948.
  Dinner, spirits, casino, and live music. 5PM–10PM, M-Thurs. Fri. and Sat.,
  5PM–2AM.

VETERINARIANS
Douglas Veterinary Clinic, P.O. Box 1766. 482-1413.
Riek Animal Clinic, P.O. Box 948. 482-3107.

SPORTING GOODS
Redwater Trader, 813 South Central Ave. 482-6737.
  Guns, ammunition, and gun parts.

AUTO REPAIR
Bloesser Auto, 1440 South Central Ave. Business 482-5508, home 482-3676.

AIR SERVICE
Richland-Sidney Airport. 482-5120. Res. 1-800-882-4475.
  Terminal—Big Sky Airlines.

MEDICAL
Community Memorial Hospital and Clinic, 216 14th Ave SW. 482-1916.

FOR MORE INFORMATION:
  Sidney Chamber of Commerce
  909 South Central Ave
  Sidney, MT 59270.
  482-1916.

GLENDIVE
AND DAWSON COUNTY

Population– 4,802
Elevation– 2,069'
County Population– 9,505
County Area– 2,373 sq. mi.

October Temperature– 45.7
Annual Precipitation– 15"
Acres in CRP– 79,942
FWP Region 7

Glendive is in eastern Montana, along the Yellowstone River, off of Interstate 94. Located on the outskirts of town is the 8,000-acre Makoshika State Park of Primitive Terrain, where dinosaurs once roamed.

Glendive is the county seat of Dawson County. The large, slow-moving Yellowstone River, with its many islands and hardwood bottoms, crosses Dawson County.

The Big Sheep Mountains in western Dawson County have hardwood draws, plains grasslands, rolling hills, and agricultural land extending to the Yellowstone River. Dawson County has irrigated land along the river and some dryland farming.

UPLAND BIRDS
sharp-tailed and sage grouse, Hungarian partridge, pheasant,

The hardwood draws and hill country of Dawson County provide good habitat for both Huns and sharptails. The Yellowstone River bottom supports a pheasant population and the northeast portion of Dawson County has pockets of sage grouse.

WATERFOWL
geese and ducks

The Yellowstone River is large and slow-moving. Its islands and backwater channels provide excellent hunting for ducks and geese during the fall migration in the Central Flyway.

ACCOMMODATIONS
Super 8, 1904 North Merrill. 365-5671.
  53 rooms. Dogs allowed. Reasonable rates.
Day's Inn, 2000 North Merrill. 365-6011.
  60 rooms. Dogs allowed. Reasonable rates.
Budget Hosts Riverside Inn, Interstate 94 and Hwy 16. 365-2349.
  36 rooms. Dogs allowed. Reasonable rates.
Parkwood Motel, 1002 West Bell. 365-8221.
  16 rooms. Dogs allowed for a $5 charge. Very reasonable.

Glendive Campground, I-94, Exit 215. 365-6721.
Open all year. 7 tent and 60 RV spaces. Full services.

RESTAURANTS
Twilite Dining, Lounge and Casino, 209 North Merrill. 365-8705.
Prime rib, steak, and seafood.
Jordan Motor Hotel and Coffee Shop, 223 North Merrill. 365-5655.
Fine dining in the Blue Room.
Trail Star Truck Stop and Trail Star II , Hwy 16, Exit 213. 365-3901.
Open 24 hours. Good, home-cooked meals.

VETERINARIANS
Glendive Veterinary Clinic and Supply, 821 North Sargent. 365-3475.

SPORTING GOODS
Friendly True Value, P.O. Box 1089. 365-8233.
Guns and ammunition.

AUTO REPAIR
Cenex, Hwy 16 and Interstate 94. 365-8404.
Open 24 hours.

AIR SERVICE
Big Sky Airlines, P.O. Box 1086. 687-3360.

MEDICAL
Glendive Medical Center, 202 Prospect Dr. 365-3306.

FOR MORE INFORMATION:
Chamber of Commerce and Agriculture
200 North Merrill, P.O. Box 930
Glendive, MT 59330.
365-5601.
Fax: 365-3302.

TERRY
AND PRAIRIE COUNTY

Population– 659	October Temperature– 43.7
Elevation– 2,251'	Annual Precipitation– 15"
County Population– 1,383	Acres in CRP– 30,519
County Area– 2,394 sq. mi.	FWP Region 7

Terry is on Interstate 94, halfway between Miles City and Glendive. This small community is nestled against the Yellowstone River between the confluence of the Powder River and O'Fallon Creek. Terry is in the heart of agate country. People come from all over the U.S. to hunt the transparent rock.

Terry is the county seat of Prairie County. The county has agricultural lands, riparian habitat along the rivers, plains grasslands with rolling hills, and famed badlands.

UPLAND BIRDS
sharp-tailed and sage grouse, Hungarian partridge, pheasant

The Yellowstone River bottom and the farm country carry established populations of pheasants. Sharp-tailed grouse, sage grouse, and Huns are located throughout the county.

WATERFOWL
geese and ducks

Prairie County supports a good population of waterfowl along the Yellowstone River system and farmlands. When the Central Flyway migration is in full swing, many ducks and geese funnel down the Yellowstone River.

ACCOMMODATIONS
Diamond Motel, 118 East Spring St, Box 446. 637-5407.
 12 rooms, campground available. Dogs allowed.
Kempton Hotel, 204 Spring St. 637-5543.
 Downtown Terry. 14 rooms, 9 apartments with kitchens.
Berg's RV Oasis, Box 375. 637-5829.

RESTAURANTS
Bud and Betty's Bar and Cafe, 204 Laundre St. 637-5879.
 Full menu, breakfast, lunch, and dinner, 6AM–8PM.
Roy Rogers Tavern, 205 Spring St. 637-9913.
 Lunch and dinner, 12PM–2AM.
Overland Restaurant, 316 East Spring St. 637-5830.

VETERINARIANS

The nearest veterinarians are in Miles City:

East Main Animal Clinic, 2719 Main St, Miles City. 232-6900.

Miles City Veterinary, west of Miles City. 232-2559.

SPORTING GOODS

Netzer Hardware, 200 Logan Ave. 637-5440.

AUTO REPAIR

Dan's Welding and Repair, 637-5724.

AIR SERVICE

County airstrip, Willis Barholomay. 637-5459

MEDICAL

Prairie County Clinic, 409 Bowen. 637-5863.

FOR MORE INFORMATION

Terry Chamber of Commerce
Box 6
Terry, MT 59349.
637-2126.

ROCKY MOUNTAIN COUNTRY

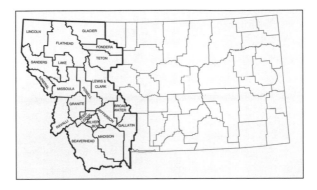

The Rocky Mountain Country occupies the western part of Montana. Some of our largest towns and resort communities (Bozeman, Missoula, Kalispell, Great Falls, and Big Sky) are located in this part of the state. The area contains vast national forests and the majority of our mountain ranges. Many of our famous blue-ribbon trout streams are in this area including the Madison, Jefferson, Clark Fork, and Missouri.

The three species of mountain grouse—ruffed, blue, and Franklin's—are the predominate gamebirds. There is also good hunting for pheasants in the beautiful valleys of the Rocky Mountain Country. The eastern fringe of the area holds pheasants and Hungarian partridge. The southwest section, centered in Beaverhead County, has good hunting for sage grouse. The many rivers and wildlife refuges provide excellent waterfowl hunting.

PHEASANT DISTRIBUTION

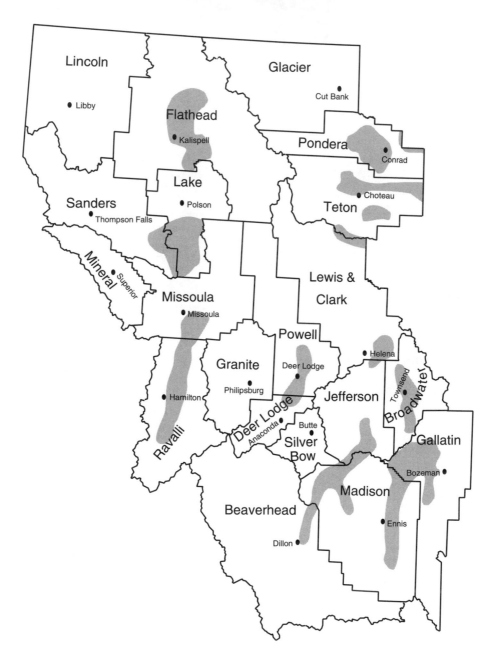

SHARP-TAILED GROUSE DISTRIBUTION

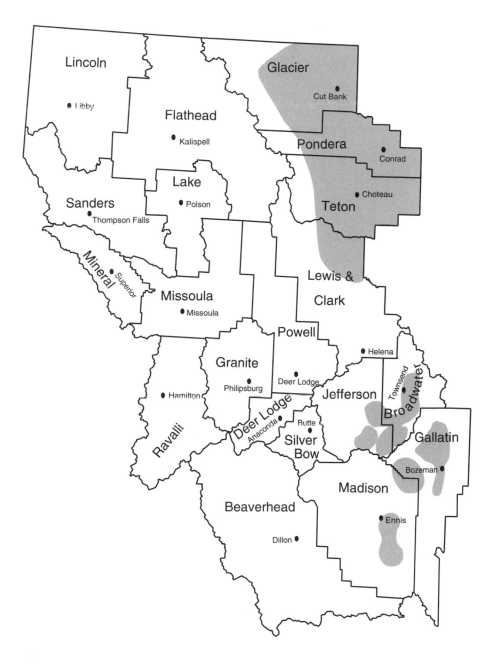

SAGE GROUSE DISTRIBUTION

GRAY (HUNGARIAN) PARTRIDGE DISTRIBUTION

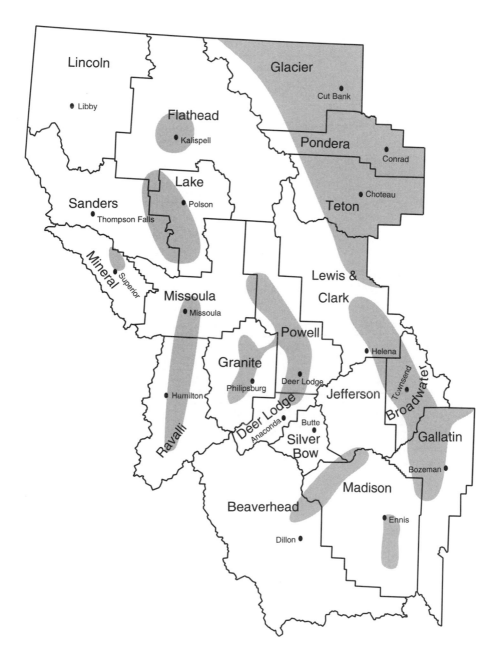

BLUE GROUSE DISTRIBUTION

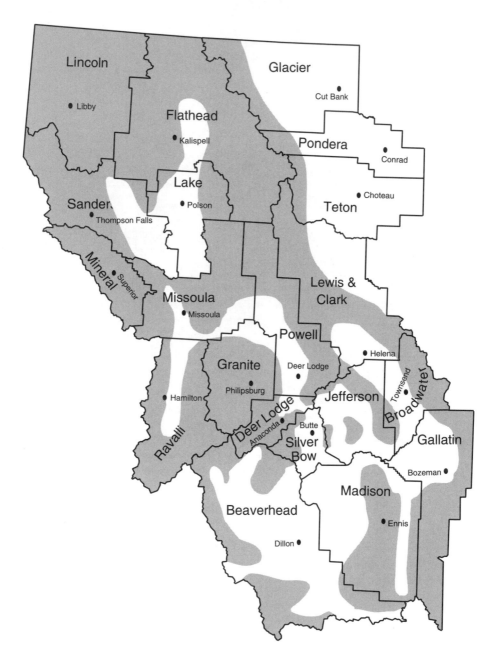

Ruffed Grouse Distribution

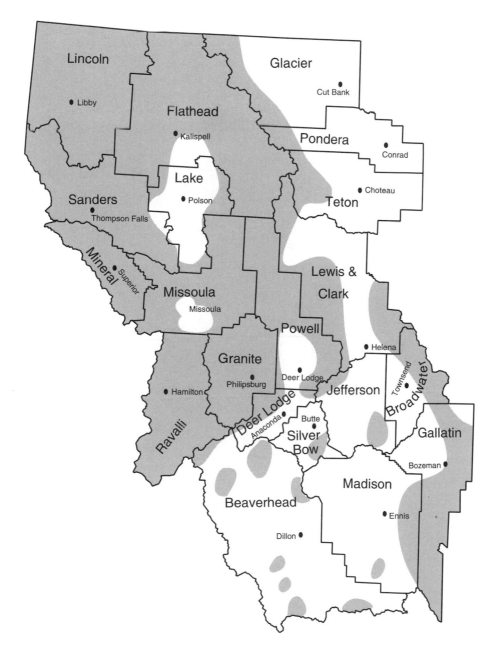

FRANKLIN'S GROUSE DISTRIBUTION

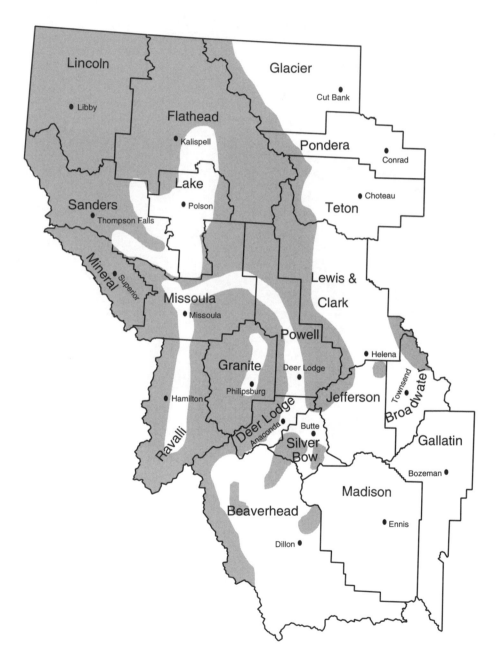

MERRIAM'S TURKEY DISTRIBUTION

Special Permit-Only Hunting Areas
Spring and Fall

Datus Proper hunts mountain grouse.

LIBBY
AND LINCOLN COUNTY

Population– 2,800	October Temperature– 48.4
Elevation– 2,066'	Annual Precipitation– 18.85"
County Population– 18,700	Acres in CRP– 0
County Area– 3,613 sq. mi.	FWP Region 1

Libby is located in a beautiful valley surrounded by the grandeur of the 2.5 million-acre Cabinet Mountain Wilderness. The blue-green Kootenai River borders the north edge of town. The Kootenai National Forest (over 2 million acres) provides extensive public hunting land in some of the most beautiful and rugged country in northwest Montana.

Lincoln County is first in the state in commercial lumber and wood products. Libby has a host of fine restaurants, motels, and services and its people are known for their friendliness. The terrain consists of montane forest.

UPLAND BIRDS
blue, Franklin's, and ruffed grouse

Mountain grouse are the predominate birds in this region. The vast Kootenai National Forest and the Cabinet Mountains provide great public hunting opportunities for grouse. The northwest part of Montana does not have a lot of bird hunting pressure and it is not uncommon to go an entire day without seeing another hunter.

WATERFOWL
Ducks

The Kootenai River and Lake Koocanusa, north of Libby, provide excellent duck hunting during the Pacific Flyway fall migration.

ACCOMMODATIONS: LIBBY

The Caboose Motel, West Hwy 2. 293-6201.
  28 rooms. Hunters and dogs welcome, $5 pet fee. Very reasonable rates.
Sandman Motel, Hwy 2 West. 293-8831.
  16 units. Hot tub, cable, microwaves and refrigerators in each room. Hunters and dogs welcome, $5 pet fee. Very reasonable rates. Your hosts are John and Christine Heinlein.
Super 8 Motel, 448 West Hwy 2. 293-2771.
  42 units. Cable, indoor pool. Hunters and dogs welcome, $5 fee. Rates reasonable.

Venture Motor Inn, 443 Hwy 2 West.
72 rooms. Cable, indoor pool, exercise room, adjoining restaurant. Hunters welcome and dogs allowed. Rates reasonable.

ACCOMMODATIONS: TROY
Yaak River Lodge, 2774 Rt 508. 295-5463.
5 rooms and a dorm room that sleeps 9. Located in the beautiful Yaak river valley. Hunters and dogs welcome. Laundry service, gourmet dining, hot tub and sauna. Hosts are Don and Gloria Belcher.
Overdale Lodge, 1076 Overdale Lodge Rd. 295-4057.
Two-story, 5 bedrooms. Fully equipped kitchen. Overlooks a pond and a lake— a beautiful, secluded setting. Hunters and dogs welcome. Hosts are Jim and Mary Jackson.

CAMPGROUNDS AND RV PARKS
Big Bend RV Park, 13 miles from Libby on Rt 37. 792-7277.
25 tent, 25 RV sites. Water, electric, sewer, dump, 10 acres on lake, restaurant, and bar.
Russell's Conoco, 2 miles west of Libby on Hwy 2. 293-4942.
5 tent, 20 RV sites. Water, electric, sewer, dump, shower, laundry, store.

OUTFITTERS
Linehan Outfitting Co., 22408 Yaak River Rd, Troy, MT 59935. 295-4872.
Tim Linehan—specializes in grouse. I have hunted with Tim and he knows his birds and the area. He will provide you with a top-notch hunt.

RESTAURANTS
Beck's Montana Cafe, 2425 Hwy 2 West. 293-6686.
Open 8AM–10PM daily. Specializing in broasted chicken. Thursday night prime rib special.
4B's Restaurant, 442 Hwy 2. 293-8751.
Open 24 hours.
Henry's Restaurant, 407 West 9th. 293-7911.
Family restaurant.
MK Steakhouse, 9948 Hwy 2 South. 293-5686.
Open for dinner 6 days, closed Mondays Beautiful log building. Cocktails, specializing in steaks and prime rib.
Venture Inn Restaurant, 443 Hwy 2 West.
Open 6AM–11PM. Family restaurant.

VETERINARIANS
Treasure Valley Veterinary Clinic, 845 Hwy 2 West. 293-7410.
Doug Griffiths, D.V.M.

Sporting Goods
Libby's Sport Center, 116 East 9th. 293-4641.
  Complete hunting supplies and licenses.

Auto Repair
Auto Haus, 808 Hwy 2 West. 293-4351.
Carr's Towing, 4063 Hwy 2 South. 293-3988.

Air Service
Libby Airport, Keith Kinden. 293-9776.

Medical
St. John's Lutheran Hospital, 350 Louisiana Ave. 293-7761.

For more information:
  Libby Area Chamber of Commerce
  905 West 9th St
  P.O. Box 704
  Libby, MT 59923-0704.
  293-4167.

Datus Proper and his German shorthair Huckleberry.

KALISPELL
AND FLATHEAD COUNTY

Population– 26,000
Elevation– 2,959'
County Population– 59,000
County Area– 5,099 sq. mi.

October Temperature– 44.2
Annual Precipitation– 23.40"
Acres in CRP– 10
FWP Region 1

Kalispell is one of the fastest growing areas in Montana. It has become a summer and winter playground. Glacier National Park is 32 miles north of Kalispell and Flathead Lake is seven miles south of town. Kalispell is a regional trade center with shopping malls and numerous stores. It is located in the broad Flathead Valley surrounded by the Flathead National Forest. The Salish Mountains lie to the west and the Whitefish and Swan Mountains are to the east. The terrain is montane forest.

UPLAND BIRDS
blue, Franklin's, and ruffed grouse and Merraim's turkey
There is excellent hunting for all three types of mountain grouse in the surrounding mountain ranges. In recent years the wild turkey population has increased dramatically. There is a spring gobbler season. Permits are available on a draw basis. Check with the Montana Department of Fish, Wildlife, and Parks for information.

WATERFOWL
ducks
There is limited duck hunting in the fall on Flathead Lake.

ACCOMMODATIONS
Blue and White Motel, 640 East Idaho St. 755-4311.
  107 rooms, sauna, hot tub, pool, and restaurant. Dogs allowed in rooms. Rates moderate.
Kalispell Super 8, 1341 1st Ave East. 755-1888.
  74 rooms. Dogs allowed in smoking rooms only. Rates moderate.

CAMPGROUNDS AND RV PARKS
Rocky Mountain "Hi" Campground, 5 miles east of Kalispell on Rt 2. 755-9573.
  Open year-round. 20 tent and 70 RV spaces. Full facilities including laundry and store.
Spruce Park RV Park, 3 miles east, Junction US 2 and 93 on Hwy 35 at Flathead River. 752-6321. Open year-round. 60 tent and 100 RV spaces. Full facilities including laundry and store.

Restaurants
Bulldog Steak House, 208 1st Ave East. 752-7522.
Spirits, beer, fine steaks, and salads. Steamed shrimp is their specialty.
Que Pasa Restaurant, 75 Woodland Park Dr. 756-8776.
Open 7AM–10PM daily. Serving breakfast, lunch, and dinner. Fine Mexican food, beer, wine, and margaritas.
Fred's Family Restaurant, 1600 Hwy 93. 257-8666.
Open 5:45AM–11PM daily. Serving breakfast, lunch, and dinner.

Veterinarians
Animal Clinic, 1408 City Airport Rd. 755-6886.
24-hour service.
Ashley Creek Animal Clinic, 3251 Hwy 93 South. 752-1330.
24-hour service.

Sporting Goods
Snappy Sport Center, 1400 Hwy 2 East. 257-7525.
Open 7 days.
Sportsman and Ski Haus, Junction of Hwy 2 and 93. 755-6484.

Auto Repair and Rental
Conoco Car Care Center, 229 3rd Ave. 755-3797.
Avis, Glacier Park International Airport. 257-2727.
National Car Rental, Glacier Park International Airport. 257-7144.

Air Service
Glacier Park International Airport, 4170 Hwy 2 East. 257-5994.

Medical
Kalispell Regional Hospital, 310 Sunnyview Lane. 752-5111.

For more information:
Montana Dept. Fish, Wildlife, and Parks
490 North Meridian
Kalispell, MT 59901.
752-5501.

Kalispell Chamber of Commerce
15 Depot Loop
Kalispell, MT 59901.
752-6166.

CUT BANK
AND GLACIER COUNTY

Population– 3,300
Elevation– 3,838'
County Population– 12,000
County Area– 2,995 sq. mi.

October Temperature– 43.9
Annual Precipitation– 22.43"
Acres in CRP– 60,843
FWP Region 4

Cut Bank is an oil and gas town that sits on the Hi-Line at the eastern edge of the Blackfeet Indian Reservation. Most of Glacier County is comprised of Glacier National Park and the Indian reservation. Hunting is limited to the reservation or the small eastern part of the county that is privately owned. The terrain consists of intermountain grasslands on the reservation and plains grasslands in the eastern part of the county.

UPLAND BIRDS
Hungarian partridge and sharp-tailed grouse
There is good hunting for Huns on the Blackfeet Reservation. Currently this is the only bird that you are allowed to hunt on the reservation. There are good numbers of both Huns and sharptails on the private land in the eastern part of the county. The birds will be in the CRP and agricultural areas.

WATERFOWL
geese and ducks
There is good waterfowl hunting on the pothole lakes in the northeast part of the county.

ACCOMMODATIONS
Glacier Gateway Inn, 1121 East Railroad St. 800-851-5541 or 873-5544.
19 rooms at the Inn, 9 more (budget) at another motel owned by the same people. Dogs allowed, $2.50 per dog. Some theme rooms, hot tub, free breakfast. Moderate prices. Your hosts are Irene and Keith Gustafson.

CAMPGROUNDS AND RV PARKS
Riverview Campground, end of 4th Ave SW. 873-5546.
Open year-round. 9 tent and 36 RV spaces. Full service except for sewer. Laundry and store.

RESTAURANTS
Maxie's, 1159 East Railroad St. 873-4220.
American fare. Prices moderate to expensive.

Golden Harvest, Main Street. 873-4010.
6AM–10PM. Breakfast, lunch, and dinner.

VETERINARIANS
Northern Veterinary Clinic, 55 Santa Rita Hwy. 873-5604.
Gary Cassel, D.V.M.

SPORTING GOODS
Many Feathers Trading Post, 519 Main St. 873-4484.

AUTO REPAIR
Auto Tune Diagnostic Center, 1122 East Main. 873-2126.
Northern Ford-Mercury, 120 West Main. 873-5541.

AIR SERVICE
County airstrip, Arnie Lindberg. 873-4722.

MEDICAL
Glacier County Medical Center, 802 2nd St SE. 873-2251.

FOR MORE INFORMATION:
The Cut Bank Chamber of Commerce
P.O. Box 1243
Cut Bank, MT 59427.
837-4041.

THOMPSON FALLS
AND SANDERS COUNTY

Population– 1,300	October Temperature– 47
Elevation– 2,463	Annual Precipitation– 22.62"
County Population– 8,669	Acres in CRP– 1,227
County Area– 2,762 sq. mi	FWP Region 1

Thompson Falls is a small, friendly town in northwestern Montana on the banks of the Clark Fork River. Timber and agriculture are the dominant industries of the area. The beautiful Cabinet Mountains are to the east of Thompson Falls and the Bitterroot Mountains frame the western border. These vast mountain ranges of the Lolo National Forest provide countless acres of public land for great hunting opportunities. Terrain consists of montane forest.

UPLAND BIRDS
blue, Franklin's, and ruffed grouse
The mountain areas provide excellent habitat and hunting for all three of Montana's mountain grouse. A map of the Lolo National Forest is a big help in locating public hunting possibilities. Most of the land bordering the Clark Fork River is privately owned and posted, however there are numerous access roads to the forest.

WATERFOWL
geese and ducks
The Clark Fork River on the Pacific Flyway has good waterfowl hunting during the annual migration.

ACCOMMODATIONS
Falls Motel, 112 South Gallatin. 827-3559.
  22 rooms. Dogs allowed, $10 per dog, per night. Rates very reasonable.
Rimrock Lodge, Hwy 200, 1 mile west of town overlooking the Clark Fork River. 827-3536. Cable, restaurant. Dogs allowed. Rates moderate.

CAMPGROUNDS AND RV PARKS
Riverfront RV Park, 1 mile west on Hwy 200. 827-3460.
  3 tent and 10 RV sites. Full facilities.

RESTAURANTS
Granny's Homecooking, 915 Main St.
  Open for breakfast, lunch, and dinner.

Rimrock Lodge , Hwy 200, 1 mile west. 827-3536.
Beautiful dining room overlooking the Clark Fork River. Open for breakfast, lunch, and dinner. Fine food and western hospitality.

VETERINARIANS
Thompson Falls Lynch Creek Vet. Clinic, 1 mile east on Hwy 200. 827-4305.

SPORTING GOODS
Krazy Ernie's, 602 Main St. 827-4898.

AUTO REPAIR
Bob's Auto Repair, 33 Prospect Creek Rd. 827-4811.
Ken's Auto Repair, Hwy 200 East. 827-3940.

AIR SERVICE
County airstrip, Frank Barbeau. 827-3536.

MEDICAL
Fork Valley Hospital, in Plains, 22 miles east. Emergency, call 911.

FOR MORE INFORMATION:
Thompson Falls Chamber of Commerce
P.O. Box 493
Thompson Falls, MT 59873.
827-4930.

Datus Proper with Tess working a side hill for mountain grouse.

POLSON
AND LAKE COUNTY

Population– 2,900	October Temperature– 46
Elevation– 2,949'	Annual Precipitation– 17.29"
County Population– 21,041	Acres in CRP– 859
County Area– 1,494 sq. mi.	FWP Region 1

Polson is located at the southern end of Flathead Lake. This is a resort community and the main agricultural crop is cherries. The county terrain consists of intermountain grasslands. There is very little land in grain crops or in CRP.

UPLAND BIRDS
pheasant, Hungarian partridge, blue, Franklin's, and ruffed grouse
The best hunting is found on the Flathead Indian Reservation in the southern part of the county. The reservation has good pheasant hunting and fair hunting for Hungarian partridge. See the section on Indian reservations, p. 247 for hunting rules and seasons. The Mission Mountains, east of Lake County, provide good hunting for blue, Franklin's, and ruffed grouse.

WATERFOWL
ducks
Flathead Lake provides some hunting for ducks.

ACCOMMODATIONS
Days Inn, 914 Rt 93. 883-3120.
  25 rooms. Dogs allowed, $10 fee. Rates are moderate.

CAMPGROUNDS AND RV PARKS
Rocking C Ranch, 7 miles north of Polson on Rt 35. 887-2537.
  Open year-round. 15 tent and 70 RV spaces. Full facilities including restaurant and casino.

RESTAURANTS
4B's Family Restaurant, Junction of Hwy 93 and 35. 883-6180.
Diamond Horseshoe Lounge and Supper Club, 820 Shoreline Dr. 883-2048.
Lake City Bakery and Eatery, 10 2nd Ave. 883-5667.
  Open for breakfast and lunch.

VETERINARIANS
Southshore Veterinary Hospital. Hwy 93, south Polson. 883-5229.

SPORTING GOODS
Coast to Coast Store, 214 1st St. 883-2011.
Polson Bay Trading Co, 320 Main St. 883-3742.

AUTO REPAIR
General Repair/Mechanics Mall, 58116 Hwy 93. 883-5497.

AIR SERVICE
Polson Aviation, Polson Airport. 883-6787.

MEDICAL
St. Joseph Hospital, Skyline Dr. 883-5377.

FOR MORE INFORMATION:
Polson Chamber of Commerce
P.O. Box 677
Polson, MT 59860.
883-5969.

SUPERIOR
AND MINERAL COUNTY

Population– 1,200
Elevation– 2,740'
County Population– 3,400
County Area– 1,200 sq. mi.

October Temperature– 45
Annual Precipitation– 16.46"
Acres in CRP– 0
FWP Region 2

Mineral County is along the Montana-Idaho border. Eighty-two percent of the land in the county is federally owned and provides abundant recreational and hunting opportunities. The famous Clark Fork River runs through the center of the county and the Bitterroot Mountains and the Lolo National Forest comprise most of the land. Terrain consists of montane forest.

Superior, the largest town in Mineral County, is on the banks of the Clark Fork, 57 miles northwest of Missoula.

UPLAND BIRDS
blue, Franklin's, and ruffed grouse

The mountain areas provide excellent hunting for all three species of mountain grouse. Since the vast majority of the land is national forest, access is not a problem.

WATERFOWL
ducks and geese

The Clark Fork and the St. Regis Rivers provide good duck hunting during the fall migration.

ACCOMMODATIONS
Bellevue Motel, 110 Mullan Rd East. 822-4692.
  22 rooms. Dogs welcome. Rates very reasonable.
Budget Host Big Sky Motel, 103 4th Ave East. 822-4831.
  24 rooms. Dogs welcome. Rates very reasonable.

CAMPGROUNDS AND RV PARKS
St. Regis Campground, 2 miles west of St. Regis and 16 miles west of Superior.
  649-2470. 25 tent and 75 RV spaces. Full facilities including showers, laundry, and store.

RESTAURANTS
Best's Kitchen, 104 West Mullan Rd. 822-9994.
JG's Family Restaurant, 204 East 4th Ave. 822-4967.

VETERINARIANS

Veterinarians in Missoula, 60 miles south:

Missoula Veterinary Clinic. 251-2400.

Pruyn Veterinary Hospital. 251-4150.

AUTO REPAIR

Carl's Auto Repair, 35 Diamond Rd. 822-4691.

Schneider Auto Service, 109 River. 822-4811.

AIR SERVICE

County airstrip, Gerald Geske. 822-4917.

MEDICAL

Mineral Community Hospital, Brooklyn and Roosevelt. 822-4841.

FOR MORE INFORMATION:

Superior Area Chamber of Commerce
Box 483
Superior, MT 59872.
822-4891.

MISSOULA
AND MISSOULA COUNTY

Population– 43,000
Elevation– 3,200'
County Population– 83,000
County Area– 2,598 sq. mi.

October Temperature– 45
Annual Precipitation– 13"
Acres in CRP– 93
FWP Region 2

Missoula is located in a broad valley in western Montana. It is at the center of five scenic valleys: the Flathead to the north, Frenchtown to the west, Bitterroot to the south, Blackfoot to the northeast, and Hellgate to the east. The Clark Fork River flows through the center of town and is joined by the famous Bitterroot River from the south. Home to the University of Montana, Missoula is a major retail and cultural center of western Montana. Terrain consists of montane forest.

UPLAND BIRDS
pheasant, Hungarian partridge, blue, Franklin's, and ruffed grouse
Pheasants are numerous on the Flathead Indian Reservation north of Missoula (*see Indian reservation section, p. 247 for game regulations and season*). The Bitterroot Valley running south of town provides good hunting for both pheasants and Huns. The Bitterroot Mountains to the west, the Rattlesnake Wilderness Area, and the Lolo National Forest to the east provide excellent hunting for all the mountain grouse.

WATERFOWL
ducks and geese
The Clark Fork and the Bitterroot Rivers provide good waterfowl hunting during the fall migration.

ACCOMMODATIONS
Bel Aire Motel, 300 East Broadway. 543-7183.
 52 rooms. Dogs allowed in smoking rooms, $5 fee. There is one non-smoking room in which dogs are allowed. Rates moderate.
Days Inn/Westgate, Rt 93 and I-90. 721-9776.
 69 rooms. Dogs allowed, $5 fee. Restaurant on premises. Rates moderate.
4B's Inn North, 4953 North Reserve. 542-7550.
 67 rooms. Dogs allowed. Restaurant on premises. Rates moderate.
4B's South, 3803 Brooks. 251-2665.
 79 rooms. Dogs allowed. Restaurant on premises. Rates moderate.

CAMPGROUNDS AND RV PARKS

Missoula El-Mar KOA, Reserve St exit, 1½ miles south. 549-0881.
36 tent and 164 RV spaces. Open year-round. Full facilities including hot tub and store.
Out Post Campground, I-90 exit 96, 2 miles north on Rt 93. 549-2016.
10 tent and 35 RV spaces. Open year-round. Full facilities.

RESTAURANTS

4B's, located at 4B's motels north and south.
Open for breakfast, lunch, and dinner.
Finnegan's Family Restaurant, 700 East Broadway. 542-2752.
Open 24 hours, 7 days for breakfast, lunch, and dinner.
McKay's on the River, 1111 East Broadway. 728-0098.
Restaurant/lounge open 7 days for breakfast, lunch, and dinner. Unique antique gun display. Steaks, prime rib, and seafood.
New Pacific Grill, 100 East Railroad Ave at the old Northern Pacific Railroad station. 542-3353. Open 7 days for lunch and dinner. Casual dining. Fresh seafood and beef.
Paradise Falls, 3621 Brooks. 728-3228.
Restaurant, lounge, casino open 6AM–2AM for breakfast, lunch, and dinner. Steaks and baby-back ribs.

VETERINARIANS

Missoula Veterinary Clinic, 3701 Old 93 South. 251-2400.
24-hour emergency service.
Pruyn Veterinary Hospital, 2501 Russell. 251-4150.
24-hour emergency service.

SPORTING GOODS

Bob Ward and Sons, 2300 Brooks. 728 3220.
Open 7 days.
Sportsman's Surplus, Temperaturer's Shopping Center. 721-5500.
Open 7 days.

AUTO RENTAL AND REPAIR

Avis, Missoula International Airport. 549-4711.
Hertz, Missoula International Airport. 549-9511.
National, Missoula International Airport. 543-3131.
Ram Towing and Repair, 3402 Grant Creek Rd. I-90 at Reserve St. 542-3636 or 800-870-3634. 24-hour auto and diesel repair.
Skip's Orange Street Sinclair, 400 West Broadway. 549-5571.
Open 7 days.

AIR SERVICE

Missoula International Airport, Hwy 93 north of town. 728-4381.
Delta, Horizon, and Northwest airlines.

MEDICAL

Community Medical Center, 28227 Fort Missoula Road. 728-4100.
St. Patrick Hospital, 500 West Broadway. 543-7271.
24-hour emergency services. Life flight.

FOR MORE INFORMATION:

The Missoula Chamber of Commerce
825 East Front St.
Missoula, MT 59802.
543-6623.

Montana Dept. of Fish, Wildlife, and Parks
3201 Spurgin Rd.
Missoula, MT 59801.
542-5500.

U.S. Forest Service
340 North Pattee
Missoula, MT 59802.
329-3511.

HAMILTON
AND RAVALLI COUNTY

Population– 2,800	October Temperature– 46
Elevation– 3,600'	Annual Precipitation– 13"
County Population– 25,000	Acres in CRP– 2,212
County Area– 2,394 sq. mi.	FWP Region 3

Hamilton is a retirement and resort community located in the beautiful Bitterroot Valley. The Bitterroot Mountains form the western border of the valley, and the Sapphire Mountains are to the east. The famous blue-ribbon Bitterroot River runs north through the valley. Logging and log home manufacturing are the main industries of Ravalli County.

UPLAND BIRDS
pheasant, Hungarian partridge, ruffed, blue, and Franklin's grouse

Hunting for pheasants and Hungarian partridge is best along the Bitterroot River and in the irrigated farmland in the valley. The Bitterroot and Sapphire Mountains provide excellent hunting for the three species of mountain grouse.

WATERFOWL
geese and ducks

The Bitterroot River and its tributaries provide hunting during the fall migration of ducks and geese. Geese can also be hunted in the adjoining grain fields. Ravalli County is located in the Pacific Flyway.

ACCOMMODATIONS

Bitterroot Motel, 408 South 1st St. 363-1142.
  10 rooms. Dogs welcome. Rates very reasonable.
Sportsman Motel, 410 North 1st St. 363-2411.
  18 rooms, restaurant. Dogs allowed in smoking rooms only. Rates very reasonable.
TownHouse Inns of Hamilton, 115 North 1st St. 363-6600.
  64 rooms, restaurant. Dogs allowed, $5 charge. Rates moderate.

CAMPGROUNDS AND RV PARKS

Angler's Roost, on Bitterroot River 3 miles south on Rt 93. 363-1268.
  15 tent and 60 RV spaces. Open year-round. Full facilities, including cabins, store, gun and tackle shop, hunting licenses, and gas.

OUTFITTERS
Fetch Inn Hunting Preserve, P.O. Drawer 1429. 800-854-6732.
   Contact Tom Fox between 8AM-6PM. Pheasant, Chukar, Huns, Turkey, Ducks, and
   Geese.

RESTAURANTS
Coffee Cup Cafe, 500 South 1st St. 363-3822.
   Home-style cooking and pastry. Breakfast served all day.
4B's Restaurant, 1105 North 1st St. 363-4620.
Staver's Restaurant, 163 South 2nd St. 363-4433.
   The Bitterroot's finest bar and grill.
Sportman Restaurant, adjacent to the Sportman Motel. 363-2411.

VETERINARIANS
Basin Veterinary Service, 58 Roaring Lion Rd. 363-4579.
Bitterroot Veterinary Clinic, 1116 North 1st St. 363-1123.

SPORTING GOODS
Bob Ward and Sons, 1120 North 1st St. 363-6204.

AUTO REPAIR
Al's Car Care Center, 324 South 1st St. 363-3700.

AIR SERVICE
Ravalli County Airport, 363-3833.

MEDICAL
Marcus Daly Hospital, 1200 Westwood Dr. 363-2211.

FOR MORE INFORMATION:
   Bitterroot Valley Chamber of Commerce
   105 East Main
   Hamilton, MT 59840.
   363-2400.

DEER LODGE
AND POWELL COUNTY

Population– 3,378	October Temperature– 44
Elevation– 4,688'	Annual Precipitation– 10.6"
County Population– 6,600	Acres in CRP– 0
County Area– 2,326 sq. mi.	FWP Region 2

The friendly community of Deer Lodge is in the heart of a beautiful mountain valley in southwestern Montana, bisected by the Clark Fork River. The Deerlodge National Forest borders the western part of the county and the Helena National Forest is to the east. Deer Lodge is situated on Interstate 90 and is home to the state prison and the Grant-Kohrs Ranch national historical site. Timber and agriculture are the main industries. Terrain consists of intermountain grassland and montane forest.

UPLAND BIRDS
pheasant, Hungarian partridge, blue, Franklin's, and ruffed grouse
The farmland adjacent to the Clark Fork River provides fair hunting for both pheasants and Huns. The mountain ranges to the west and east of the valley provide good hunting for the three species of mountain grouse.

WATERFOWL
geese and ducks
There is fair duck hunting along the Clark Fork River. Geese can be found in the agricultural fields in the valley.

ACCOMMODATIONS
Deer Lodge Super 8, 1150 North Main St. 846-2370.
 54 rooms. Dogs allowed in smoking rooms only, $5 per dog. Rates very reasonable.
Scharf Motor Inn, 819 Main St. 846-2810.
 44 rooms. Dogs allowed. Restaurant on premise. Rates very reasonable.

CAMPGROUNDS AND RV PARKS
Riverfront RV Park, Garrison Mtn, off I-90, 10 miles north. 800-255-1318.
 Open year-round. 12 tent and 16 RV spaces. Full facilities including store.

RESTAURANTS
4B's Restaurant, I-90 interchange. 846-2620.
 Breakfast, lunch, and dinner. 24 hours.

Country Village, I-90 interchange. 846-1442.
  Open 7:30AM–9PM, 7 days.
RJ's Steakhouse and Casino, 317 Main. 846-3400.
  Open for dinner 7 days a week.
Scharf's Family Restaurant, 819 Main. 846-3300.
  Serving breakfast, lunch, and dinner 7 days a week. Family style dining.

VETERINARIANS
Clark Fork Veterinary Clinic, 390 North Frontage Rd. 846-1925.
  Paul Bissonette, D.V.M. 9AM-5PM M–F, 9AM-1PM Sat.

SPORTING GOODS
Hiatts Sporting Goods, 101 Milwaukee Ave.
Ace Hardware, 506 Second St. 846-2461.

AUTO REPAIR
Riverside Service Center, 228 Mitchell. 846-3113.

AIR SERVICE
County airstrip, Ralph Besk. 846-2238 or 846-1771.

MEDICAL
Powell Co. Memorial Hospital, 1101 Texas Ave. 846-1722.
Deer Lodge Clinic, 1101 Texas. 846-2212.

FOR MORE INFORMATION:
  Powell County Chamber of Commerce
  P.O Box 776
  Deer Lodge, MT 59722.
  846-2094.

PHILIPSBURG
AND GRANITE COUNTY

Population– 940	October Temperature– 43.8
Elevation– 5,195'	Annual Precipitation– 21.13"
County Population– 2,548	Area in CRP– 0
County Area– 1,728 sq. mi.	FWP Region 2

Philipsburg is a small mining town located 74 miles southeast of Missoula in the Flint Creek Valley. The Sapphire Mountains are located in the western part of the county and the Flint Mountains form the eastern front of the county. The terrain consists of montane forest and intermountain grasslands.

UPLAND BIRDS
blue, Franklin's, and ruffed grouse, Hungarian partridge

The Sapphire and Flint Mountains located in the Deerlodge National Forest provide excellent mountain grouse hunting. There are some scattered Huns located in the Flint Creek Valley.

WATERFOWL
geese and ducks

There is limited waterfowl hunting on the Flint River during the fall.

ACCOMMODATIONS
The Inn at Philipsburg, P.O. Box 392. 859-3959.

11 rooms. Dogs allowed. Reservations recommended. Rates moderate.

FOR SERVICES, SEE ANACONDA OR DEER LODGE COUNTIES

ANACONDA
AND DEER LODGE COUNTY

Population– 10,700	October Temperature– 44.6
Elevation– 5,331'	Annual Precipitation– 21.16"
County Population– 10,200	Acres in CRP– 0
County Area– 737 sq. mi.	FWP Regions 2 and 3

Anaconda, a town built by copper magnate Marcus Daly, was once home to one of the largest copper smelters in the world. Anaconda is bisected by the Flint River and sits in the middle of Flint Creek Valley.

Deer Lodge County is comprised of montane forest and intermountain grass-lands. Georgetown Lake and the Anaconda-Pintler Wilderness are located in the western part of the county.

UPLAND BIRDS
blue, Franklin's, and ruffed grouse, and pheasant

Grouse are the major upland birds available. The mountain areas in the western and southern part of the county provide good hunting for all three species of mountain grouse. There is some pheasant hunting along the Flint River.

WATERFOWL
geese and ducks

Georgetown Lake provides excellent hunting for both geese and ducks.

ACCOMMODATIONS
Georgetown Lake Lodge, Restaurant and Lounge, Denton's Point Rd. 563-7020.
   11 rooms. Dogs allowed. Rates moderate.
Seven Gables Inn Restaurant and Lounge, Georgetown Lake. 563-5052.
   10 rooms and one cabin that sleeps 8. Dogs allowed. Very reasonable rates.
Trade Winds Motel, 1600 East Commercial. 800-248-3428.
   24 rooms. Kitchenettes available. Dogs allowed. Rates moderate.

CAMPGROUNDS AND RV PARKS
Georgetown Lake KOA, 14 miles west on MT 1, 2 miles south at lake. 563-6030.
   Open year-round. 10 tent and 48 RV spaces. Full services except for sewer. Store and laundry.

RESTAURANTS
Barclay II Supper Club, 1300 East Commercial. 563-5541.
   Open for dinner. Italian food.

Georgetown Lake Lodge, Denton's Point. 563-7020.
Granny's Kitchen, 1500 East Commercial. 563-2349.

VETERINARIANS
Anaconda Veterinary Clinic, 1501 East Park. 563-2440.

SPORTING GOODS
Don's Sport Center, 1310 East Commercial. 563-3231.
Rainbow Sporting Goods, 605 East Park. 563-5080.

AUTO REPAIR
Anaconda Automotive, 1400 East Commercial. 563-8126.

AIR SERVICE
Bowman Field, Warm Springs, MT. Contact John McPhail, 563-8112 or 563-9984.

MEDICAL
The Community Hospital of Anaconda, 401 West Penn. 563-5261.

FOR MORE INFORMATION:
Anaconda Chamber of Commerce
306 East Park Ave.
Anaconda, MT 59711.
563-2400.

BUTTE
SILVER BOW AND JEFFERSON COUNTIES

Population– 34,800
Elevation– 5,750'
County Population– 33,300
County Area– 718 sq. mi.

October Temperature– 55
Annual Precipitation– 17.95"
Acres in CRP– 0
FWP Region 3

For many years, Butte was a booming mining center. Located at the crossroads of Interstates 15 and 90, Butte is now a diversified commercial city. The terrain in Silver Bow and Jefferson Counties is primarily montane forest. The Beaverhead National Forest forms the western part of the county and the Deerlodge National Forest is east and north of the county.

UPLAND BIRDS
blue, Franklin's, and ruffed grouse
The Beaverhead and Deerlodge National Forests provide good hunting for all three species of mountain grouse.

ACCOMMODATIONS
TownHouse Inns of Butte, 2777 Harrison Ave. 494-8850.
  150 rooms. Dogs allowed, $5 fee. Rates moderate.
War Bonnet Inn, 2100 Cornell Ave. 494-7800.
  134 rooms. Dogs allowed, $10 fee. Restaurant on site. Rates expensive.

CAMPGROUNDS AND RV PARKS
Fairmont RV Park, 17 miles west of Butte off I-90. 797-3535.
  84 RV spaces. Full facilities including showers, laundry, store, and cabins.

RESTAURANTS
4B's Family Restaurant, 1905 Dewey and Rocker Interchange. 494-1199.
Perkins Family Restaurant, 2900 Harrison Ave. 494-2490.
  Open 24 hours.
The Uptown Cafe, 47 East Broadway. 723-4735.
  One of the finest restaurants in Montana.

VETERINARIANS
Animal Hospital, 2330 Amherst Ave. 494-4044.
Butte Veterinary Service, 6000 Harrison Ave. 494-3656.

SPORTING GOODS
Bob Ward and Sons, 1925 Dewey. 494-3445.
Fran Johnson's Sports Shop, 1957 Harrison Ave. 782-3322.

AUTO REPAIR
Mark's Sinclair, 1200 South Montana, 3 blocks north of I-90. 723-3351.
Open 7 days.

AIR SERVICE
Bert Mooney Field, Harrison Ave South.
Delta (Sky West), 494-4001.
Horizon, 494-1402.

MEDICAL
St. James Hospital, 400 South Clark St. 782-8361.

FOR MORE INFORMATION:
Butte Chamber of Commerce
2950 Harrison Ave
Butte, MT 59701.
800-735-6814, Ext. 10.

DILLON
AND BEAVERHEAD COUNTY

Population– 3,991	October Temperature– 45.8
Elevation– 5,057'	Annual Precipitation– 16.55"
County Population– 8,424	Acres in CRP– 5,216
County Area– 5,551 sq. mi.	FWP Regions 2 and 3

Dillon is a friendly college town located in southwestern Montana, surrounded by four mountain ranges—the Beaverhead, Tendoy, Centennial, and Pioneer. The famous blue-ribbon Beaverhead River flows through Dillon. The Big Hole River flows west to east across the northern part of the county. These two rivers join and eventually become part of the Missouri River. Clark Canyon Dam and Clark Canyon Lake, located 20 miles south of town, provide excellent hunting for waterfowl.

Beaverhead County is Montana's largest producer of cattle and is one of the largest counties in the nation, with an area larger than Connecticut and Rhode Island combined. Much of the surrounding terrain consists of plains and sagebrush.

John Huges shoots a sharp-tailed grouse in sagebrush flats.

UPLAND BIRDS
sage, blue, and Franklin's grouse

The vast areas of sagebrush in Beaverhead County are ideal habitat for sage grouse. Much of this land is BLM with easy public access.

The four mountain ranges provide very good mountain grouse hunting.

WATERFOWL
ducks and geese

Clark Canyon Lake provides superb hunting for ducks and geese. The Beaverhead and Big Hole Rivers are excellent places for jump shooting and float hunting.

ACCOMMODATIONS

Sundowner Motel, 500 North Montana. 683-2375.
  32 rooms, cable. Dogs allowed. Reasonable rates.
Super 8 Motel, 550 North Montana. 683-4288.
  46 rooms, cable. Refrigerators and microwave ovens in some rooms. Dogs allowed. Reasonable rates.
TownHouse Inns of Dillon, 450 North Interchange. 683-6831.
  46 rooms, cable. Laundry, indoor pool. Dogs allowed in rooms for a $3 fee.

CAMPGROUNDS AND RV PARKS

Beaverhead Marina and RV Park, 20 miles south on I-15, exit 44 on Clark Canyon Reservoir. 683-5556. 2 tent and 31 RV spaces. Full facilities including docks, gas, and boat ramp.
Skyline RV Park, 3 miles north of Dillon on Hwy 91. 683-4903.
  5 tent, 38 RV spaces. Full facilities.

RESTAURANTS

Anna's Oven, 120 Montana St. 683-5766.
  7AM–4PM. Breakfast and baked goods.
Buffalo Lodge, I-15 20 miles south of Dillon at Clark Canyon. 683-5088.
  Open 10:30AM–9PM. Features burgers and steaks.
Lion's Den, 725 North Montana. 683-2051.
  11AM–10PM. Steak, prime rib, cocktails.
The Mine Shaft, 26 South Montana. 683-6611.
  11AM–11PM. Wide variety of steaks.
Town Pump, 625 North Montana. 683-5097.
  Open 24 hours for breakfast, lunch, and dinner.

VETERINARIANS

Veterinary Hospital, 935 South Atlantic. 683-2385.
  Dr. Knorr and Dr. Nelson.

SPORTING GOODS
Hitchin Post Sporting Goods, 125 North Montana. 683-4881.

AUTO REPAIR
B&L Auto Repair, 250 North Railroad. 683-6733.
Dillon Auto Repair, 624 East Glendale. 683-5214.

AIR SERVICE
Iverson Aviation. 683-4447.
   Call for information.

MEDICAL
Barrett Memorial Hospital, 1260 South Atlantic. 683-2323.

FOR MORE INFORMATION
   Dillon Chamber of Commerce
   Box 425
   Dillon, MT 59725.
   683-5511.

ENNIS
AND MADISON COUNTY

Population– 790	October Temperature– 45.6
Elevation– 4,927'	Annual Precipitation– 17.32"
County Population– 5,900	Acres in CRP– 8,080
County Area– 3,587 sq. mi.	FWP Region 3

Ennis is located on the banks of the famous blue-ribbon Madison River trout stream. It is a small ranching and tourist community situated in a broad valley between the Gravelly and Tobacco Root Mountains to the west and the Madison Range to the east. The terrain consists of montane forest and intermountain and shrub grasslands.

UPLAND BIRDS
blue, ruffed, and sage grouse, Hungarian partridge

There is good hunting for blue and ruffed grouse in the mountain ranges. The northern part of Madison County has fair hunting for Huns and the shrub grasslands in the southern part of the county have some sage grouse.

WATERFOWL
geese and ducks

The Madison River and Ennis Lake provide good hunting for ducks during the fall migration. The agricultural lands in the area provide good field hunting for geese and ducks. Madison County is on the Pacific Flyway.

ACCOMMODATIONS

Riverside Motel, 346 Main St. 682-4240, 800-535-4139.
Open May–December. Cabins, some with kitchens. All have cable, refrigerator, picnic table, and gas grill. Located on the Madison River, only 12 miles from a bird hunting preserve. Hunters and dogs are welcome, $3 per dog. Reservations are necessary. Your host is Robert Hines.

The Sportsman's Lodge, P.O. Box 305. 682-4242.
18 lodgepole pine cabins, 11-unit motel. Cable, restaurant, and lounge on premises. Dogs allowed, $5 per dog. Reservations recommended.

CAMPGROUNDS AND RV PARKS

Elkhorn Store and RV Park, ½ mile south on Hwy 287. 682-4273.
Open year-round. 12 tent and 13 RV spaces. Full facilities except for laundry.

OUTFITTERS
Diamond J Ranch, REC Orvis Outfitter, P.O. Box 816, Ennis, MT 59729.
Call M-F 8-5, 682-7404 or 682-4867 after 5. Pheasant and chukar shooting preserve. 1,200 private ranch acres.

RESTAURANTS
Continental Divide Restaurant. Downtown Ennis. 682-7600.
Open for dinner summer through mid-fall. One of Montana's finest restaurants. Your hosts are Jay and Karen Bentley.
Ennis Cafe, 682-4442.
Breakfast, lunch, and dinner.
Kathy's Wild Rose Restaurant, 682-4717.

VETERINARIANS
White and White Veterinary Hospital and Supply, 5098 Hwy 287, 682-7151.
Douglas B. Young, D.V.M. 682-7956.

SPORTING GOODS
True Value, 682-4210.

AUTO REPAIR
D&D Auto, 682-4234.

AIR SERVICE
Ennis Airport, 8 miles south of town. Contact Madison Valley Aircraft. 682-7431.

MEDICAL
Madison Valley Hospital, 682-4274. Emergency, 682-4222.

FOR MORE INFORMATION:
Ennis Chamber of Commerce
P.O. Box 297
Ennis, MT 59729.
682-4388. If no answer try Ed Williams, Chamber President, 682-4264.

BOZEMAN
AND GALLATIN COUNTY

Population– 25,000	October Temperature– 46.2
Elevation– 4,793'	Annual Precipitation– 23.51"
County Population– 50,465	Acres in CRP– 12,268
County Area– 2,507 sq. mi.	FWP Region 3

Known for its blue-ribbon trout fishing and great skiing, Bozeman is a rapidly growing resort and college town. There has been a recent population boom, resulting in crowded conditions and high prices. In spite of this, Bozeman has a lot to offer the sportsman. There is still a small-town atmosphere with big city amenities: good air service, shopping, fine restaurants, and outdoor activities. The terrain consists of montane forests and intermountain plains. The Gallatin Valley economy is based on agriculture. Bozeman is bordered by the Bridger Mountains northeast of town, the Gallatin National Forest and Gallatin Mountains to the south, and the Madison Range to the southwest.

UPLAND BIRDS
blue and ruffed grouse, pheasants and Hungarian partridge
The three mountain ranges provide very good hunting for both blue and ruffed grouse. Numerous Forest Service roads make access easy. A map of the national forests will show you the access points. Pheasants and Huns are found along the Gallatin River and the adjacent farmlands in the northern part of the county. Almost all of this land is privately owned and it is often difficult to get permission to hunt.

WATERFOWL
geese and ducks
Gallatin County is located in the Pacific Flyway. The Gallatin and nearby Madison River provide excellent duck hunting. The many spring creeks in the northern part of the valley are also very good for ducks, however, access to the creeks can be difficult. The farmlands provide good hunting for geese. Again, access is the main problem.

ACCOMMODATIONS
Days Inn, 1321 North 7th Ave. 587-5251.
　80 rooms, cable, continental breakfast. Dogs allowed, $25 deposit. Moderate rates.
Fairfield Inn, 828 Wheat Dr. 587-2222.
　57 rooms, 12 suites w/kitchenettes. Continental breakfast, pool, and jacuzzi. Dogs allowed, no restrictions. Rates moderately expensive.

Holiday Inn, 5 Baxter Lane. 587-4561.
178 units, restaurant, bar, pool and jacuzzi, cable. Dogs allowed, but not unattended in rooms. Rates expensive.
Super 8, 800 Wheat Dr. 586-1521.
108 rooms, cable. Dogs allowed, no restrictions. Budget rates.
The Bozeman Inn, 1235 North 7th Ave. 587-3176.
45 rooms, outdoor pool, sauna, cable. Mexican restaurant and lounge. Dogs allowed for a $5 fee. Moderate rates.

CAMPGROUNDS AND RV PARKS
Bozeman KOA , 8 miles west on US 91. 587-3030.
Open year–round. 50 tent and 100 RV spaces. Full services including laundry and store.

OUTFITTERS
Montana Bird Hunts, P.O. Box 5031, 587-5923.
Contact Dennis Kavanagh, 7AM-9PM. Ruffed, sage, and sharp-tailed grouse, pheasant, ducks, and Huns.

RESTAURANTS
Bacchus Pub and Rocky Mountain Pasta Co., 105 East Main. 586-1314.
Breakfast, lunch, dinner. Bacchus 7AM–10PM. Sandwiches, burgers, salads, soups, and daily special entrees. Moderate prices.
Pasta Company, 5:30PM–10PM. Fine dining, pasta and seafood. Expensive.
John Bozeman's Bistro, 242 East Main. 587-4100.
International and regional specialties. Breakfast and lunch moderate, dinner expensive.
Mackenzie River Pizza Company, 232 East Main. 587-0055.
M-Sat. 11:30AM–10PM, Sun 5-9PM.
Fancy pizzas, pasta, salad. Moderate prices.
O'Brien's, 312 East Main. 587-3973.
M-Sun 5PM–9PM. Continental cuisine. Expensive.
Crystal Bar, 123 E. Main. 587-2888.
Open seven days. Beer Garden, will pack lunches for hunters. Reasonable.
Spanish Peaks Brewery, 120 North 19th. 585-2296.
M-F, lunch 11:30AM-2:30PM, M-Sun., dinner 5:30–10:30PM, Sat-Sun, brunch 11AM-2PM. Italian cuisine, microbrewed ales. Moderate to expensive.

VETERINARIANS
All West Veterinary Hospital, 81770 Gallatin Rd. 586-4919.
Gary Cook, Honor Nesbet, David E. Catlin, D.V.M.s. 24-hour emergency service.
Animal Medical Center, 216 North 8th Ave (behind Kentucky Fried Chicken). 587-2946. Sue Barrows, D.V.M. Emergency service.

Sporting Goods
Bob Ward and Sons, 2320 West Main. 586-4381.
Powder Horn Sportsman's Supply, 35 East Main. 587-7373.
The River's Edge, 2012 North 7th Ave. 586-5373.

Auto Rental and Repair
Budget Rent-A-Car of Bozeman, Gallatin Field. 388-4091.
Avis Rent-A-Car, Gallatin Field. 388-6414.
Hertz Rent-A-Car, Gallatin Field. 388-6939.
College Exxon Service, 723 South 8th Ave. 587-4453.
Frank Manseau Auto Clinic, 715 East Mendenhall. 586-4480.
E.J. Miller Service and Towing, 28373 Norris Rd. 587-0507.

Air Service
Gallatin Field Airport, 8 miles west of Bozeman. 388-6632.
Served by Delta, Horizon, Skywest, and Frontier Airlines. Charter service available.

Medical
Bozeman Deaconess Hospital, 915 Highland Blvd. 585-5000.

For more information:
Bozeman Chamber of Commerce
1205 East Main
P.O. Box B
Bozeman, MT 59715.
800-228-4224.

TOWNSEND
AND BROADWATER COUNTY

Population– 1,635	October Temperature– 45
Elevation– 3,833'	Annual Precipitation– 16.21"
County Population– 3,300	Acres in CRP– 25,091
County Area– 842 sq. mi.	FWP Region 8

Known as the "First City on the Missouri," Townsend is in the heartland of excellent waterfowl and upland bird hunting. Townsend is located on Rt 287 between Three Forks and Helena. It is 5 miles south of Canyon Ferry Lake and 1 mile east of the Missouri River. There is a great deal of public land around the lake. The terrain consists of intermountain grasslands and montane forests.

UPLAND BIRDS
pheasant, Hungarian partridge, sharp-tailed, sage, blue, Franklin's, and ruffed grouse

The Missouri River runs north through the center of Broadwater County. The grasslands along the river and Canyon Ferry Lake provide good hunting for pheasants. The farmland in the broad valley has good hunting for sharp-tailed grouse and Hungarian partridge. There is some sage grouse hunting available in the southern part of the county. The Big Belt Mountains in the eastern section have good hunting for blue, ruffed, and Franklin's grouse.

WATERFOWL
geese and ducks

The Missouri River and Canyon Ferry Lake provide excellent hunting for both ducks and geese. Both the lake and this part of the Missouri are on the Pacific Flyway.

ACCOMMODATIONS
The Bedford Inn, 3 miles north of Townsend on Hwy 287. 266-3629.
  5 units in a large home. Dogs allowed.
Mustang Motel, Hwy 287. 266-3491.
  22 units. Dogs allowed, but they cannot be left unattended.
Lakeside Motel, Hwy 287. 266-3461.
  12 units. Dogs allowed for a $10 deposit, some housekeeping units.

CAMPGROUNDS AND RV PARKS
Road Runner and Fireside RV Campground, 2 miles east of Townsend on Hwy 12.
  266-9900. Showers, laundry, phone, hook ups, tent spots, and pull-through.
Goose Bay Marina RV park, Hwy 284 on the east side of Canyon Ferry Lake.
  266-3645. Sanitary dump, tent camping, store, showers, propane, ice, beer.

RESTAURANTS

Jasper's Pub and Pizza, North 287.
Lunch and dinner.

A&W Townsend, North 287. 266-3814.
Open year-round with drive-up and inside seating. Good sandwiches for lunch and dinner.

Horseshoe Family Dining, 550 North Front St. 266-3800.
Unbeatable breakfasts. Open all week for breakfast, lunch, and dinner.

Deep Creek Restaurant, 11 miles east of town on Rt 12. 266-3718.
Gourmet dining in a rustic log cabin. Excellent Sunday brunch.

VETERINARIANS

Elkhorn Vet Clinic, Rt 287 just north of town. 266-5794.
Erik Sorensen, D.V.M. The clinic also boards dogs.

AUTO REPAIR

Valley Sales, 266-5207.

Townsend Muffler and Welding, 266-3935.

AIR SERVICE

City/County Airport, one mile east of town. Contact Vern Spanfill, 266-3218.

MEDICAL

Townsend Community Hospital, on North Oak near the center of town. 266-3186.

FOR MORE INFORMATION:

Townsend Chamber of Commerce
Box 947
Townsend, MT 59644.
266-3911.

HELENA
AND LEWIS AND CLARK COUNTY

Population– 24,569	October Temperature– 43
Elevation– 4,157'	Annual Precipitation– 11.7"
County Population– 47,495	Area in CRP– 7,391
County Area– 3,451 sq. mi.	FWP Region 8

Helena is the capital of Montana. It is a thriving commercial center, bordered on the west by the Helena National Forest. The Missouri River flows east of town. The Big Belt Mountains and the Gates of the Mountains Wilderness Area are east of the Missouri. A number of reservoirs along the river provide outstanding hunting and recreational opportunities. The terrain is comprised of montane forest and inter-mountain grasslands.

UPLAND BIRDS
blue, Franklin's, ruffed, and sharp-tailed grouse, pheasant, and Hungarian partridge

The national forests surrounding the county provide very good hunting for all three species of mountain grouse. Pheasants can be found along the Missouri River and its tributaries. Sharptails are located in the northeastern part of the county. Huns are located along the Missouri River and in the northeast.

WATERFOWL
geese and ducks

The Missouri River, its tributaries, and the adjacent farmland provide very good hunting for geese and ducks.

ACCOMMODATIONS
Aladdin Motor Inn, 2101 East 11th Ave. 443-2300 or 800-541-2743.
  13 rooms, indoor pool, sauna, steam, health club. Dogs allowed, $5 fee. Rates moderate.
Days Inn, 2001 Prospect Ave. 442-3280.
  Dogs allowed with $40 deposit, smoking rooms only. Rates moderate.
Lamplighter Motel, 1006 Madison. 442-9200.
  Large units, 13 with kitchens, suites with up to 4 bedrooms. Dogs allowed, $4 per day (no dogs left unattended in rooms).
Super 8 Motel, 2201 11th Ave. 443-2450.
  Dogs allowed with $25 deposit in smoking rooms only.

CAMPGROUNDS AND RV PARKS
Helena KOA, 3 miles north of city limits on Montana Ave. 458-5110.
  Open year-round. Full service including laundry and store.

RESTAURANTS

Frontier Pies, 1231 Prospect Ave. 442-7437.
Family dining, specialty pies. Open 7AM–10PM daily.
The Pasta Pantry, 1220 11th Ave. 442-1074.
Windbag Saloon and Grill, 19 South Main. 443-9669.

VETERINARIANS

Big Sky Animal Clinic, 1660 Euclid Ave. 442-0980.
Gary Erickson, D.V.M. 24-hour emergency service.
Animal Center Veterinary Clinic, 1301 Cedar St. 442-3160. If no answer, 442-7094.
Arla Barkemeyer, Julie Kappes, Ed Newman, George Bates, D.V.Ms. 24-hour
emergency service.

SPORTING GOODS

Bob Ward and Sons, 1401 Cedar St. 443-2138.
CrossCurrents an Orvis Full-Line Dealer, 326 North Jackson St. 449-2292.
Capitol Sports and Western Wear, Hustad Center. 443-2978.

AUTO REPAIR AND RENTAL

Prestige Service Center, 1140 11th Ave. 442-2724.
Al Rose Garage and Wrecking Service, 2801 North Cook. 442-9965 or 442-3400.
9AM–6PM Mon-Sat.
Hertz Rent-a-Car, at the Helena Regional Airport. 442-8169.

AIR SERVICE

Helena Regional Airport, 2850 Skyway Dr. 442-2821.
Serviced by Delta and Horizon. Charter service available.

MEDICAL

St. Peter's Community Hospital, 2475 Broadway. 442-2480.

FOR MORE INFORMATION:

Helena Area Chamber of Commerce
201 East Lyndale Ave.
Helena, MT 59601.
442-4120.

CHOTEAU
AND TETON COUNTY

Population– 1,741
Elevation– 3,800'
County Population– 6,271
County Area– 2,273 sq. mi.

October Temperature– 48.8
Annual Precipitation– 11.26"
Acres in CRP– 74,151
FWP Region 4

Choteau is a friendly ranching community located near the eastern edge of the Rocky Mountain Front. Southeast of town is the Freezeout Lake Waterfowl Refuge, noted for its outstanding duck and goose hunting. The Boone and Crockett Club has a ranch northeast of town and the Pine Butte Swamp stretches west of town from the plains to the mountains across a wetland. One of the largest dinosaur sites, "Egg Mountain," is southwest of town. Tours of the dinosaur fields are available.

UPLAND BIRDS
pheasant, Hungarian partridge, sharp-tailed, blue, Franklin's, and ruffed grouse

West of Choteau, in the foothills of the Rocky Mountain Front, there are good populations of sharptails. The mountains in the extreme western part of the county provide hunting for blue, Franklin's, and ruffed grouse. East of Choteau, the plains grasslands and the Teton River provide excellent hunting for pheasants and fair hunting for Huns. This area is predominately private ranches and gaining access can be difficult. Southeast of Choteau on Hwy 89 is the Freezeout Lake Waterfowl Refuge. Here you will find public hunting opportunities for pheasants, Hungarian partridge, and sharptails.

WATERFOWL
geese and ducks

Freezeout Lake Wildlife Management Area offers excellent duck and goose hunting on its 12,000 acres. As many as 300,000 snow geese and 10,000 tundra swans have been observed here at one time. A special permit is required to hunt swan. Priest Lake, which lies 7½ miles north on Hwy 89 also has good opportunities for waterfowl hunting.

ACCOMMODATIONS
Western Star Motel, 426 South Main Ave. 466-5737.
   18 rooms, cable, coin laundry next door. Dogs allowed, $5 per night. Rates reasonable.
Big Sky Motel, 405 South Main Ave. 466-5318.
   12 rooms, dogs allowed for a $5 charge.

Hensley 287 Motel, 466-5775.
Dogs allowed in rooms. Rates reasonable.

RESTAURANTS
Circle N, 925 North Main Ave. 466-5331.
Lunch and dinner. Prime rib on weekends.
John Henry's Pizza, 215 North Main Ave. 466-5642.
Lunch and dinner.
Log Cabin Drive-in, 102 South Main Ave. 466-2888.
6AM–6PM daily.

VETERINARIANS
Double Arrow Veterinary Clinic, North of Choteau. 466-5333.
Robert Lee, D.V.M.

AUTO REPAIR
Dirke's Chevrolet-Pontiac-Oldsmobile-GMC Trucks, 302 South Main Ave.
466-2061.

AIR SERVICE
Choteau Flying Service, east of Choteau. 466-2968.

MEDICAL
Teton Medical Center Hospital and Nursing Home, 915 4th St NW. 466-5763.

FOR MORE INFORMATION:
Choteau Chamber of Commerce
Rt 2, Box 256
Choteau, MT 59422.
466-5332.

CONRAD
AND PONDERA COUNTY

Population– 3,200	October Temperature– 46
Elevation– 3,537'	Annual Precipitation– 19"
County Population– 6,433	Acres in CRP– 37,250
County Area– 1,626 sq mi.	FWP Region 4

Conrad, a small ranching and farming community, is located on I-15 just south of the Hi-Line and east of Glacier National Park.

The eastern half of Pondera County is comprised of plains grasslands. The western half is mostly intermountain grassland. The major agricultural crop is wheat.

UPLAND BIRDS
Hungarian partridge, sharp-tailed, blue, Franklin's, and ruffed grouse, pheasant

Huns are numerous in the agricultural lands in central and eastern Pondera County. Sharptails can be found in the eastern two-thirds of the county especially in the CRP. Pheasants are found in CRP and in irrigation ditches near wheat fields. All three types of mountain grouse can be found in the Lewis and Clark National Forest in the western part of the county.

WATERFOWL
ducks and geese

Geese are abundant in the wheat stubble. Ducks can be jump shot along the irrigation ditches. Lake Frances, near the town of Valier in the southwest part of Pondera County, also has duck hunting opportunities.

ACCOMMODATIONS
Conrad Motel, 210 North Main. 278-7544.
  23 rooms, some with kitchenettes. Dogs allowed for a small fee.
Northgate Motel, 5 North Main. 278-3516.
  6 rooms. Hunters welcome and dogs are allowed in rooms at no charge. Very reasonable rates.
Conrad Super 8 TownHouse Inns, 215 North Main. 278-7676.
  48 rooms, suites with kitchenettes, laundry. Dogs allowed in smoking rooms only. Small charge per dog.

CAMPGROUNDS AND RV PARKS
Sunrise Trailer Court, 3½ blocks east of stop light in Conrad. 278-5901.
  20 RV spaces, water, electric, sewer, dump.

RESTAURANTS

Durango Dining Room, 404 South Main. 278-5477.
Open for lunch and dinner. Cocktails.
Home Cafe, 408 South Main, Conrad. 278-5922.
Open 6AM–7PM for breakfast, lunch, and dinner.
Keg Family Restaurant and Drive-In, 616 South Main. 278-7731.
Open Noon–11PM.
Town Pump, 215 North Main next to Super 8 motel.
Open 24 hours.

VETERINARIANS

Conrad Veterinary Hospital, 307 North Main. 278-3236.

SPORTING GOODS

Coast to Coast Hardware, 2 4th Ave SE.

AUTO REPAIR

Marbel's Repair, 302 4th Ave SE. 278-5361.

AIR SERVICE

County airstrip, Steve Becker. 278-5672.

MEDICAL

Pondera Medical Center, 805 Sunset Blvd. 278-3211.

FOR MORE INFORMATION:

Conrad Chamber of Commerce
406½ South Main
Conrad, MT 59425.
278-7791.

YELLOWSTONE COUNTRY

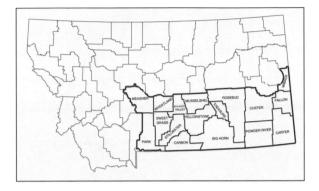

The Yellowstone River, the largest free-flowing river in the U.S., flows through the center of Yellowstone Country. Ranching is the main industry in this part of Montana and the plentiful rangeland provides great habitat for sharptails, Hungarian partridge, and sage grouse. There is excellent pheasant hunting along the Yellowstone River. The Custer National Forest in the southeastern section offers the best opportunity for a Merriam's wild turkey. The mountainous regions in the south provide excellent hunting for ruffed and blue grouse.

The entire length of the Yellowstone River has excellent hunting for ducks and Canada geese. The Bighorn River and the Yellowstone are both blue-ribbon trout streams. An early season trip can provide you with an opportunity to hunt birds and fish for trout—a Montana "cast and blast."

PHEASANT DISTRIBUTION

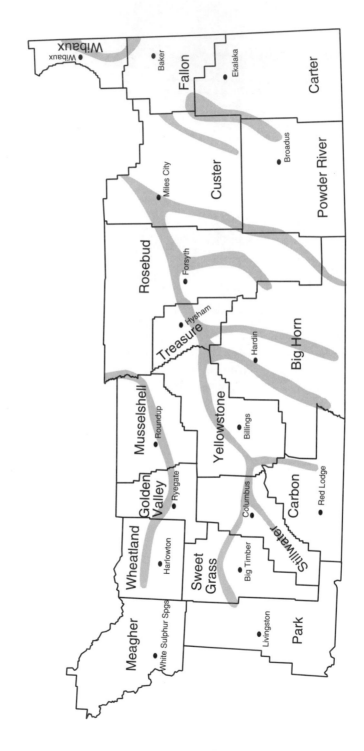

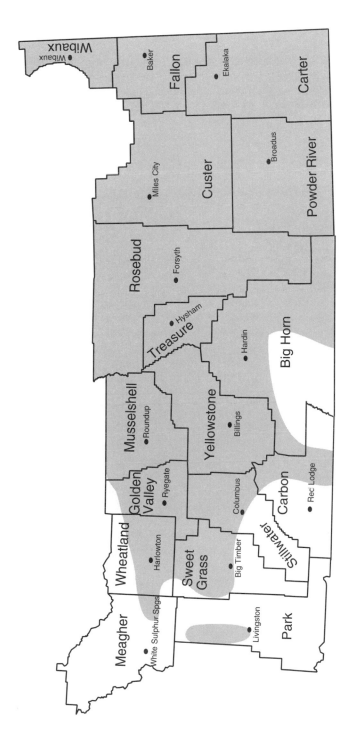

SHARP-TAILED GROUSE DISTRIBUTION

SAGE GROUSE DISTRIBUTION

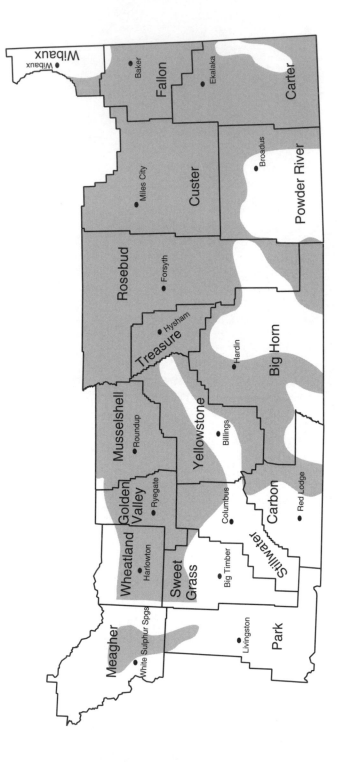

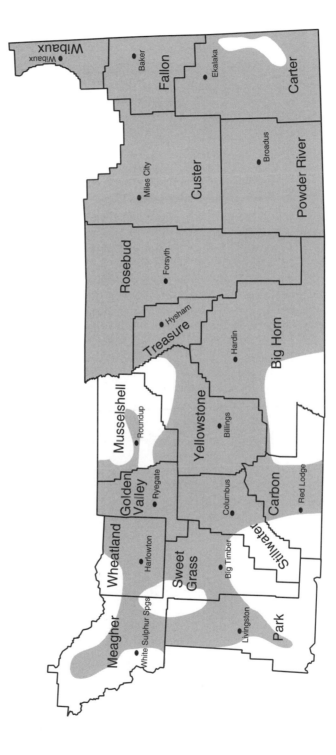

GRAY (HUNGARIAN) PARTRIDGE DISTRIBUTION

BLUE GROUSE DISTRIBUTION

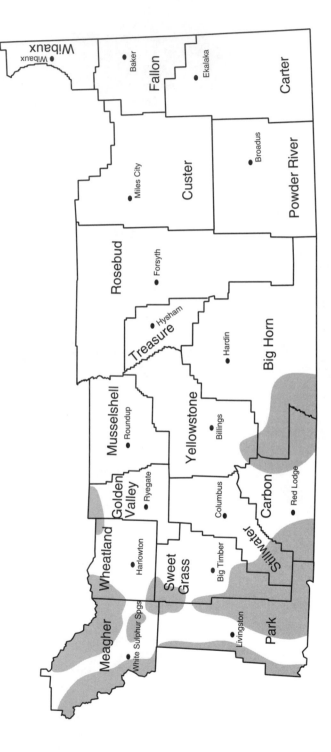

RUFFED GROUSE DISTRIBUTION

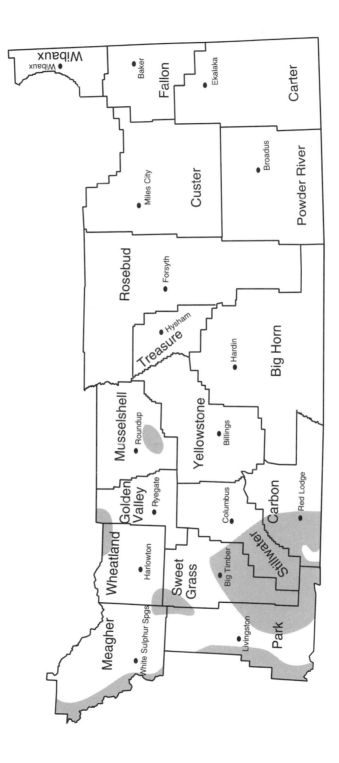

Wibaux
• Wibaux

• Baker

Fallon

• Ekalaka

Carter

• Broadus

Powder River

• Miles City

Custer

Rosebud

• Forsyth

• Hysham

Treasure

• Hardin

Big Horn

Musselshell

• Roundup

Yellowstone

• Billings

Golden
Valley

• Ryegate

• Columbus

Carbon

• Red Lodge

Stillwater

Wheatland

• Harlowton

Sweet
Grass

• Big Timber

Meagher

• White Sulphur Spgs

• Livingston

Park

FRANKLIN'S GROUSE DISTRIBUTION

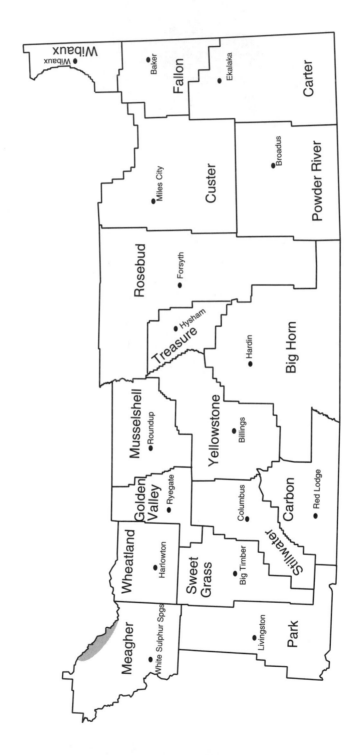

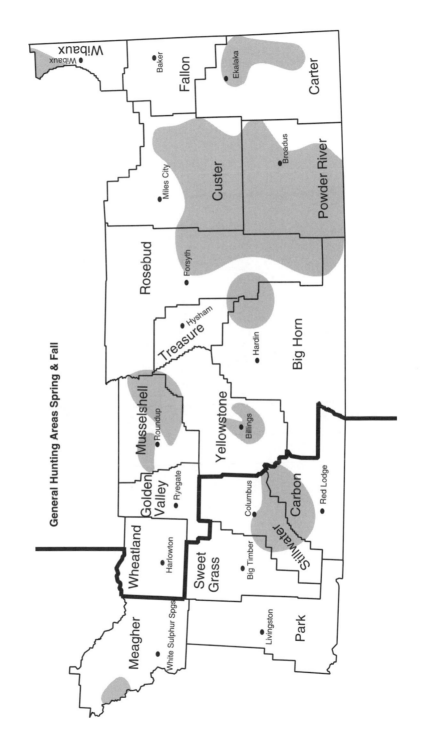

MERRIAM'S TURKEY DISTRIBUTION

General Hunting Areas Spring & Fall

Wibaux • Wibaux

Baker •

Fallon

Ekalaka •

Carter

Miles City •

Custer

Broadus •

Powder River

Rosebud

Forsyth •

Hysham •

Treasure

Hardin •

Big Horn

Roundup •

Musselshell

Billings •

Yellowstone

Ryegate •

Golden Valley

Columbus •

Red Lodge •

Carbon

Stillwater

Wheatland

Harlowton •

Sweet Grass

Big Timber •

Meagher

White Sulphur Spgs •

Livingston •

Park

Late season hunting can be productive.

WHITE SULPHUR SPRINGS AND MEAGHER COUNTY

Population– 1,002
Elevation– 5,200'
County Population– 1,857
County Area– 3,392 sq. mi.

October Temperature– 45.2
Annual Precipitation– 15"
Acres in CRP– 5,966
FWP Region 4

White Sulphur Springs is located halfway between Yellowstone and Glacier National Parks on US 89 and US 12. The town is named for the mineralized, thermal waters located in the city park. The heated water is used in the Spa Hot Springs Motel's pool. White Sulphur Springs sits in a high mountain valley with the Big Belt, Little Belt, and Castle Mountains surrounding its perimeter.

It is a full-service community and the county seat of Meagher (pronounced "marr") County. There is a wealth of recreational opportunities, wide open spaces, and thousands of areas to explore in the Lewis and Clark and Helena National Forests. The headwaters of the Smith River are in the Castles and the Little Belts and the river flows through the county to meet the Missouri at Ulm. The Smith is a famous floating river that passes through 61 miles of beautiful natural canyons cut in limestone formations. Although Meagher County is surrounded by mountains the valley is vast and flat with shrub grasslands and croplands.

UPLAND BIRDS
ruffed, blue, sage, Franklin's, and sharp-tailed grouse, Hungarian partridge

Meagher County has three major mountain systems that provide habitat for mountain grouse. There is good public access to federal lands. The Smith River's wide valley supports a Hungarian partridge population in areas where the proper type of cover is located *(see Gray Partridge p. 24)*. Sharp-tailed grouse are limited to a small corner of eastern Meagher County. Sage grouse are in the isolated big sage flats that have not been farmed.

WATERFOWL
geese and ducks

The Smith River, reservoirs, potholes, and marshes have local duck populations. Most of the waterfowl hunting is early in the season due to Meagher County's high elevation and early freeze-up.

ACCOMMODATIONS
The Tenderfoot Motel, 301 West Main St. 547-3303.
20 units, kitchenettes. Dogs allowed. Reasonable rates.

Spa Hot Springs Motel, 202 West Main St. 547-3366.
   21 rooms. Dogs allowed. Reasonable rates.

CAMPGROUNDS AND RV PARKS
The Spring Campground, on Hwy 89. 547-3921.
   Open 5/1-12/1. 8 RV spaces. Water, electric, and sewer.

RESTAURANTS
The Truck Stop Cafe, 511 East Main St. 547-3825.
   Full menu, 5:30AM–10PM.
Dori's Cafe, 112 East Main St. 547-2280.
Cow Palace, 547-9994.
   Steaks, seafood, and cocktails.
Mint Bar, 27 East Main St. 547-3857.

VETERINARIANS
William H. Schender, D.V.M., 404 East Hampton. 547-3857.

SPORTING GOODS
Lone Wolf Sporting Goods Stores, 105 West Main St. 547-2176.

AUTO REPAIR
Berg Chevrolet Garage, 11 West Main St. 547-3514.

AIR SERVICE
Airport, south of White Sulphur Springs. 547-3511.
   Prop aircrafts and small jets.

MEDICAL
Mountain View Memorial Hospital, 16 West Main St. 547-3384.

FOR MORE INFORMATION:
   Chamber of Commerce
   P.O. Box 356
   White Sulphur Springs, MT 59645.
   547-3932.

HARLOWTON
AND WHEATLAND COUNTY

Population– 1,049
Elevation– 4,167'
County Population– 2,246
County Area– 1,423 sq. mi.

October Temperature– 45.3
Annual Precipitation– 15"
Acres in CRP– 32,129
FWP Region 5

Harlowton is located at the intersection of US Hwy 12 and Hwy 191, 93 miles northwest of Billings. It is nestled among three mountain ranges near the geographic center of the state. The Graves Hotel and other buildings on Main Street still have the native sandstone of a frontier town. The Upper Musselshell Historical Society Museum on Central Avenue contains interesting memories of the local past.

Harlowton is the county seat of Wheatland County. Hwy 12 follows the Musselshell River with its many sandstone buttes and cottonwood bottomlands across the county. North of the river is intermountain grassland. There is plains grassland on the south side. The agricultural land along the Musselshell is mainly irrigated crops. The rest of the agriculture in the county is dryland farming.

UPLAND BIRDS
sharp-tailed and sage grouse, pheasant, and Hungarian partridge
Sharp-tailed grouse, sage grouse, and Hungarian partridge are in the lower three-quarters of Wheatland County. Clean dry farming and other farming practices have decreased much of the habitat for these species of upland birds. The pheasant population is confined to the river and its adjacent agricultural land.

WATERFOWL
geese and ducks
Wheatland County has several large reservoirs, small lakes, and ponds, but the Musselshell River is the main waterway for ducks and geese. During migration the big reservoirs can be hunted before freeze-up, but the shallow-water lakes are tough to hunt due to lack of cover.

ACCOMMODATIONS
Graves Hotel, 106 South Central Ave. 632-5855.
Built in 1908. 45 rooms. Bar 11AM–2AM, restaurant 6AM–10PM. No dogs allowed. Reasonable rates.
Corral Motel, Junction US 12 and 191 east of Harlowton, P.O. Box 721.
20 rooms, 3 kitchenettes. Dogs allowed. Reasonable rates.

County Side Inn, 309 3rd St NE, P.O. Box 72.
  11 rooms. Dogs allowed. Reasonable rates.
Troy Motel, 106 2nd Ave NE, P.O. Box 779. 632-4428.
  7 rooms. Dogs allowed. Reasonable rates.

RESTAURANTS
Graves Hotel Dining Room, 106 South Central Ave. 632-5855.
  Dining room open 5–10PM. Coffee shop open all day.
Cornerstone Inn, 11 North Central Ave. 632-4600.
  Breakfast and lunch.
Wade's Cafe, 632-4533.
  Open 7 days.

VETERINARIANS
Holloway Veterinary Hospital, P.O. Box 274. 632-4371.

SPORTING GOODS
Ray's Sports and Western Wear, Hwy 12 and Hwy 191. 632-4320.
  Guns, sporting equipment, clothing, and source for hunting guides and outfitters.

AUTO REPAIR
Leary's Exxon Service, 632-5814.
  Open 7AM–5PM.

AIR SERVICE
County airstrip, Will Morris. 632-4545.

MEDICAL
Wheatland Memorial Hospital, 530 3rd St NW. 632-4351.

FOR MORE INFORMATION:
  Harlowton Chamber of Commerce
  P.O. Box 694
  Harlowton, MT 59036.
  632-5523.

RYEGATE
AND GOLDEN VALLEY COUNTY

Population– 260	October Temperature– 47.1
Elevation– 3,550'	Annual Precipitation N/A
County Population– 912	Acres in CRP– 33,778
County Area– 1,175 sq. mi.	FWP Region 5

Ryegate is nestled under the rimrocks of the Musselshell River on Hwy 12, 29 miles east of Harlowton. Deadman's Basin Recreation Area is a few miles west of the town. Ryegate is in the central Montana sheep, cattle, and farming country. This small community has a grocery store, a cafe, two bars, a gas station, and post office. Lavina, 17 miles west on Hwy 3, 45 miles northwest of Billings, is also on the Musselshell River. Lavina's accommodations include a cafe, service station, two bars, and a post office. Lavina began as a stage station and trading post on the route between Lewistown and Billings. Ryegate, Cushman, and Lavina are the only towns in Golden Valley County.

Ryegate is the county seat. The county was named for the colored trees along the Musselshell River. Golden Valley's habitat is plains grassland, mixed cropland, and riparian forest along the river. The northern part of the county has some inter-mountain grassland and montane forest.

UPLAND BIRDS
sharp-tailed and sage grouse, pheasant, Hungarian partridge
The county supports Hungarian partridge and sharp-tailed grouse, but farming and ranching practices limit their distribution. Sage grouse are limited to big sage cover. The Musselshell River bottomlands and adjacent fields carry a limited pheasant population.

WATERFOWL
geese and ducks
Early in the waterfowl season, the Musselshell River with its oxbows, marshes, and potholes holds local and early migrating waterfowl. Puddle ducks can be numerous at times along the river system. Later in the season, when migration is in full swing, these small waterways can freeze and move waterfowl south.

ACCOMMODATIONS
See Roundup or Harlowton.

RESTAURANTS
Ryegate Cafe, 107 1st St, Ryegate. 568-9995.

Richard's Cafe, South of Hwy 3, Lavina.
Open 6AM–8PM.

AUTO REPAIR
Lanes Service, Inc. Lavina. 636-2722
Conoco Station.

ROUNDUP
AND MUSSELSHELL COUNTY

Population– 1,808	October Temperature– 47.4
Elevation– 3,184'	Annual Precipitation– 15"
County Population– 4,106	Acres in CRP– 14,759
County Area– 1,867 sq. mi.	FWP Region 5

Roundup is located 46 miles north of Billings on Hwy 87 in a valley near the Musselshell River. Long known for its natural geographic design useful for rounding-up livestock, one of the highlights of the year is the annual Roundup cattle drive, a truly western adventure lasting six days and five nights in August. Not a single motorized vehicle is seen during the drive. Roundup is also famous for its Musselshell Valley Historical Museum, open May through September.

Roundup is the county seat of Musselshell County. The Musselshell River, named for the oblong mollusks found there, was an important waterway for the early fur traders and hunters. The river flows east through the county, turns north at Melstone, and carries on to Fort Peck Lake in the C.M. Russell National Wildlife Refuge.

The county has widely varied terrain and habitat. The Bull Mountains and the surrounding area, in the southern part of the county, is plains forest. Northern Musselshell County is plains grassland mixed with shrub grassland, and the river bottom is riparian habitat.

UPLAND BIRDS
sharp-tailed and sage grouse, Hungarian partridge, pheasant, Merriam's turkey

The riparian habitat of the Musselshell and cropland along the river hold a pheasant population. Sage grouse are found north and south of the river wherever there is sagebrush. Most of the area supports sharp-tailed grouse, while Hungarian partridge are more isolated because of the intermountain grasslands. Wild turkey can be found along the river and in the Bull Mountains, but access can be difficult due to the lack of public lands.

WATERFOWL
geese and ducks

The Musselshell River complex has many small islands, backwater ponds, oxbows, marshes, and potholes. Puddle duck hunting can be productive, although later in the season most of the water freezes, sending the ducks farther south to open water.

ACCOMMODATIONS
Big Sky Motel, 740 Main. 323-2303.
   22 rooms. Dogs allowed. Reasonable rates.
Sage Motel, 630 Main. 323-1000.
   20 rooms. No dogs allowed. Reasonable rates.

CAMPGROUNDS AND RV PARKS
Ideal Motel and RV Park, 926 Main. 323-3371.
   10 rooms, 9 RV spaces, no tents. No dogs in rooms. Reasonable rates.

RESTAURANTS
Busy Bee, 317 1st Ave West. 323-2204.
   Diner, open 24 hours.
Stella's Supper Club, 123 Hwy 87 North. 323-1155.
   Good steaks. 11AM–10PM.
Pioneer Cafe, 229 Main. 232-2622.
   Full menu and spirits. 6AM–8PM.
Arcade, 230 Main. 232-1304.
   Bar and sporting goods.

VETERINARIANS
Roundup Vet Clinic, 56 Tumbleweed Rd. 323-2287.

SPORTING GOODS
Enjoy Sports, 342 Main. 232-1977.
Bull Mountain Trading, 136 Main. 232-1333.

AUTO REPAIR
A&A, 102 2nd St East. 323-1708.

AIR SERVICE,
County airstrip, Orville Moore. 323-1011.

MEDICAL
Roundup Memorial Hospital, 1202 3rd St West. 323-2301.

FOR MORE INFORMATION:
   Musselshell Valley Chamber of Commerce
   P.O. Box 751
   Roundup, MT 59072.
   323-1966.

FORSYTH
AND ROSEBUD COUNTY

Population– 2,178
Elevation– 2,515'
County Population– 10,505
County Area– 5,012 sq. mi.

October Temperature– 46.2
Annual Precipitation– 13"
Acres in CRP– 41,058
FWP Region 7

Forsyth is located in southeastern Montana on the banks of the Yellowstone River at the junction of Interstate 94 and Hwy 12, 100 miles east of Billings and 46 miles west of Miles City. Forsyth, a friendly small town, provides full services and has many recreational opportunities.

Forsyth is the county seat of Rosebud County, which is the third largest county in Montana, four times larger than the state of Rhode Island. The Yellowstone River runs east to west across the center of the county and provides rich agricultural land along the waterway. Rosebud Creek and the Tongue River are the other main water systems. Part of the southern portion of the county is the Northern Cheyenne Reservation.

UPLAND BIRDS
sharp-tailed and sage grouse, Hungarian partridge, pheasant, Merriam's turkey

Southern Rosebud County contains a part of the Custer National Forest with rolling hills of mixed hardwoods and ponderosa pine. This is ideal habitat for wild turkey and sharp-tailed grouse. South of the river is plains forest and grassland which sustains good habitat for sharp-tailed grouse, Hungarian partridge, sage grouse, and wild turkey. The three major waterways and adjacent farmland support fine cover for pheasants. North of Forsyth is plains grasslands with shallow coulees holding good populations of grouse and Huns.

WATERFOWL
geese and ducks

The Yellowstone River in Rosebud County is wide with many islands and gravel bars holding migrating waterfowl from the Central Flyway. The river is not open to waterfowl hunting, but creates excellent waterfowl shooting in the big grain fields along the system. Rosebud Creek and the Tongue River offer opportunities for waterfowl hunting early in the season.

ACCOMMODATIONS

Best Western Sundowner Inn, Interstate 90, Exit 93, 1018 Front St. 356-2115. Reservations: 800-332-0921. 40 rooms, in-room coffee bars, refrigerators. Dogs allowed (vacant lot adjacent for exercise). Reasonable rates.

Rails Inn Motel and Cafe, Intestate 94, Exit 93, 3rd and Front. 354-2242.
50 rooms, Side Track Lounge. Dogs allowed. Reasonable rates.
Rest Well Motel, 810 Front Street, Interstate 94, Exit 93. 356-2771.
Reservations: 800-548-3442. 18 rooms. Continental breakfast, refrigerators, 5 kitchenettes. Dogs allowed with restrictions. Reasonable rates.

CAMPGROUNDS AND RV PARKS
Wagon Wheeling Campsite, Interstate 94, Exit 95.
Open 4/1-10/31. 10 RV and 10 tent spaces. Full services.

RESTAURANTS
Speedway Diner, 811 Main St. 356-7987.
Home cooking. Open 24 hours.
Rails Inn Cafe and Side Track Lounge, 3rd and Front.
Family dining, homemade soups, daily specials. 6AM–8PM.
Blue Spruce Cafe, 109 South 10th. 356-7955.
Family dining, homemade soups, daily specials. 6AM–8PM.

VETERINARIANS
Animal House Veterinarian Service, 100 Prospect Ave. 356-7731.

SPORTING GOODS
Clark Hardware, 1195 Main. 356-2529.
Forsyth Hardware. 356-2405.

AUTO REPAIR
Art's Tire Service, 1487 Main St. 356-7718.

AIR SERVICE
Tillet Field Airport, Rosebud County. 356-9950.

MEDICAL
Rosebud Health Care Center, 383 North 17th. 356-2916.

FOR MORE INFORMATION:
Forsyth Chamber of Commerce
P.O. Box 448
Forsyth, MT 59327.
Contact Cal MacConnel at 356-2529.

MILES CITY
AND CUSTER COUNTY

Population– 8,461	October Temperature– 46.8
Elevation– 2627'	Annual Precipitation– 15"
County Population– 11,697	Acres in CRP– 23,522
County Area– 3,783 sq. mi.	FWP Region 7

Miles City, "Cowboy Capital of Montana," is just off Interstate 94. The community's many services have made it the hub of southeastern Montana. This is an up-to-date community that still retains its western culture.

Miles City is the county seat of Custer County. The Tongue River from the south meanders by the western edge of Miles City where it joins the Yellowstone River. The wide Powder River, with its cottonwood bottoms, flows the length of the county. Good access roads follow the major creeks and rivers in Custer County. Custer County's terrain provides a diversity of land patterns, with its vast, wide-open plains grasslands carved with an array of topographical extremes.

UPLAND BIRDS
sharp-tailed and sage grouse, Hungarian partridge, pheasant, Merriam's turkey

The cultivated lands along the two main rivers support pheasants and Huns. All parts of Custer County produce pockets of prairie grouse and partridge. Turkeys can be found in the pine forest area south of Miles City.

WATERFOWL
geese and ducks

Southeast Montana lies in the Central Flyway, playing host to thousands of waterfowl along the Yellowstone River system. The Tongue and Powder Rivers offer waterfowl hunting as do the stubble fields and small potholes.

ACCOMMODATIONS
Motel 6, 1314 South Haynes Ave. 232-7040. Interstate 90, Exit 138.
  113 rooms. Dogs allowed. Reasonable rates.
The Olive Hotel, 501 Main St. 232-2450.
  34 rooms, lounge. Dogs allowed. Rates expensive.
Buckboard Motel, 1006 South Haynes Ave. Interstate 90, Exit 138. 232-3550.
  58 rooms, continental breakfast. Dogs allowed. Reasonable rates.
Best Western War Bonnet Inn, Interstate 90, Exit 138, Hwy 312. 232-4560.
  54 units, indoor pool, continental breakfast. Dogs allowed. Reasonable rates.

RESTAURANTS
Louie's Olive Dining Room, 501 Main St. 232-7621.
  Steaks and seafood, nightly specials. Cocktails.
Club 519, 519 Main Street. 232-5133.
Cellar Casino and Bar, 719 Main St. 232-5611.
  Daily lunch and dinner specials, full menu.
600 Lounge and Cafe, 19 South 7th St. 232-3860.
Hole in the Wall, 602 Main St. 232-9887.
  Dinner specials, 5PM–10PM. Sunday buffet, 11AM–3PM.

VETERINARIANS
East Main Animal Clinic, 2719 Main St. 232-6900.
Miles City Veterinary, west of Miles City. 232-2559.

SPORTING GOODS
Red Rock Sporting Goods, 2900 Valley Dr East. 232-2716 or 800-367-5560.
  Complete sporting needs. 9AM–5:30PM.
Coast to Coast Hardware, 818 Main St. 232-4168.
  Sporting goods, M-Sat, 8AM–6PM. Sun, 1PM–5PM.

AUTO RENTAL AND REPAIR
Mac's Frontierland Ford, Mercury, and Lincoln, 3016 Valley Drive East. 232-2456.
  Rentals and service.
Jack's Body Shop, 700 7th St. 232-1661.
  Complete car care, 24-hour towing.

AIR SERVICE
Miles City Airport, East Hwy 59. 232-1354.
  Big Sky Commuter Service.

MEDICAL
Holy Rosary Hospital, 2101 Clark St. 232-2540 or 800-843-3820.
Garberson Clinic, 2200 Box Elder St. 232-0790 or 800-862-9823.

FOR MORE INFORMATION:
Miles City Chamber of Commerce
901 Main St
Miles City, MT 59301.
232-2890.

BAKER
AND FALLON COUNTY

Population– 1,818	October Temperature– N/A
Elevation– 2,929	Annual Precipitation– 15"
County Population– 3,103	Acres in CRP– 64,784
County Area– 1,620 sq. mi.	FWP Region 7

Baker is 81 miles east of Miles City on Hwy 12, just inside the Montana-North Dakota border. This friendly city serves as a market town for the surrounding grazing and farming area. Baker, the county seat of Fallon, has a museum and a new trapshooting and target range. The Medicine Rocks State Park is west of town. The county has no major rivers, but does have Fallon Creek to the south. Fallon County terrain is primarily plains grasslands with agricultural land interspersed.

UPLAND BIRDS
sharp-tailed and sage grouse, Hungarian partridge
All of Fallon County supports sharp-tailed grouse and Hungarian partridge. Good habitat and cover play an important part in determining the location of the birds. Sage grouse are in strong numbers in the county everywhere except the northeast corner.

WATERFOWL
geese and ducks
Good rains in the spring can fill reservoirs, potholes, and marshes producing good duck populations for early season waterfowl hunting.

ACCOMMODATIONS
Montana Motel, 716 East Montana Ave. 778-3315.
  12 rooms. Reasonable rates.
Sagebrush Inn, 518 US 12, Box 1157. 778-3341.
  40 rooms. Dogs allowed. Reasonable rates.
Roy's Motel, 327 Montana Ave. 778-3321.
  40 rooms. Dogs allowed. Reasonable rates.

RESTAURANTS
Sakelaris Kitchen, Lake City Shopping Center. 778-2202.
  Full family dining, 5:30AM–8PM. Sun., 7AM–3PM.
Corner Bar, 11 South Main. 778-3278.
  1PM–Midnight. Lunch and dinner.

Lost Steak House, 19 South Main. 778-3557.
Supper club and bar. 5PM–Midnight.

VETERINARIANS
Fallon County Vet, North of Baker. 778-3532.

SPORTING GOODS
Gunrunner Gun Shop, 113 South Main. 778-3443.
Guns and ammunition.

AUTO REPAIR
The Body Shop, east of Baker. 778-2263.

AIR SERVICE
Baker Municipal Airport. 778-3508.

MEDICAL
Fallon Medical Complex, 202 South 4th St West. 778-3331.

FOR MORE INFORMATION
Baker Chamber of Commerce
P.O. Box 849
Baker, MT 59313.
778-2266.

WIBAUX
AND WIBAUX COUNTY

Population– 628	October Temperature– 43.4
Elevation– 2,671'	Annual Precipitation– 19.29"
County Population– 1,191	Acres in CRP– 45,994
County Area– 889 sq. mi.	FWP Region 7

Wibaux (pronounced *wee-bo*) is the eastern gateway to Montana. In downtown Wibaux, visitors will find many historic places. There is a public pond with a picnic area located at the edge of the town on Hwy 7.

Wibaux is the county seat of Wibaux County. Beaver Creek with its many oxbows and turns meanders throughout the county. The cultivated and pasture land mix with the plains grassland, rolling hills, and badlands of Wibaux County.

UPLAND BIRDS
sharp-tailed and sage grouse, Hungarian partridge, pheasant

Sharp-tailed grouse, Hungarian partridge, and sage grouse are well established in many parts of the county. The thickest concentrations are along the water courses, and in the agricultural lands and foothills. Beaver Creek provides pheasant habitat. A small area in southwestern Wibaux County has sage grouse.

WATERFOWL
geese and ducks

The far northeastern corner of Wibaux is on the Yellowstone River, but there isn't an access road to the river. Wibaux County, at times, has some field shooting for waterfowl. Potholes, reservoirs, and Beaver Creek hold a few puddle ducks early in the season.

ACCOMMODATIONS
Wibaux Motel Super 8, Interstate 94 Exit 241 West and Exit 242 East. 795-2666.
  35 rooms. Dogs allowed. Reasonable rates.
W-V Motel, 106 West 2nd Ave. 795-2446.
  9 rooms, 4 kitchenettes. Dogs allowed with restrictions. Reasonable rates.

RESTAURANTS
Shamrock Club, 101 South Wibaux. 795-8250.
  Bar and cafe. Steaks, shrimp, sandwiches.
Palace Cafe, 125 South Wibaux. 795-2426.
  Homemade soups and pastries. Daily specials.

Tastee Hut, Exit 241 or Exit 242, I-94.
Full meals. Sandwiches, take-out or eat in.

VETERINARIANS
Terry Hall, D.V.M., P.O. Box 259. 795-2624.

AUTO REPAIR
Jim Bacon Auto Repair, 309 North Wibaux. 795-8118.

MEDICAL
Medical care is in Baker. For ambulance call 911.

FOR MORE INFORMATION:
Wibaux Chamber of Commerce
Box 159
Wibaux, MT 59353.

LIVINGSTON
AND PARK COUNTY

Population– 6,700	October Temperature– 44
Elevation– 4,503'	Annual Precipitation– 18"
County Population– 14,786	Acres in CRP– 14,759
County Area– 2,626 sq. mi.	FWP Regions 3 and 5

    Livingston is located in southcentral Montana, on the big bend of the Yellowstone River, 53 miles north of Yellowstone National Park and 25 miles east of Bozeman. It is in the lovely Paradise valley, surrounded by the Absaroka-Beartooth Wilderness, and the Gallatin, Bridger, and Crazy mountain ranges. Livingston is a hospitable western town. Its hotels, motels, and bed and breakfasts have over 600 rooms and there are many fine restaurants.

    Livingston is the county seat of Park County. Here, as in several other counties in Montana, the Great Plains and the rolling foothills give way to the Rocky Mountain Front. There are campgrounds, scenic areas, and fishing accesses along the Yellowstone River. Some of the best trout fishing in the country is found here in the rivers, small streams, spring creeks, and lakes.

UPLAND BIRDS
ruffed, blue, sharp-tailed, and sage grouse, Hungarian partridge

Most of Park County is mountain country, but there is a small amount of varied terrain—prairies, agricultural land, and foothills—along the two major waterways, the Yellowstone and Shields Rivers. The mountain habitat with its aspen and evergreen forests offers good ruffed and blue grouse populations. Most of this is federal land with decent public access. The foothills and farmland offer upland bird hunting for sharp-tailed grouse and Hungarian partridge.

WATERFOWL
geese and ducks

The Yellowstone and Shields Rivers, with their side-channels, creeks, springs, potholes, and marshes, offer good waterfowl shooting. Early in the waterfowl season, Park County has a strong population of local ducks and geese. As the hunting season progresses, there are large concentrations of ducks and geese from the northern provinces of Canada streaming down the Pacific Flyway to rest along the Yellowstone River. The Yellowstone has good public access for fishing and waterfowl hunting.

ACCOMMODATIONS

The Murray Hotel, 201 West Park. 222-1350.
Located downtown, next to Dan Bailey's Fly Shop. Newly renovated, deluxe, turn-of-the century hotel. 40 charming guest rooms with or without adjoining baths. The Winchester Cafe, The Murray Bar, and large lounge are adjoining. Dogs allowed. Reasonable rates.

Paradise Inn, P.O. Box 684. 800-437-6291.
Off Interstate 90, Exit 333. 42 rooms, all ground floor. Lounge, indoor pool, jacuzzi, and restaurant. Dogs allowed, some restrictions. Reasonable rates.

Parkway Motel-Budget Host, 1124 West Park St. 222-3840.
Reservations: 800-727-7217. Interstate 90, Exit 333. 28 rooms, 8 kitchenettes, 3 two-bedroom rooms. Dogs allowed, $3 charge. Reasonable rates.

Livingston Inn and Campground, Box 3053-A, Rogers Lane. Interstate 90, Exit 333, ½ block north. Motel: 222-3600. 16 rooms. Campground: 222-1122. 26 hookups, pull-through spaces, showers, and laundry. Reasonable rates.

Chico Hot Springs Lodge, Pray, Montana. 333-4933.
Located 23 miles south of Livingston on route 89. Inn has 50 Rooms, motel has 24 rooms, 4 cabins, 3 cottages with kitchens, log house with kitchen, 2 condos with kitchens. Mineral hot springs pool. **Chico Inn** gourmet dining room, **Poolside Grill, Saloon.** Dogs allowed,$2 charge. Moderate rates.

RESTAURANTS

Winchester Cafe and Murray Bar, 201 West Park. 222-1350.
Downtown Livingston. Full-service restaurant—breakfast, lunch, dinner, and a Sunday brunch. Homemade desserts, espresso, fine wine selection.

Chico Inn, Pray. 333-4933.
23 miles south of Livingston on Route 89. Fine dining, reservations recommended. Great wine list. **Poolside Grill** has great homemade food, bar.

Stockman, 118 North Main St. 222-8455.
Bar and restaurant. Lunch and dinner—steaks, prime rib, seafood, and burgers.

Livingston Bar and Grill, 130 North Main St. 222-7909.
Antique bar. Steak, seafood, and buffalo burgers.

The Sport, 114 South Main St. 222-3533.
BBQ ribs, chicken, burgers, cocktails, and wine.

Martin's Cafe, 108 West Park St. 222-2110.
Open 24 hours, 7 days. Carry-out, breakfast specials, smorgasbord on Sundays.

VETERINARIANS

Colmey Veterinary Hospital, P.O. Box 521. 222-1700.
Duane Colmey, D.V.M., ½ mile south of Livingston on Rt 89. Pet food, supplies, grooming, kennel.

Shields Valley Veterinary Service, Rt 85 Box 4321. 222-6171.
Donald Smith, D.V.M.

SPORTING GOODS

Dan Bailey's Fly Shop, 209 West Park St. 222-1673 or 800-356-4052.
Flies, fishing equipment, clothing, and accessories.

George Anderson's Yellowstone Angler, Rt 89 South, P.O. Box 660. 222-7130.
Flyfishing specialties, outdoor clothing.

Wilderness Outfitters, 1 mile south of town on Rt 89. 222-6933.
Guns, shells, clothing, and accessories.

AIR SERVICE

Mission Field, east of Livingston. 222-6504.

AUTO RENTAL AND REPAIR

Livingston Ford-Lincoln-Mercury, 1415 West Park St. 222-7200.
All models, 4WD and vans.

MEDICAL

Livingston Memorial Hospital, 504 South 13th St. 222-3541.

FOR MORE INFORMATION:

Livingston Area Chamber of Commerce, Depot Center, Baggage Room
212 West Park Street
Livingston, MT 59047.
222-0850.

Many ducks and geese migrate down the big rivers in Montana.

BIG TIMBER
AND SWEET GRASS COUNTY

Population– 1,557
Elevation– 4,100'
County Population– 3,154
County Area– 1,855 sq. mi.

October Temperature– 47.3
Annual Precipitation– 15.43"
Acres in CRP– 3,482
FWP Region 5

Tucked between the Yellowstone and the Boulder Rivers, in the shadow of the Crazy Mountains, is the town of Big Timber. It is located halfway between Bozeman and Billings off I-90.

Big Timber is the county seat of Sweet Grass County. The Boulder River leads south into the spectacular Absaroka-Beartooth Wilderness. To the north are the Crazy Mountains. There are many Forest Service campgrounds in the area. In addition to wingshooting, fine fishing abounds here.

UPLAND BIRDS
ruffed, blue, sage, and sharp-tailed grouse, Hungarian partridge

The mountain habitat in the Absaroka-Beartooth Wilderness and the Crazy Mountains provide ruffed and blue grouse hunting. The foothills and the agricultural land to the north offer sharp-tailed grouse, sage grouse, and Hungarian partridge hunting.

WATERFOWL
geese and ducks

Sweet Grass County is in the Central Flyway. The Yellowstone River and Big Timber Creek, with their side channels, marshes, and potholes, offers good waterfowl shooting. Sweet Grass Creek north of Big Timber also provides waterfowling. Later in the season, there is fine goose hunting along the Yellowstone River.

ACCOMMODATIONS
Big Timber Super 8 Motel, Interstate 90 and Hwy 1. 932-8888.
  39 rooms. Dogs allowed with a $15 deposit. Reasonable rates.
The Grand Hotel, Box 1242, McLeod Street. 932-4459.
  Recently restored with high ceilings and Victorian atmosphere, 10 rooms. No dogs. Moderate rates. A hearty breakfast is included with your room.
Lazy J Motel, P.O. Box 1096, on old Hwy 10. 932-5533.
  15 rooms. Dogs allowed for a small fee. Reasonable rates.

CAMPGROUNDS AND RV PARKS
Spring Creek Camp & Trout Ranch, 2 miles south on Rt 298. 932-4387.
Open 4/1-11/30. 50 RV and 50 tent spaces. Full services.

RESTAURANTS
Frye's Cafe and Lounge, Hwy 10 West. 932-5242.
Breakfast, lunch, and dinner.
The Grand Hotel, 139 McLeod St.
Breakfast, lunch, and dinner. Fine dining and full beverage service. Expensive but elegant.
Country Pride Restaurant, Old Hwy 10 West. 932-4419.
Breakfast, lunch, and dinner.
Timber Bar, 116 McLeod St. 932-9211.
Breakfast, lunch, and dinner. 10AM–Midnight.

VETERINARIANS
All Creatures Veterinarian Service, 21 North Bramble. 932-4324.

SPORTING GOODS
The Fort, Hwy 10 East. 932-5992.
Guns and ammunition.
Bob's Sport Shop, 230 McLeod St. 932-5464.
Guns and ammunition.

AUTO REPAIR
Stetson Ford, 403 McLeod St. 932-5732.

AIR SERVICE
County airstrip, Justin Ferguson. 932-4389.

MEDICAL
Sweet Grass Family Medicine, 5th Ave and Hooper. 932-5920.

FOR MORE INFORMATION
Sweet Grass Chamber of Commerce
Box 1012
Big Timber, MT 59011.
932-5131.

COLUMBUS
AND STILLWATER COUNTY

Population– 1,573	October Temperature– 43.7
Elevation– 3,585'	Annual Precipitation– 16.5"
County Population– 3,154	Acres in CRP– 61,157
County Area– 1,795 sq. mi.	FWP Region 5

Columbus is located off Interstate 90, 40 miles south of Billings, where the Stillwater River meets the Yellowstone River. Columbus, the county seat of Stillwater County, offers a quiet, peaceful, and friendly atmosphere with full-service facilities. The town is situated along the Yellowstone at the foothills of the Beartooth Mountains. North of the river there are open foothills, grasslands, and cultivated fields.

UPLAND BIRDS
ruffed, blue, sharp-tailed, and sage grouse, Hungarian partridge, pheasant

Ruffed and blue grouse are found from the Stillwater drainage south to the mixed hardwood and evergreen forests of the mountains. Much of this is federal land with public access. North of the Yellowstone River is where the sharp-tailed grouse and Hungarian partridge are located. A few pheasants can be found along the Yellowstone drainage.

WATERFOWL
geese and ducks

In Stillwater County the Yellowstone River is large and has many side channels, potholes, and sloughs that offer good waterfowl shooting. To the north are smaller ponds, reservoirs, and alkali lakes.

ACCOMMODATIONS
Super 8 TownHouse Inn, 602 8th Ave North. 322-4101.
   72 rooms. Kitchenette, spa, sauna, guest laundry, coffee and toast bar. Dogs allowed. Reasonable rates.
Riverside Cabins and Fly Shop, 44 West Pike. 322-5472.
   7 cabins, 3 with kitchens. Fishing guide service, licensing agent. No dogs in cabins and no smoking. Reasonable rates.

RESTAURANTS
Town Pump, Exit 408, Interstate 90 and Hwy 78, 8th Ave North. 322-4535.
   Lucky Lil's Casino, buffet breakfast, lunch, and dinner. Open 24 hours.

Apple Village Cafe, I-90, Exit 408. 322-5939.
Breakfast, lunch, and dinner.
Air Bowl Steakhouse, 142 South Pike Ave. 322-4340.
Daily breakfast, lunch, and dinner specials. Prime rib. 6AM–10PM.
Branding Iron Cafe, downtown Columbus.
A taste of the Old West. 6AM–10PM, 7 days.

VETERINARIANS
Cloverleaf Veterinarian Service, Frontage Road. 322-4581.
Kevin Homewood, D.V.M.

SPORTING GOODS
Stillwater Hardware, 508 Pike St. 322-4436.
Guns, ammunition, and licenses.

AUTO REPAIR
Ken's I-90 Repair. 322-4730.
Bob Kem Auto Repair. 322-5996.

AIR SERVICE
Columbus Airport, Rickman Field. 322-5974.

MEDICAL
Stillwater County Hospital, 322-5316.
24-hour emergency service.

FOR MORE INFORMATION:
Columbus Chamber of Commerce
Box 783
Columbus, MT 59019.
322-4505.

BILLINGS
AND YELLOWSTONE COUNTY

Population– 81,151	October Temperature– 47.5
Elevation– 3,567'	Annual Precipitation– 15"
County Population– 113,419	Acres in CRP– 51,266
County Area– 2,635 sq. mi.	FWP Region 5

Billings, located in the southcentral portion of the state, is the industrial, commercial, and agricultural hub of the region. Accommodations range from casual to elegant with over 3,000 rooms and 150 restaurants to meet every taste and budget.

Billings is the county seat of Yellowstone County. The Yellowstone River Valley covers a large portion of the county with riparian habitat along the waterway. The agricultural land fans out across the valley floor to the rimrocks and foothills. To the north is plains forest, plains grassland, and dryland farming.

UPLAND BIRDS
ruffed, blue, sage, and sharp-tailed grouse, Hungarian partridge, pheasant

Yellowstone County has an abundance of agricultural lands and a long growing season by Montana standards. Along the river valley are a variety of crops useful to Hungarian partridge, sharp-tailed grouse, and pheasants. The northern part of Yellowstone County offers good hunting for sharp-tailed grouse, Huns, and sage grouse. Blue and ruffed grouse are found in the plains forest and mountain forests.

WATERFOWL
geese and ducks

Yellowstone County is in the Central Flyway. The Yellowstone River is big, with many side channels and numerous potholes. There is good waterfowl shooting on the river as well as in the adjacent agricultural lands.

ACCOMMODATIONS
Ramada Limited, 1345 Mullowney Lane. 252-2584, 800-272-6232.
Off I-90, Exit 446, one block south. The Best Rest in the West Lounge, continental breakfast. Dogs allowed. Reasonable rates.
Kelly Inn, 5425 Midland Road. 252-2700.
Off I-90, Exit 446, three blocks east. 88 rooms, indoor whirlpool and sauna, continental breakfast. Dogs allowed. Reasonable rates.
Motel 6, 5400 Midland Road. 252-0093.
Off I-90, Exit 446, 3 blocks east. 99 rooms. Dogs allowed. Reasonable rates.

CAMPGROUNDS AND RV PARKS
Trailer Village, I-90 exit 447. 6 blocks north on South Billings Blvd. 248-8685.
Open year-round. 35 RV spaces. Full services.

RESTAURANTS
Olive Garden Restaurant, 220 Grand Road. 652-1395.
Fine Italian dining, bar. Serving lunch and dinner, 10AM–11PM.
Tiny's Tavern, 323 North 24th, Exit 450. 259-0828.
Bar. Serving lunch and dinner, 10AM–11PM.
Billings Club-Sports Pub, 2702 1st Ave North, Exit 450. 245-2262.
Serving lunch and dinner 10AM–11PM. Bar open until 2AM.

VETERINARIANS
Moore Lane Veterinary Hospital, 50 Moore Lane. 252-4159.
Emergency 252-4159 or 656-1910. Boarding services, office hours 8AM–Noon.
Shepard-Huntley Animal Care Center, ½ mile east of Shepard. 373-6642.

SPORTING GOODS
Big Bear Sports Center, Rimrock Mall. 656-0285.
Complete sporting goods store, guns, ammunition, clothing.
Scheel's, 233 24th St West. 656-9220.
Complete sporting goods at affordable prices.
Sir Michael's Sport Shoppe, 21 North Broadway. 446-1614.
Guns, ammunition,clothing, maps, licenses. Open 7 days.

AUTO RENTAL AND REPAIR
Budget Rent-A-Car, Logan International Airport. 259-4168.
Hertz Rent-A-Car, Logan International Airport. 248-9151 or 800-654-3131.
Custom Auto Repair, 4840 Laurel Rd. 245-9912, Mobile 698-2897.
Complete repair service, American and foreign. 24-hour towing.

AIR SERVICE
Logan International Airport, 245-9449.
The region's busiest airport. Seven airlines.

MEDICAL
Deaconess Medical Center, 2800 10th Ave North. 657-4000.
Full-service regional medical center.
Billings Clinic, 2825 8th Ave North. 238-2500.
85 physicians. Over 25 specialists.

FOR MORE INFORMATION:
Billings Area Chamber of Commerce and Visitor Center
815 South 27th St
Billings, MT 59107.
800-735-2635.

HYSHAM
AND TREASURE COUNTY

Population– 361	October Temperature– 46.1
Elevation– 2,660	Annual Precipitation– 15"
County Population– 871	Acres in CRP– 3,658
County Area– 979 sq. mi.	FWP Region 7

Hysham is halfway between Miles City and Billings off I-94. Dropping down the hills toward the Yellowstone River, you have a panoramic view of this agricultural community—green fields, pasture land, and strips of golden grain.

Hysham is the county seat of Treasure County, where the Yellowstone River meanders from west to east with many access sites. To the south are beautiful rolling hills. Treasure County has some outstanding historical sites.

UPLAND BIRDS
sharp-tailed and sage grouse, Hungarian partridge, pheasant

Most of the agricultural land along the Yellowstone River has well established populations of pheasants. All of Treasure County has sharp-tailed grouse, Hungarian partridge, and pockets of sage grouse.

WATERFOWL
geese and ducks

The Yellowstone River is large and has many channels and sandbars that make good resting places for ducks and geese. Birds from the northern providences of Canada in the Central Flyway spend considerable time resting on the river and feeding in the agricultural fields. Even though the river is closed to waterfowl hunting, the agricultural land is open with landowner permission. Be sure to consult the waterfowl hunting regulations.

ACCOMMODATIONS
Treasure County Motel, P.O. Box 469, I-94, Exit 67. 342-5627.
  4 rooms. Dogs allowed. Very reasonable.

RESTAURANTS
Town and Country Lounge and Hysham Hills Supper Club, I-94, Exit 67. 342-5434.
  M-Th, 10AM–9PM, Fri-Sat, 10AM–10PM, Sun, 8AM–8PM. Sunday buffet, family dining. Entrees range from burgers to lobster.
Brunswick Bar, Interstate 95, Exit 67.
  Mixed drinks, beer, wine, burgers, and pizza. 10AM–2PM.

VETERINARIANS
Treasure Veterinarian Service, I-94, Exit 67. 342-5224.

SPORTING GOODS
Hysham Hardware. 342-5285.
Ammunition.

AUTO REPAIR
Farmer's Union, I-94, Exit 67. 342-5221.
Gas and service.
Gene's Auto AAA. 342-5368.
Approved towing service and repair.
Friendly Corner, I-94, Exit 67. 342-5888.
Food, gas, and travel shop.

AIR SERVICE
County airstrip, Glen White. 342-5563.

MEDICAL
Medical service is in Forsyth. For ambulance call 911.

FOR MORE INFORMATION
Hysham Chamber of Commerce
P.O. Box 312
Hysham, MT 59038.
Contact Cora Marks, secretary, Chamber of Commerce, 342-5457.

RED LODGE
AND CARBON COUNTY

Population– 1,875
Elevation– 5,555'
County Population– 8,080
County Area– 2,048 sq. mi.

October Temperature– 42.6
Annual Precipitation– 22"
Acres in CRP– 14,893
FWP Region 5

The majestic Beartooth Mountains form the backdrop for Red Lodge, the former summer camp of the Crow Indians. It is located on Rock Creek in the middle of a triangle formed by Billings, Cody, WY, and Yellowstone National Park, each approximately 65 miles away. Red Lodge offers a variety of lodging including motels, condominiums, a historic hotel, and bed and breakfasts. There are two private campgrounds and numerous public campsites in the surrounding national forest areas.

The county seat for Carbon County, Red Lodge is the starting point for what is arguably the most beautiful drive in America, the 69-mile Beartooth Highway that reaches a height of almost 11,000 feet as it climbs through the Beartooth Mountains to Yellowstone National Park. This highway is usually open from Labor Day to at least Memorial Day, depending on snow depth. Fine fishing can be found in nearby streams and mountain lakes. Red Lodge Mountain is a well-known ski area.

UPLAND BIRDS
ruffed, blue, sharp-tailed, and sage grouse, pheasant, Hungarian partridge
Carbon County has a mixed terrain of mountains, foothills, prairies, and agricultural land. Blues and ruffed grouse are found in the foothills and mountains of the county. Prairie birds abound in the riparian forest, foothills, prairie grasslands, and agricultural lands. Pheasants are mostly in the agricultural lands.

WATERFOWL
geese and ducks
Early in the season, Carbon County has a good population of local ducks and geese in the potholes and streams. Later in the season, waterfowl will be feeding in the fields. Carbon County is in the Central Flyway.

ACCOMMODATIONS
Red Lodge Super 8, 1223 Broadway. 446-2288.
  50 units, kitchenettes, indoor pool. Dogs allowed. Reasonable rates.
Eagles Nest Motel, 702 South Broadway. 446-2312.
  16 units, 2 with kitchens. Dogs allowed. Reasonable rates.

Yodeler Motel, 601 South Broadway. 446-1435.
22 rooms, in-room steam bath. Dogs allowed. Reasonable rates.
Red Lodge Inn, 1223 South Broadway. 446-2030.
12 units. Dogs allowed. Reasonable rates.

RESTAURANTS
Bogart's Restaurant, 11 South Broadway. 222-1784.
Great atmosphere, bar, Mexican food, pizza, sandwiches, Italian dishes.
Old Pitney Dell, south of Red Lodge. 446-1196.
Gourmet dining. Mon–Sat, 5–10PM.
Red Lodge Cafe, 16 South Broadway. 446-1619.
Breakfast, buffalo burgers, homemade pie, soup. Full-service bar and lounge.
The Pollard, 2 North Broadway.
Newly renovated, full-service restaurant and bar.

VETERINARIAN
Red Lodge Veterinary Clinic, Rt 1, Box 4025. 446-2815.
John Beud, D.V.M.

SPORTING GOODS
Outdoor Adventure, 110½ South Broadway. 446-3818.
Sir Michael's Sport Shoppe, 21 North Broadway. 446-1613.
Hunting licenses.
True Value Hardware and Variety, 101 North Broadway. 446-1847.
Hunting licenses.

AUTO REPAIR
Buffalo Bob's, north of Red Lodge. 446-3000.

AIR SERVICE
County airstrip, Amos C. Clark. 466-2537.

MEDICAL
Billings Clinic, 10 South Oaks. 446-2412.
8AM–5PM. Walk-in care available.
Carbon County Memorial Hospital, 600 West 20th St. 446-2345.

FOR MORE INFORMATION:
Red Lodge Chamber of Commerce
P. O. Box 988
Red Lodge, MT 59068.
446-1718.

HARDIN
AND BIG HORN COUNTY

Population– 2,940   October Temperature– 47.6
Elevation– 2,905'   Annual Precipitation– 19"
County Population– 11,337   Acres in CRP– 27,270
County Area– 4,995 sq. mi.   FWP Regions 5 and 7

Hardin is located 46 miles east of Billings just off Interstate 90, and lies at the northern edge of the Crow Indian Reservation in southern Montana. Hardin has a multitude of attractions including the gateway to the Bighorn Canyon Recreation Area, Yellowtail Dam, and the Bighorn River, a blue-ribbon trout stream.

Hardin is the county seat of Big Horn County. The county is large, stretching from the Yellowstone River south to the Wyoming border, and from the Pryor Mountains in the east beyond the Tongue River Reservoir. A large portion of the county is in the Crow Reservation. The major waterways are the Bighorn Reservoir, the Bighorn River, and the Little Bighorn River.

UPLAND BIRDS
ruffed, blue, sharp-tailed, and sage grouse, Hungarian partridge, pheasant

The mixed hardwood and evergreen forests of the Bighorn Mountains support mountain grouse. Along the major waterways there is riparian habitat and croplands with good populations of pheasant and Hungarian partridge. The county consists of intermountain grasslands, shrub, and plains grassland ideal for sharp-tailed grouse and Huns.

WATERFOWL
geese and ducks

The Bighorn River and the Little Bighorn River offer some outstanding waterfowl hunting. On the Bighorn River you can trout fish and waterfowl hunt while drifting from a boat — a real cast and blast.

Note: The Crow Indian Reservation lies within Big Horn County.
Please be aware of Reservation hunting regulations.

ACCOMMODATIONS
Super 8 Motel, I-90, Exit 495. 665-1700.
Peaceful, quiet atmosphere. Guest laundry, free coffee and toast. Non-smoking rooms available. Dogs with permission. Reasonable rates.
Western Motel, I-90, Exit 495 or 497. 665-2296.
Single or two-family units, room coffee. Dogs allowed with restrictions. Reasonable rates.

American Inn, 324 Crawford. 665-1870 or 800-582-8094.
42 units. Swimming pool, hot tub, coffee and toast. Dogs allowed with restrictions. Reasonable rates.

OUTFITTERS
Phil Gonzalez's Bighorn River Lodge, P.O. Box 7756, Ft. Smith.
666-2368 or 800-235-5450. Complete facilities, 6 comfortable rooms for 12 guests, fine dining. Flyfishing, upland birds, and waterfowl. A great place to stay.
Eagle Nest Lodge Bighorn River, P.O. Box 470, Hardin. 665-3799.
Lodge has 6 bedrooms with baths, cabin retreat hosting 4 persons, fine dining. Orvis-endorsed, flyfishing and bird hunting.

RESTAURANTS
Merry Mixer, 317 North Center Ave. 665-3736.
Restaurant and lounge. Breakfast, lunch, and dinner. Daily specials, wide selection of steaks.
Purple Cow, Rt. 1, Box 1003. 665-3601.
Family restaurant, homemade soups and pies. 7AM–10PM.
Corner Pocket, 920 West 3rd. 665-2024.
Full bar. Handmade pizza and sandwiches.

VETERINARIANS
Animal Care Center, ½ mile west of Hardin. 665-3456.
Call day or night. Boarding.
Bighorn Veterinary Hospital, 1224 North Crawford Ave. 665-2405.
Emergency, 665-1815. 24-hour emergency care.

SPORTING GOODS
Bighorn Fly and Tackle Shop, 1426 North Crawford Ave. 665-1312.

AUTO REPAIR
Conoco Bob's Interstate Service, I-90, Exit 495.

AIR SERVICE
Hardin Airstrip, Larry Romine. 665-2301.

MEDICAL
Big Horn County Memorial Hospital, 17 North Miles Ave. 665-2310.

FOR MORE INFORMATION:
Hardin Chamber of Commerce
200 North Center Ave.
Hardin, MT 59034.
665-1672.

BROADUS AND
POWDER RIVER COUNTY

Population– 571
Elevation– 3,027'
County Population– 2,090
County Area– 2,329 sq. mi.

October Temperature– 46.2
Annual Precipitation– 15"
Acres in CRP– 23,209
FWP Region 7

Broadus is located on Hwy 212, 79 miles south of Miles City in the southeastern corner of the state, near the junction of the Powder and the Little Powder Rivers. The Powder River starts in Wyoming and travels north across the county. It has been described as "a mile wide and an inch deep, too wet to plow and too thick to drink." Broadus is the gateway to the Black Hills in South Dakota and is often called the biggest little town in the west.

Broadus is the county seat of Powder River County. Custer National Forest is in the western portion of the county. Powder River County offers a smorgasbord of rugged landscape—picturesque cottonwood, creeks, river bottoms, and agricultural lands.

UPLAND BIRDS
sharp-tailed and sage grouse, Hungarian partridge, pheasant, Merriam's turkey

Custer National Forest, with its hardwood draws and ponderosa pine, is one of the more popular places for turkey hunting in the state. The Powder River cottonwood bottoms also hold good populations of wild turkey. Sharp-tailed grouse and Huns are interspersed throughout the county, but not always in high numbers. The Powder River system provides some pheasant hunting. Sage grouse are distributed in the north and east sections of the county.

WATERFOWL
geese and ducks

Powder River County and most of the southeastern quarter of the state has a shortage of resting and feeding water and does not hold migrating waterfowl long. However, early in the season, if the water is available, potholes, reservoirs, and waterways can be good for small concentrations of puddle ducks.

ACCOMMODATIONS
C-J Motel, US 212, west side. 436-2671.
30 rooms. Dogs allowed for a $5 fee. Reasonable rates.

Quarterhorse Motor Inn, US 212, center of town. 436-2626.
  10 rooms. Dogs allowed for a $5 fee. Reasonable rates.
Buckskin Inn, 436-2929.
  11 rooms. Dogs allowed for a $5 fee. Reasonable rates.

OUTFITTERS
Oakwood Lodge, South Pumpkin Creek, 25 miles west of Broadus, 3 miles south of Hwy 212. 427-5474. Three spacious rooms with individual baths, homemade breakfast, peaceful and quiet. Professional guide for big game, spring and fall turkey, and upland gamebirds.

RESTAURANTS
Montana Bar and Cafe, 436-2454.
  Breakfast, lunch, and dinner. Red Velvet dining room, homemade rolls and pies.
Homestead Inn, 436-2615.
  Full menu, restaurant and lounge. 7 days, 6:30AM–10PM.
Chuck's Tastee Freez, west side of Broadus. 436-2818.
  Complete menu.

VETERINARIANS
Broadus Veterinary Clinic, 436-2401.

SPORTING GOODS
Cobbs True Value Hardware, 436-2811.
  Guns and ammunition.

AUTO REPAIR
Powder River Rebuild, 436-2889.
Alderman Oil Conoco, south end. 436-2898.
  Open 7 days, 5:30AM–10PM.

AIR SERVICE
Fly West Air Inc, 436-2966.

MEDICAL
Powder River Medical Clinic, 436-2651.

FOR MORE INFORMATION:
  Broadus Chamber of Commerce
  P.O. Box 484
  Broadus, MT 59317.
  436-2611.

EKALAKA
AND CARTER COUNTY

Population– 439
Elevation– 4,806'
County Population– 1,503
County Area– 3,340

October Temperature– 44
Annual Precipitation– 15"
Acres in CRP– 38,837
FWP Region 7

Ekalaka is 116 miles south of Miles City. Known as "the town at the end of the road," Ekalaka has only one paved road. Though small, it meets all the needs for a pleasant stay. The primary industries are sheep and cattle production.

Ekalaka is the county seat of Carter County, located in the southeastern corner of Montana. The county is comprised of wide open spaces where arid prairie and shrub grassland rise to meet the Chalk Buttes, Ekalaka Hills, and the Long Pines which are part of Custer National Forest. Carter County is a mixture of sagebrush prairie, grassland prairie, and agriculture. Ponderosa pine, juniper breaks, and hardwood bottoms are found along Box Elder Creek and the Little Missouri.

UPLAND BIRDS
sharp-tailed and sage grouse, Hungarian partridge, Merriam's turkey

The southeast corner of the the state is the land of climatic extremes. Bird populations can fluctuate considerably. Most of Carter County carries established populations of sharp-tailed grouse, sage grouse, and Huns. The Custer National Forest has wild turkeys.

WATERFOWL
geese and ducks

Early season hunting for waterfowl is best. During wet springs the potholes, reservoirs, and marshes will fill, producing a good population of puddle ducks.

ACCOMMODATIONS
Guest House, 4 Main St, P.O. Box 296. 775-6337.
 5 rooms. Dogs allowed with restrictions. Reasonable rates.
Midway Motel, Main St, P.O. Box 484. 775-6619.
 6 rooms, some dogs allowed. Reasonable rates.

CAMPGROUNDS AND RV PARKS
Cline Camper Court, West of town near fairgrounds. 775-6231.
 Open 5/1-12/1. 15 RV and 6 tent spaces. Water, electric, sewer, showers.

Restaurants
B&B Grill and Bar, Main St. 775-6484.
 Breakfast, lunch, and dinner. Full menu, 7AM–10PM.
Wagon Wheel Cafe, Main St. 775-6639.
 Full menu, 6AM–8PM.
Old Mill Cafe, Main St. 775-6684.
 Full menu.

Veterinarians
James G. Tooke, D.V.M., north of town on Hwy 7. 775-6494 office, 775-6493 home.

Sporting Goods
W&S Propane, 775-6221.
 Guns and ammunition.

Auto Repair
Fruit Repair, Main Street. 775-6542.
 Full service and repair.

Air Service
Ekalaka Airport, Ernest Tooke. 775-6542.

Medical
Dahl Memorial Hospital, Park Ave. 775-8730.

For more information:
 Chamber of Commerce
 P.O. Box 297
 Ekalaka, MT 59324.
 775-6658.

MONTANA FORESTS, PARKS, AND INDIAN RESERVATIONS

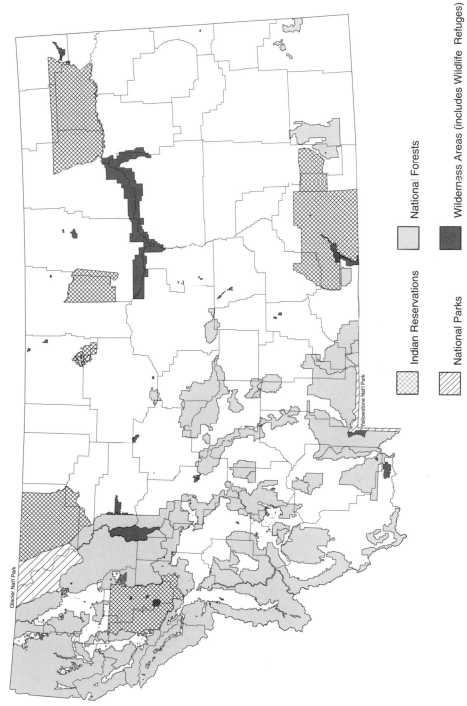

Glacier Nat'l Park

Yellowstone Nat'l Park

Indian Reservations

National Forests

National Parks

Wilderness Areas (includes Wildlife Refuges)

HUNTING ON INDIAN RESERVATIONS

Montana is home to seven reservations representing 11 tribes. Each features a wealth of cultural institutions and historical sites. Together, the reservations cover over 7 million acres, much of it excellent bird habitat.

The type and quality of hunting on each reservation varies greatly. Some tribes do not permit hunting. Only one reservation, the Flathead, has a joint hunting program set up with the Montana Dept of Fish, Wildlife, and Parks. It will be necessary to contact the reservation you are interested in hunting before you plan your trip for current regulations.

When traveling on reservations, be particularly respectful of the people you encounter. Many tribes work to attract visitors, but others feel that tourists invade their privacy and compromise the integrity of their traditional culture.

In order to make your visit to a reservation pleasant for everyone, be sensitive to your surroundings and obey all tribal laws and regulations.

Indian Reservations in Montana

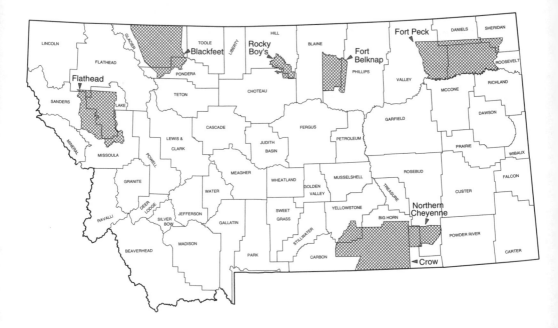

Flathead Indian Reservation

1.2 million acres
Confederated Salish & Kootenai Tribes
Tribal Fish and Game Conservation Program
P.O. Box 278
Pablo, MT 59855.
675-4700 or 1-800-634-0690.
Species allowed: Hungarian partridge, pheasant, ducks, and geese.

The Flathead Reservation is located north of I-90 between Missoula and Kalispell in the beautiful Mission Valley. It is the only reservation to have a cooperative agreement with the Montana Fish, Wildlife, and Parks for hunting and fishing. They welcome hunters and have established seasons and management programs. The valley is known for its excellent pheasant hunting. There are good populations of Huns in the grasslands and agricultural areas. Ducks and geese are plentiful on the rivers and lakes, and in the fields. The Mission Valley is in the Pacific Flyway.

Special permits and licenses are required to hunt the reservation. Season and three-day permits are available. A Federal duck stamp is required to hunt waterfowl, however a Montana hunting license is not needed. For a complete set of regulations, limits, and season dates, write the Tribal Fish and Game Conservation Program at the address above.

See Missoula, p. 167 for accommodations.

Blackfeet Reservation

1.5 million acres
Blackfeet Nation, Glacier County
Box 850
Browning, MT 59417.
338-7276.
Species allowed: Hungarian partridge, ducks, and geese.

The Blackfeet Reservation is located in northwestern Montana along the eastern slopes of the Rocky Mountains. It is bordered on the north by Canada and on the west by Glacier National Park. The nearest town with accommodations is Cut Bank (see page 159).

Hunting is good to excellent for Huns. The rivers and the many pothole lakes provide good waterfowl hunting. The reservation is located in the Pacific Flyway. The limits are the same as the state. There is a license fee in 1995 of $10. A federal and state waterfowl stamp is required to hunt waterfowl. All waterfowl hunting is steel shot only. A Montana hunting license is not needed to hunt on the reservation. The terrain is comprised of plains and shrub grassland.

The reservation is also known for its outstanding trout fishing. Call for regulations.

Joe Kipp offers guided bird hunts and fishing trips. He also can provide lodging and meals. You can hunt over his Gordon setter or bring your own dogs.

Joe Kipp, Morning Star Troutfitters
P.O. Box 968
Browning, MT 59417.
338-2785.

Rocky Boy's Reservation

108,000 acres
The Chippewa-Cree Business Committee
Box 544, Rocky Boy Route
Box Elder, MT 59521.
395-4282.
Species allowed: pheasant, Hungarian partridge, sharp-tailed and sage grouse, ducks and geese

The Rocky Boy's Reservation is located on the Hi-Line in Hill County, about 20 miles south of Havre. The terrain consists of plains grasslands and montane forest. The Bear Paw Mountains grace the southern part of the reservation. Hunting licenses are available at the police station located on Lower Box Elder Rd. The nearest accommodations are in Havre (see page 103).

Hunting is excellent for pheasants on the reservation. The best hunting spots are the grassland areas, but they can also be found in the CRP and along the creek bottoms. There is also good hunting for Huns and sharptails. Some sage grouse can be found in the sagebrush areas.

The many creeks and ponds have superior duck hunting. The grain fields provide field shooting for both ducks and geese. Rocky Boy's is located in the Central Flyway.

Fort Belknap Reservation

705,000 acres
Fort Belknap Tourism Office
RR 1, Box 66
Fort Belknap Agency
Harlem, MT 59526.
353-2205.
Species allowed: sage and sharp-tailed grouse, Hungarian partridge, pheasant, ducks, and geese

Fort Belknap is home to the Assiniboine and the Gros Ventre tribes. It is located on the Hi-Line in northcentral Montana, bounded on the north by the Milk River and south by the Little Rocky Mountains. The terrain consists of shrub and plains grasslands. The principal use of the land is grazing and dryland farming.

The reservation offers a wide variety of hunting opportunities. In addition to upland bird and waterfowl hunting, they offer prairie dog shooting and the unique opportunity to hunt bison. Fort Belknap has one of the only free-ranging herds of wild bison in the country.

The reservation has good to excellent hunting for all upland birds. Sharptails and Huns are located in the plains grasslands. There are large areas of sagebrush that hold sage grouse. Pheasant are most abundant along the Milk River. The 1995 license fee is $40. The seasons and limits are the same as the state.

Fort Belknap is located in the Central Flyway. The Milk River and the pothole lakes provide good hunting for both ducks and geese. A separate $40 waterfowl license is required along with a federal waterfowl stamp. Steel shot must be used. The season and limits are the same as the state.

The tribe has licensed hunting partners that provide guide services. You must negotiate services and fees individually. These services are optional for upland and waterfowl hunting. The reservation will provide you with a list of hunting partners.

Fort Peck Reservation

2 million acres
P.O. Box 1027
Poplar, MT 59255.
768-5305.
Species allowed: pheasant, sharp-tailed and sage grouse, ducks and geese

The Fort Peck Reservation is home to the Assiniboine and Sioux tribes. It is located on the Hi-Line in northeastern Montana, 50 miles south of the Canadian border.

The Missouri River forms the southern border of the reservation. The terrain consists of plains and shrub grassland.

The reservation has both an upland bird and a waterfowl license. A conservation permit is also required. CRP tracts and the plains grassland are prime areas for pheasants and sharptails. Sage grouse can be found wherever there is a large concentration of sagebrush.

The reservation is located in the Central Flyway. The Poplar and Missouri Rivers and the pothole lakes provide good waterfowl hunting. Steel shot, as well as a tribal hunting permit and a federal waterfowl stamp, is required when hunting ducks and geese.

Crow Reservation

2.4 million acres
Crow Agency, MT 59022.
638-2601.

The Crow Reservation is located in southeastern Montana. The northern boundary is just south of Billings and the reservation continues down to Wyoming. The famous Little Bighorn River, noted for its fabulous trout fishing and the Little Bighorn battlefield, flows through the center of the reservation.

The Crow Reservation is not open to hunting by non-tribal members.

Northern Cheyenne Reservation

445,000 acres
P.O. Box 328
Lame Deer, MT 59043.
477-6253.

The reservation is located in southeastern Montana. It is bounded on the east by the Tongue River and on the west by the Crow Reservation.

The Northern Cheyenne is not open to hunting by non-tribal members.

NATIONAL AND STATE WILDLIFE REFUGES

Montana has seven national refuges and one state wildlife management area that provide protection for 1.2 million acres of vital habitat. These areas all have excellent waterfowl hunting. Most also have good populations of pheasants, Huns, and prairie grouse. Hunting pressure is very light in most of these areas.

Each refuge has their own set of regulations and seasons. Beginning in 1996, steel shot will be required for hunting all game including upland birds. Some of the refuges already have a steel shot only requirement in effect. Addresses have been provided for each refuge. Please write to request maps and copies of the hunting regulations.

Both a federal and state duck stamp are required in addition to a state hunting license.

There are many waterfowl production areas ranging from 15 to 1,000 acres that are managed by each refuge. Write the refuge you would like to hunt to receive a map showing waterfowl production areas (WPAs).

WILDLIFE REFUGES THAT ALLOW HUNTING

MEDICINE LAKE NATIONAL WILDLIFE REFUGE
223 N. Shore Road
Medicine Lake, MT 59247.
789-2305, fax: 789-2350.

31,000 acres
Central Flyway
FWP Region 6

Medicine Lake is located in northeastern Montana in Sheridan County, 20 miles south of the town of Plentywood.

The refuge contains sharp-tailed grouse, pheasant, and Hungarian partridge as well as Canada geese and several species of duck.

Medicine Lake Refuge consists of three areas. Area 2 is open to hunting for the duration of the upland gamebird and waterfowl season and includes the 8,700-acre Medicine Lake, several smaller lakes, and numerous potholes. Area 1, containing Katy's Lake, and Area 3, containing the 1,280-acre Homestead Lake, open on November 15th and remain open until the end of the season.

Hunting and fishing are allowed on the refuge in accordance with state and federal regulations and state season dates apply. There are no additional license fees. Hunting of tundra swans and sandhill cranes is prohibited. A steel shot only regulation is in effect for both waterfowl and upland birds.

BOWDOIN NATIONAL WILDLIFE REFUGE
HC 65, Box 5700
Malta, MT 59538.
654-2863.

15,500 acres
Central Flyway
FWP Region 6

Bowdoin National Wildlife Refuge is located on the Hi-Line along Rt 2, seven miles east of Malta in Phillips County.

The entire refuge is 15,500 acres, with Bowdoin Lake covering 4,000 acres. The surrounding area is a mixture of marsh and plains grasslands. The western section of the refuge is open to hunting for waterfowl, upland birds, mourning dove, and sandhill cranes. Steel shot is required. All state and federal hunting regulations apply and some special regulations are also in effect. All hunters are required to check in and out at refuge headquarters.

Bowdoin is located in the Central Flyway, although waterfowl from the Pacific Flyway also use this refuge. During the fall migration up to 100,000 ducks and geese congregate here. The major waterfowl species are Canada geese, snow geese, gadwall, mallard, and blue-winged teal. White pelicans, California gulls, double-crested cormorants, great blue herons, coots, eared grebes, and other species are also present.

Pheasants are the major upland birds on the refuge. There are also some sharp-tailed grouse, but they are not present in huntable numbers.

Many ducks and geese rest in refuges along their migration routes.

CHARLES M. RUSSELL NATIONAL WILDLIFE REFUGE

P.O. Box 110
Lewistown, MT 59457.

1 million acres
Central Flyway
FWP Regions 4,6,7

The CMR refuge spreads across 1 million acres and extends for 125 miles along the Missouri River from northcentral Montana to the Fort Peck Reservoir. The area is characterized by spectacular breaks, forested coulees, prairie grasslands, and cottonwood river bottoms. Motels, restaurants, and services are available at the following towns near the refuge: to the north, Malta, Glasgow, and Fort Peck; to the south, Lewistown and Jordan.

Camping is allowed anywhere on the refuge and there are a number of designated primitive camping areas. Many roads on the refuge are not maintained and on some stretches it is necessary to have a vehicle with a high center or a 4-wheel drive. Boating is permitted, however the Wild and Scenic section of the Missouri upstream of the CMR has a no-motor restriction.

Sage grouse, sharp-tailed grouse, pheasants, and Hungarian partridge live on the refuge. Numbers fluctuate considerably from year to year. Sharptails are the most abundant bird on the CMR. Look for them in the brushy coulees and the grasslands. Sage grouse are plentiful in the large areas of sagebrush. Pheasants can be found in good numbers along the tributaries. Huns are available in the grasslands.

Good populations of ducks and geese can be found along the Fort Peck Reservoir and the Missouri River. The CMR is part of the Central Flyway, however, many birds from the Pacific Flyway occupy the area. Most hunting

Don Williams and his Lab field shoot snow geese.

opportunities are in the fields where birds feed. The many islands on the free-flowing portions of the Missouri River also provide good hunting.

The CMR is an great place to plan a combination deer, antelope, and bird hunt. The mule deer population is excellent. The best place to hunt deer is the brushy coulees along the river. Many birds are usually flushed during a deer drive. Antelope can be found on the prairie and sage grass areas, along with the sage grouse and sharptails.

BENTON LAKE NATIONAL WILDLIFE REFUGE
P.O. Box 450
Black Eagle, MT 59414.
727-7400.

12,383 acres
Pacific Flyway
FWP Region 4

Benton Lake Refuge is located 12 miles north of Great Falls in Cascade County. It is on the western edge of the northern Great Plains. The 5,000-acre lake is actually a shallow marsh created by the last continental glacier.

The gentle rolling terrain is dominated by native shortgrass prairie and surrounded by mountain ranges on three sides—the Highwood Mountains to the east, the Big Belt Mountains to the south, and the Rocky Mountains to the west.

To get to the refuge follow Hwy 87 north out of Great Falls about a mile and turn left onto Bootlegger Trail which leads to the refuge.

About one-third of the refuge is open to hunting during the fall. Sharp-tailed grouse, pheasants, and Hungarian partridge are present in huntable numbers. Hunting is excellent for both geese and ducks. There are over 40,000 snow geese that pass through the refuge. Canada geese are also plentiful. Up to 100,000 ducks inhabit the refuge. Steel shot is required for both waterfowl and upland birds. Write the refuge for seasons and special regulations.

FREEZEOUT LAKE WILDLIFE MANAGEMENT AREA
4600 Giant Springs Rd.
Great Falls, MT 59406 .
454-3441.

12,000 acres
Pacific Flyway
FWP Region 4

Freezeout Lake is a state-owned management area designed to increase waterfowl production and provide the public with superior waterfowl hunting opportunities.

Freezeout Lake is located halfway between Choteau and Great Falls on Hwy 89 in Teton County. The terrain surrounding the lake is shrub grassland.

Pheasants are plentiful and can be found in the marshy areas around the lake. Huns and sharptails are found in the prairie grasslands adjacent to the lake.

Snow geese arrive near the end of October and are present in spectacular numbers. Canada geese are also abundant. There are a limited number of permits for tundra swans. Up to 400,000 ducks may be found during peak migration.

The closest town with accommodations is Choteau in Teton County (see page 195).

RED ROCK LAKES NATIONAL WILDLIFE REFUGE
Monida Star Route, Box 15
Lima, MT 59739.
276-3536.

44,100 total acres, 9,000 acres of lakes
Pacific Flyway
FWP Region 3

Red Rock Lakes is located in scenic and isolated Centennial Valley, a remote section of Beaverhead County in southwestern Montana. It is 50 miles west of West Yellowstone off of Hwy 20. The refuge has a vast array of habitat, ranging from high elevation prairie at 6,600 feet to montane forest at 10,000 feet. Red Rock was established in 1935 to protect the trumpeter swan. Today it is one of the most important habitats in North America for this rare and beautiful bird.

Hunting is permitted for waterfowl and big game on about half of the refuge. There is an abundance of ducks, geese, and coots during the fall migration, although hunting is allowed on the lower lake only. Steel shot is required. There is no hunting for upland birds. Write for information and maps on seasons and special regulations.

Ennis and West Yellowstone are the closest towns with accommodations (see page 185).

LEE METCALF NATIONAL WILDLIFE REFUGE
P.O. Box 257
Stevenville, MT 59870.
777-5552.

2,800 acres
Pacific Flyway
FWP Region 2

The Lee Metcalf Refuge lies along the Bitterroot River, 25 miles south of Missoula and just east of Hwy 93 in Ravalli County. Public hunting for deer and waterfowl is permitted on portions of the refuge and is subject to federal and state regulations. One waterfowl and two deer hunter access points are wheelchair accessible. For more hunting information and maps contact the refuge.

Canadian geese, mallard, teal, and wood ducks are the most abundant birds. Wigeon, pintail, redhead, and scaup are also present. Hunting is done from assigned blinds. There is a maximum of five hunters per blind. Blind selection is on a first-come, first-serve basis with the exception of opening weekend when a drawing is held. Shell limit is 15 per day. Only steel shot is permitted.

John Tomlin and Muffy hunt waterfowl.

Hamilton, in Ravalli County, is the closest town with accommodations (see page 171).

BLM INDEX MAP

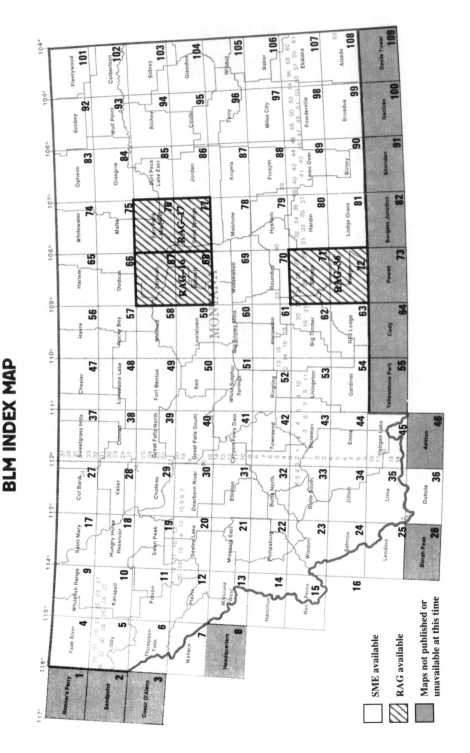

To order BLM maps, write or call: BLM Map Sales, P.O. Box 36800, Billings, MT 59107, 255-2888.

SME available

RAG available

Maps not published or unavailable at this time

ACCESS GUIDE TO
FEDERAL AND STATE LANDS

About 35% of Montana's total land area, some 31.3 million acres, is owned by the public and managed by state and federal agencies. The rules and regulations for public land use are complex. Plan your hunt with accurate maps and make sure that you understand the regulations. There is a listing of all state and federal agencies at the end of this section. We strongly urge you to get the regulation guides and maps. To hunt state lands you need a special state lands recreational use permit and a Montana hunting license. One of the best guides to public lands is the Montana Access Guide, available from the Montana Dept of Fish, Wildlife, and Parks, 1420 East 6th Ave, Helena, MT 59620. 444-2535.

U.S. Dept of the Interior Fish, Wildlife, and Parks.

The FWP manages 1.1 million acres of national wildlife refuges and waterfowl production areas in Montana. See pages 251-257 for a description of the state's wildlife refuges.

Bureau of Land Management

The BLM manages some 8.1 million acres of federal lands in Montana. Most of this land is in eastern Montana. There is excellent hunting on BLM lands, especially for sharptails, sage grouse, and Hungarian partridge. However, access to many of the acres of BLM can be difficult. We suggest that you obtain the BLM section maps for the areas that you plan to hunt. These maps are available from: BLM Map Sales, P.O. Box 36800, Billings, MT 59107. The phone number is 255-2888.

Orders can be placed by phone and Mastercard and Visa are accepted. Maps are currently $4 each. An index map like the one on page 258 is available free of charge.

Block Management: A Program for Landowners and Sportsman

The block management program, a cooperative effort between landowners and the Montana Dept of Fish, Wildlife, and Parks (FWP) to provide recreational opportunities on private lands, was started in 1985. At present there are over 4 million acres enrolled in the program.

The main focus of block management is to provide hunters with public access to private lands. There is no charge to hunters utilizing any of the block management units. The landowner receives monetary incentives for cooperating with the FWP. The program is funded through hunting license sales and federal matching dollars.

FISH, WILDLIFE, AND PARKS REGIONS

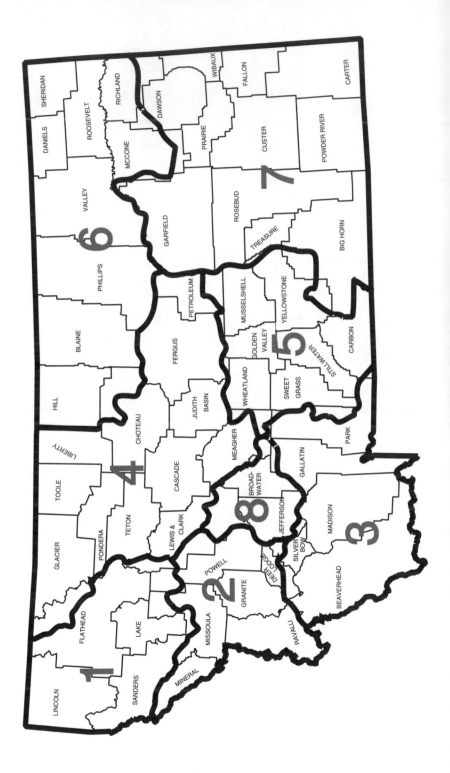

Regulations vary for each block management area (BMA). On some you may be required to obtain written permission from either the landowner or the FWP. A few landowners restrict vehicle use. Some areas only allow certain types of hunting and others limit the number of hunters allowed. BMAs change from year to year. Do not assume that an area you hunted one year will necessarily be available the next.

There is no statewide list of landowners and land enrolled in the block management program. The eight regional fish and game offices coordinate and run the block management for their region. Each region will have a list of BMAs with type of hunting offered, species, and location maps. These lists are available after September 1 from each regional office. To find out what land and hunting opportunities are available, write to the region or regions that you are interested in hunting. The BMAs in regions 6 and 7 offer the hunter an opportunity for a combination hunt for deer, antelope, and upland birds.

Montana FWP Offices

STATE HEADQUARTERS
1420 East 6th Ave
Helena, MT 59620
444-2535.

REGION 1
490 N. Meridian
Kalispell, MT 59901.
752-5501.

REGION 2
3201 Spurgin Rd
Missoula, MT 59801.
542-5500.

REGION 3
1400 S. 19th
Bozeman, MT 59715.
994-4042.

REGION 4
4600 Giant Springs Rd
Great Falls, MT 59406.
454-3441.

REGION 5
2300 Lake Elmo Dr
Billings, MT 59105.
252-4654.

REGION 6
Route 1-4210
Glasgow, MT 59230.
228-9347.

REGION 7
P.O. Box 1630-1
Miles City, MT 59301.
232-4365.

REGION 8
1404 8th Ave
Helena, MT 59620.
444-4720.

State Lands

Montana has 5.2 million acres of state lands. Most of these acres are trust lands granted to Montana when it was admitted to the Union. These lands are managed to produce income to support schools and public institutions. Legally accessible state lands are open for hunting and fishing unless closed or restricted by the Dept. of State Lands.

To hunt on state lands you must purchase and carry on your person a recreational use license. Any one accompanying you must also have a state recreational use license even if they are not hunting. This license is available from the Fish, Wildlife, and Parks. It is also available at any of the many stores that sell hunting and fishing licenses. You are required to have a state hunting license as well.

Montana Department of State Lands Offices

MT Dept. of State Lands
P.O. Box 201601
Helena, MT 59620.
444-2074.

Forestry Division Headquarters
2705 Spurgin Rd
Missoula, MT 59801.
542-4300.

Area Offices

Central Land Office
8001 N. Montana Ave
Helena, MT 59601.

Eastern Land Office
P.O. Box 1794, 321 N. Main
Miles City, MT 59301.

Northeastern Land Office
1401 South Moore Land
Billings, MT 59101.
259-3264.

Southwestern Land Office
1401 27th Avenue
Missoula, MT 59801.
542-4200.

ACCESS TO PRIVATE LAND

Montana Trespass Law

Privilege to enter or remain upon private land is extended either by the explicit permission of the landowner, or by failure of the landowner to post notice denying entry onto the land. You are required to obtain landowner permission to hunt big game. Even though bird hunters may legally hunt on unposted private land without explicit permission, we highly recommend, as a matter of courtesy, that you ask first before entering any private property.

Land may be posted by signs or by painting fence posts with orange paint.

Public access to streams and rivers

Montana law states that all surface waters capable of recreational use may be so used by the public without regard to the ownership of the land underlying the waters. An informational brochure entitled "Stream Access in Montana" is available from Montana Dept. of Fish, Wildlife, and Parks, 1420 East 6th Ave, Helena, MT 59620. 444-2535.

OTHER SOURCES OF INFORMATION

OUTFITTERS & GUIDES

Fishing Outfitters Association of Montana
P.O. Box 67
Gallatin Gateway, MT 59730.

Montana Board of Outfitters
Department of Commerce
111 N. Jackson
Helena, MT 59620.
444-3738.

Montana Outfitters and Guides Association
P.O. Box 1248
Helena, MT 59624.
449-3578.

TOPOGRAPHICAL MAPS

U.S. Geological Survey
Federal Center
Box 25286
Denver, CO 80225.
303-236-7477.

TRAVEL INFORMATION

Montana Dept. of Commerce
Tourism Office
1424 S. 9th Ave
Helena, MT 59620-0533.
1-800-VISIT MT or 444-2654.

WEATHER REPORTS

Statewide: 449-5204.
Billings: 657-6335.
Glasgow: 228-4042.
Great Falls: 453-2081.
Kalispell: 755-4829.
Missoula: 329-4842.

NATIONAL FORESTS

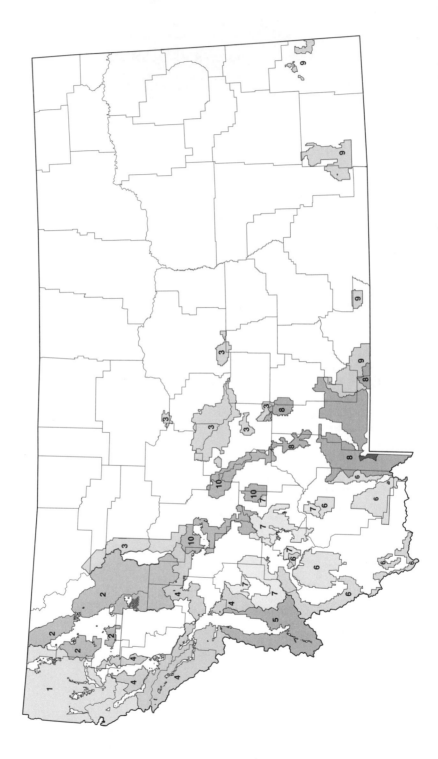

NATIONAL FOREST HEADQUARTERS

Ten national forests, covering 16.7 million acres, are available for public use in Montana. Within the national forest land there is some 2.4 million acres of privately owned land. Write the national forest you intend to hunt and purchase a map of the area. The maps contain information on land ownership, roads, trails, lakes, streams, and campgrounds.

NORTHERN REGION HEADQUARTERS
USDA—Forest Service
P.O. Box 7669
Missoula, MT 59807.
329-3511.

(1) KOOTENAI NATIONAL FOREST
506 US Hwy 2 West
Libby, MT 59923.
293-6211.

(2) FLATHEAD NATIONAL FOREST
1935 3rd Ave East
Kalispell, MT 59901.
755-5401.

(3) LEWIS & CLARK NATIONAL FOREST
1935 3rd Ave East
Kalispell, MT 59901.
755-5401.

(4) LOLO NATIONAL FOREST
Building 24, Ft. Missoula
Missoula, MT 59801.
329-3750.

(5) BITTERROOT NATIONAL FOREST
1801 N. First
Hamilton, MT 59840.
363-3131.

(6) BEAVERHEAD NATIONAL FOREST
P.O. Box 1258
Dillon, MT 59725.
683-3913.

(7) DEER LODGE NATIONAL FOREST
400 North Main
Butte, MT 59701.
496-3400.

(8) GALLATIN NATIONAL FOREST
P.O. Box 130
Bozeman, MT 59771.
587-6701.

(9) CUSTER NATIONAL FOREST
(Headquarters for all National Grasslands in the Northern Region)
P.O. Box 2556
Billings, MT 59103.
657-6361.

(10) HELENA NATIONAL FOREST
2880 Skyway Dr
Helena, MT 59626.
449-5201.

APPENDIX I

TRAVELING WITH DOG AND GUN

The regulations for taking dogs and firearms on a plane vary from airline to airline. Listed below are some basic guidelines, but it will be necessary for you to ask about specific policies when you make your reservation.

Insurance is available for both animals and firearms. Check with your airline for costs and limits.

Dogs

1. Your dog will have to be checked as baggage. Most airlines charge an extra fee per dog (usually around $50).
2. You will need a travel kennel for each dog accompanying you. Kennels are available at most pet supply stores and sometimes at the airport. It is best to familiarize your dog with the kennel 2-3 weeks prior to the trip so that he will be comfortable. Your dog must be able to stand up, turn around, and lie in a comfortable position. There must be absorbent material in the bottom of the kennel (a towel or black-and-white newspaper is acceptable). Two empty dishes for food and water must be accessible from the outside. Also, don't forget to label your dog's kennel with your name, address, phone number, and final destination. It is necessary to attach certification that the animal has been fed and watered within four hours of departure time. Label the kennel with signs stating "Live Animal" and "This Side Up" with letters at least one inch high.
3. You will need a certificate of health from your veterinarian, including proof of rabies vaccination. Tranquilizers are not recommended because high altitude can cause dangerous effects. If you must sedate your dog, be sure to discuss it with your vet first.
4. Federal regulations exist regarding safe temperatures for transport of your dog.
   - Animals will not be accepted if the temperature is below 10 degrees Fahrenheit at any point in transit.
   - If the temperature at your destination is below 45 degrees Fahrenheit, a certificate of acclimation stating that your dog is used to low temperatures will be necessary. This is available from your vet.
   - Temperatures above 85 degrees Fahrenheit can be dangerous for animals in transit. Many airlines will not accept dogs if the temperature at any transit point is more than 85 degrees.

The temperature during the fall in Montana varies widely. September can be quite hot; December is generally very cold. It is good idea to check with the reservation desk regarding current temperatures and make your reservations accordingly. If you run into difficulty transporting your dog, remember these regulations are for your dog's safety.

Guns and Ammunition

1. Firearms and ammunition must be checked as baggage and declared by the passenger. You will be required to fill out a declaration form stating that you are aware of the federal penalties for traveling with a loaded firearm and that your gun is unloaded.

2. Guns must be packed, unloaded, in a hard-sided crushproof container with a lock, specifically designed for firearm air transport. If you do not already have a case, they are usually available at the airport. Call your airline for details about dimensions. If your gun does not arrive on the baggage carousel you may be required to claim it at a special counter in the baggage claim area.

3. Ammunition must be left in the manufacturer's original packaging and securely packed in a wood or metal container separate from the firearm. In most cities in Montana a large variety of ammunition is available in sporting good stores. It might be easier to purchase shells at your destination rather than traveling with them. If you use a rare or special type of ammo, you can pre-ship it through a service like UPS.

APPENDIX II

HUNTER CONDITIONING AND EQUIPMENT

Hunting the western prairies is dramatically different than hunting your favorite grouse or woodcock cover back east. Montana is nicknamed the "Big Sky Country" with good reason. In eastern Montana, you can drive for miles between ranches and towns without spotting any evidence of civilization. The prairies are characterized by dry, open spaces. Water is scarce. The elevation is 3,000–6,000 feet, and the sky is normally bright blue and sunny.

A normal hunt for Huns, sharptails, and sage grouse starts in the early morning. when the temperature will be in the 20s. Early in the season (September-October), the temperature may climb into the 60s, or even as high as the 90s by noon. Coveys of birds, while numerous, are spread over great distances. I usually leave the truck quite early and return in the late afternoon or evening. In the course of the day I cover 10-16 miles of open prairie. In order to enjoy your hunt, you need to be well conditioned and properly equipped.

Conditioning

I recommend that you start a walking or running program at least four months before you plan to hunt in Montana. You should be able to walk about three miles an hour on level ground. Try walking with a weighted pack. Remember you will be walking with a shotgun, vest, and shells when hunting. Walk in the boots you intend to wear hunting.

You don't have to be a marathon runner to have a productive hunt in Montana, however, if you are in good shape you can cover more ground.

Clothes

I wear lightweight ankle-high hunting boots. Unless you are hunting for waterfowl or are near a high stream, waterproof boots are not necessary. I wear two pairs of socks—an inner polypropylene sock to wick away moisture and a heavy wool outer sock for support.

Briars are not normally a problem in Montana. I like to wear a light pair of canvas pants during the early part of the season. During the late season I wear double-faced pants.

It is important to layer clothing on your upper body because of the wide range of temperatures you could encounter in a typical fall Montana day. Wear two or more layers of lightweight clothing that can be easily removed as temperatures climb. I normally wear a polypropylene undershirt and a canvas or wool overshirt.

Sunburn is a common problem in the West. I always wear sunscreen and a billed hat while hunting. A bandana provides protection from the sun and can be used as a tourniquet for emergency purposes.

In the early season I wear a hunting shell bag. During the late season I use a hunting vest. If the weather is cold and snowy, I will wear an oilcloth coat and a vest over the coat. Make sure that you order a vest big enough to fit over all of your outer garments.

I always carry a pair of light leather shooting gloves. Finally, I have a good pair of shooting glasses for sun and eye protection and earplugs to protect my hearing.

Dave Meisner, Steve Smith, and Chuck Johnson take a break with their pointing dogs.

Equipment

I carry a small folding knife in a sheath on my belt, along with a 24-inch dog lead. I have a wristwatch that also has a compass on the band. I carry a whistle and a hemostat around my neck. We have huge porcupines in Montana and unfortunately dogs only learn to avoid them the hard way. The hemostat is also great for picking out cactus needles. I always carry at least one quart of water for my dogs. When it is especially hot and water is scarce, I carry several quarts, because I have come close to losing dogs to heat prostration. I normally wear a small fanny pack that holds water, lunch, a camera, and other miscellaneous items. Finally, I carry a small amount of honey for my dogs. Honey can rejuvenate an exhausted dog.

Following is an equipment list for clothes, dogs, and supplies. Make copies and use it as a checklist when packing for your trip.

EQUIPMENT CHECKLIST

CLOTHING

____ polypropylene underwear
____ inner socks
____ wool socks
____ long sleeve canvas/chamois
     shirt
____ pants—double-faced
____ hunting boots
____ billed hat

____ bandana
____ shooting gloves
____ shooting glasses
____ ear protectors
____ hunting vest/coat
____ down vest/coat
____ chaps/raingear
____ hip boots/waders for waterfowl
     hunting

DOG SUPPLIES

____ food, bowls
____ beeper collar
____ lead
____ dog boots, pad toughener
____ hemostat
____ whistle

____ water bottles
____ *Field Guide to Dog 1st Aid*
____ dog 1st aid kit
____ record of dog vaccinations
____ scissors
____ toenail clippers

HUNTING SUPPLIES

____ shotgun/shells
____ cleaning kit
____ maps
____ knife
____ fanny pack
____ water bottle
____ camera, film
____ binoculars
____ game shears

____ license
____ matches
____ axe, shovel
____ sunscreen
____ twine
____ decoys
____ compass
____ flashlight
____ bird calls
____ spare choke tubes

APPENDIX III

CONDITIONING OF HUNTING DOGS

Dogs, like people, must be in top physical condition to hunt day after day. As for any athlete, proper food and exercise is the key to good health. The best performing dogs are those that are in training year-round.

Many hunting dog owners are not willing or able to devote enough time to exercising their dog throughout the year. Even if you are pressed for time, you should start working your dog regularly at least four or five weeks before hunting season. You and your dog will start getting into shape and have more stamina throughout the season.

Proper feeding of a hunting dog is important and a good grade of dog food certainly helps. Feeding once a day is sufficient, but I feed my dogs smaller amounts of moistened food twice a day. If they are working hard, animals should be given all the moistened food they want.

A dog should not be fed just prior to a workout, so feed them early in the morning before going hunting. I don't subscribe to the old adage, "A hungry dog fights best." I believe I hunt better and harder after having a good breakfast and so do my dogs. I recommend that red meat be added to the dog's diet during hunting season. It increases the palatability of the food and encourages the dog to eat more, which in turn will increase nutritional intake and energy reserves.

Ben Williams and friends take a rest after hunting sage grouse country.

The benefits of a well-trained dog for bird hunting are many. Considerable time and money is required to maintain hunting dogs, but in the long run it will add a new dimension to your life. Keep your dogs in good physical condition; they expect it of you.

Eliza Frazer caring for Shoe after the hunt.

John Huges hunts a CRP field with his dogs.

Alex Burks with his two English setters.

- Exercise your dog all year long if possible.
- Exercise your dog at least one month before hunting season.
- Feed a good grade of dog food that is high in protein.
- Do not let your dog get overweight. (An obese dog in the field can collapse quickly due to lack of conditioning.)
- When transporting dogs make sure your vehicle is well-ventilated. Don't smoke around your dog in close quarters.
- Carry ample supplies of water in the field and in the vehicle.
- Dogs should be watered often which helps with stamina and scenting ability.
- Dog boots and tummy savers are useful when hunting in prickly pear country or stubble fields.
- Let dogs rest occasionally.
- Give your dogs a small nutritional treat from time to time. (They deserve it.)
- In the field, dogs come first. See to any needs immediately: thorns, burrs, cuts, etc...
- Feed, care for, and make your dogs comfortable before you take care of yourself.

Charles F. Waterman waters Shoe.

APPENDIX IV

THE PRAIRIE WAGON

Almost any vehicle can be used for upland gamebird or waterfowl hunting, but a four-wheel drive rig does give you an advantage in rough country. I have a 4x4 pick-up truck, with an extra cab and a fiberglass topper (white to keep the dogs cool) designed with six dog compartments that can hold up to a dozen dogs. It has a fan and a drain system that allows for dry storage beneath the topper with ample room for hunting needs.

These are the things I keep in my hunting rig at all times:

shovel, axe
come-along
jumper cables
tow rope
paper towels

flashlight
small air compressor
fencing tool (for fixing fence only)
extra key taped under the chassis

for the dogs:
5 gallons of water
several 1-gallon water jugs
lead
beeper collars
whistles

two different sizes of hemostats
duct tape
water bottle
first aid kit
Seven 5™ dust for use against ticks

for the hunter:
water bottle
first aid kit
cooler
knife
toilet paper

extra socks
soap, towel
binoculars
extra warm fleece pullover
extra set of keys for a partner

APPENDIX V

PREPARING A BIRD FOR MOUNTING IN THE FIELD

by Web Parton, Taxidermist

The art of taxidermy has made considerable advances in recent years. This is especially true in the realm of bird taxidermy. Ho!!w you take care of your birds in the field determines the finished quality of your mounts. This crucial step is out of the control of the taxidermist. However, with a modicum of preparation, you can proceed confidently when you are holding a freshly taken bird destined for the book-shelf.

Start by putting together a small kit to be carried with you in the field. Use a small plastic container, such as a plastic traveler's soap box. Throw in some cotton balls, a few wooden toothpicks, a dozen or so folded sheets of toilet paper, and a pair of panty hose.

After shooting a bird, examine it closely. First, look for pin feathers. If there are any present, you will notice them on the head directly behind the beak or bill and on the main side coverts below the bird's wing. If there are even a few pinfeathers, the specimen may not be worth mounting. By all means, save it and let your taxidermist make the decision. However, it wouldn't hurt to examine additional birds to find one with better plumage. The taxidermist can always use extra birds for spare parts.

The next step is to check for any bleeding wounds in order to prevent the taxidermist from having to wash the bird before mounting. Plug any visible wounds with cotton. Use a toothpick as a probe to push the cotton into the holes. Now pack the mouth and nostrils, remembering that the body is a reservoir of fluids that can drain down the neck. Make a note or take a photo of any brightly colored soft tissue parts (unfeathered areas) for the taxidermist's reference later. Fold several sheets of toilet paper and lay them between the wings and the body. Should the body bleed, this will protect the undersides of the wings from being soiled. Slide the bird head-first into the nylon stocking. Remember that the feathers lay like shingles: they slide forward into the stocking smoothly, but will ruffle if you pull the bird back out the same end. The taxidermist will remove it by cutting a hole in the material at the toe and sliding the bird forward. When the specimen is all the way down, knot the nylon behind its tail. Now you are ready to slide the next one in behind it.

Place the wrapped bird in an empty game vest pocket, allow it to cool, and protect it from getting wet. When you return to your vehicle, place the bird in a cool spot. At home, put it in a plastic bag to prevent freezer burn, and freeze it solid. You can safely wait several months before dropping it off at the taxidermist.

For the traveling hunter, there is the option of next-day air shipping. Provided that you can find a place to freeze the birds overnight, even a hunter on the other side of the nation can get birds to his taxidermist in good shape. Wrap the frozen birds, nylons and all, in disposable diapers. Line a shipping box with wadded news-papers. Place the birds in the middle with dry ice. Dry ice is available in some major supermarkets. Call your taxidermist to be sure someone will be there, and then ship the parcel next-day air. Be sure to contact them the next day so that a search can be instituted in the event that the parcel did not arrive.

Mounted birds are a beautiful memory of your days in the field. With just a little bit of advance preparation, you can be assured of a top-quality mount.

Recommended Reading

American Game Birds of Field and Forest. Frank C. Edminste. New York: Castle Books, 1954.

American Wildlife & Plants: A Guide to Wildlife Food Habits. Alexander C. Martin, Herbert S. Zim, Arnold L. Nelson. New York: Dover Publishing, Inc., 1951.

The Audubon Society Encyclopedia of North American Birds. John K. Terres. New York: Alfred A. Knopf, 1980.

•*Best Way to Train Your Gun Dog: The Delmar Smith Method.* Bill Tarrant. New York: David McKay Company, Inc., 1977. $20.00

•*Bill Tarrant's Gun Dog Book: A Treasury of Happy Tails.* Bill Tarrant. Honolulu: Sun Trails Publishing, 1980. A great collection of fireside dog stories. $25.00

Ducks, Geese & Swans of North America. Frank C. Bellrose. Harrisburg, PA: Stackpole Books, 1976.

•*A Field Guide to Dog First Aid.* Randy Acker, D.V.M. and Jim Fergus. Bozeman, MT: Wilderness Adventures Press, 1994. An indispensible pocket guide. It could save your dog's life. $15.00

•*Fool Hen Blues: Retrievers, Shotguns, & the American West.* E. Donnal Thomas, Jr. Bozeman, MT: Wilderness Adventures Press, 1995. Don hunts sharptails, Huns, sage grouse, mountain grouse, pheasants, and waterfowl against the wild Montana sky. $29.00

Game Birds of North America. Leonard Lee Rue, III. New York: Harper & Row, 1973.

Game Management. Aldo Leopold. Madison, WI: University of Wisconsin Press,1933.

•*Good Guns Again.* Steve Bodio. Bozeman, MT: Wilderness Adventures Press, 1994. A survey of fine shotguns by an avid gun collector and trader. $29.00

Grasslands. Lauren Brown. New York: Alfred A. Knopf, 1985.

Grouse and Quails of North America. Paul A. Johnsgard. Lincoln, NB: University of Nebraska Press, 1973.

•*Gun Dogs and Bird Guns: A Charlie Waterman Reader.* Charles F. Waterman. South Hamilton, MA: Gray's Sporting Journal Press, 1986. To be reprinted in the fall of 1995.

•*Hey Pup, Fetch it Up: The Complete Retriever Training Book.* Bill Tarrant. Mechanicsburg, PA: Stackpole Books, 1979. $25.00

•*How to Hunt Birds with Gun Dogs.* Bill Tarrant. Mechanicsburg, PA: Stackpole Books, 1994. Bill covers all the birds, what dogs to use and how to hunt each game bird. $21.00

•*A Hunter's Road.* Jim Fergus. New York: Henry Holt and Co., 1992. A joyous journey with gun and dog across the American Uplands. A hunter's *Travels with Charlie.* $25.00

•*Hunting Ducks and Geese.* Steve Smith. Harrisburg, PA: Stackpole Books, 1984. A bit dated, but still the best how-to book on hunting waterfowl. $20.00

Hunting Upland Birds. Charles F. Waterman. New York: Winchester Press, 1972.

•*Kicking Up Trouble.* John Holt. Bozeman, MT: Wilderness Adventures Press, 1994. John takes you on a delightful bird hunting trip through Montana. $29.00

Life Histories of North American Gallinaceous Birds. Arthur Cleveland Bent. New York: Dover Publishing, Inc., 1963.

•*Meditations on Hunting.* José Ortega y Gasset. Bozeman, MT: Wilderness Adventures Press, 1995. The classic book on hunting. Special edition. $60.00

Peterson Field Guides: Western Birds. Roger Tory Peterson. Boston: Houghton Mifflin, 1990.

•*Pheasants of the Mind.* Datus C. Proper. Bozeman, MT: Wilderness Adventures Press, 1990. Simply the best book ever written on pheasants. $25.00

•*Problem Gun Dogs.* Bill Tarrant. Mechanicsburg, PA: Stackpole Books, 1992. $20.00

Prairie Ducks. Lyle K. Sowls. Lincoln, NB: University of Nebraska Press, 1978.

A Sand County Almanac. Aldo Leopold. New York: Oxford University Press, 1949.

•*Training the Versatile Retriever to Hunt Upland Birds.* Bill Tarrant. Bozeman, MT: Wilderness Adventures Press, 1996.

Waterfowl Identification in the Central Flyway. Central Flyway Council, 1974.

Waterfowl Tomorrow. United States Department of the Interior. Washington, DC: US Government Printing Office, 1964.

Western Forests. Stephen Whitney. New York: Alfred K. Knopf, 1985.

•Available from Wilderness Adventures.

INDEX

A WINGSHOOTER'S GUIDE TO MONTANA

If you would like to order additional copies of this book, or any other Wilderness Adventures Press, Inc. publication, please fill out the order form below or call **1-800-925-3339** or **fax: 406-763-4911**.

Mail to:

Wilderness Adventures Press, P.O. Box 1410, Bozeman, MT 59771.

Ship to:

Name: _____

Address: _____

City: _____ State: _____ Zip Code: _____

Home Phone: _____ Work Phone: _____

Payment: ☐Check   ☐Visa   ☐Mastercard   ☐Discover

Card Number: _____ Exp. Date: _____

Signature: _____

Quantity	Title of Book & Author	Price	Total
	Total Order + shipping & handling		

Please add $3.00 per book for shipping and handling.

Coming in 1996 from Wilderness Adventures Press

Wingshooter's Guide to South Dakota AND *Wingshooter's Guide to Arizona*

Reserve Your Copy Now!